Exploring Developmental Theories:

Toward a Structural/Behavioral Model of Development

D0933406

Exploring
Developmental Theories:

Toward a
Structural/Behavioral
Model of Development

Frances Degen Horowitz

The University of Kansas

LEA LAWRENCE ERLBAUM ASSOCIATES, PUBLISHERS

1987   Hillsdale, New Jersey   London

Lawrence Erlbaum Associates, Inc., Publishers
365 Broadway
Hillsdale, New Jersey 07642

Library of Congress Cataloging-in-Publication Data

Horowitz, Frances Degen.
  Exploring developmental theories.

  Bibliography: p.
  Includes index.
  1. Developmental psychology—Philosophy.   2. Child
development—Philosophy.   I. Title.
[BF713.H67   1987]   155.4   86-24315
ISBN 0-89859-737-7
ISBN 0-89859-938-5 (pbk.)

Printed in the United States of America
10 9 8 7 6 5 4 3 2 1

This book is dedicated to
Floyd R. Horowitz
with love and respect

Contents

Preface

In the last 50 years, and more especially, in the last 30 years, we have learned an enormous amount about behavioral development. Our journals and textbooks are filled with facts about the behavioral capabilities of infants and young children, with concepts and theories about how these behavioral capabilities develop, and with discussions of the practical implications of our knowledge for child rearing. The lay-public is eager to discover what we know and to learn what it means for the everyday life of individuals.

As behavioral scientists laboring in the vineyards of developmental psychology we readily acknowledge that we now have more facts about the behavior of infants and young children. Our knowledge has led to mini-revolutions in our conception of the behavioral capabilities of infants and in how we characterize the cognitive sophistication of young children. We also know much about the laws of learning. This knowledge has been applied with great benefit to the handicapped and the retarded and in educational settings for normal children. We have identified a large number of behavioral phenomena and have enlarged our descriptive lexicon considerably.

The increase in our knowledge, however, has not been accompanied by concomitant advances in developmental theory. The basic theoretical umbrellas that currently guide most developmental research have their roots in the 1920s and 1930s. The era of grand developmental schemes is acknowledged as past, yet the concepts and orientations associated with these theories continue to permeate our discussions of behavioral development. Mini-theories designed to address specific phenomena, behavioral domains, or individual developmental periods supplement the concepts and ideas associated with the grander developmental theories but are not intended to replace them. Attempts to study developmental theory in the light of these circumstances have been few and far between.

This book is intended for fellow developmental psychologists and for those who consider themselves now and forever students of human behavioral development. It is designed to explore the theoretical concepts and schemes that underlie the research enterprise of developmental psychology via a series of essay-like chapters. The historical and contemporary threads that link theory and research are discussed and evaluated. From these discussions there emerges a proposal for a structural model of behavioral development to serve a research agenda for understanding behavioral development. The model is simple in concept, complex in implications. The model is more than a heuristic and less than a theory. It incorporates ideas related to stages and systems; it gives a role to the laws that account for the acquisition of behavior; it provides a theoretical arena for the function of individual difference parameters in behavioral development.

The purpose of this book was not ecumenical in nature. However, the proposed model draws liberally from a variety of theories and models that might otherwise be thought of as competing accounts of human behavioral development. The working premise that has been adopted is that any model or theory being proposed at this time in the history of developmental psychology should include as much of the replicated data base and as many of the heuristically attractive concepts that are abroad as can be logically accommodated.

In writing this book I have benefited from a number of things. First, I had the good fortune to combine a sabbatical leave from the University of Kansas with an invitation to take up residence as a Fellow at the Center for Advanced Study in the Behavioral Sciences at Stanford University during the 1983–1984 academic year. While at the Center I was a member of a study group on cultural transmission and found that the weekly meetings with Marcus Feldman, Luca Cavalli-Sforza, William Wang and Ellen Messer— mathematical biologist, geneticist, linguist, and anthropologist, respectively— enlivened my thinking as I read and wrote. Threads of these influences are detectable throughout the book. The support from the John D. and Catherine T. MacArthur Foundation that made my Fellowship year at the Center possible is gratefully acknowledged. The congenial personal and intellectual atmosphere of the Center lent a serenity to my work that is, alas, not replicable anywhere else.

Second, I have for many years taught a graduate level course in "Developmental Theories" at the Unviersity of Kansas. The students have come from a number of different departments reflecting a variety of theoretical biases ranging from radical behaviorism to cognitivism, with interests in a broad range of basic and applied research problems. The questions, arguments, and dialogues I have had with these students over the years in class and in responding to their papers on the relevance of the different theories to their research have made important contributions to my thinking about developmental theory and analyzing the issues.

Third, I have been fortunate to have been a member of the Department of Human Development and Family Life at the University of Kansas, the Department of Psychology, and the Bureau of Child Research. Among my colleagues have been Donald Baer, Todd Risley, Montrose Wolf, Barbara Etzel, Jim Sherman, John Wright, Howard Rosenfeld, Paul Gump, and Richard Schiefelbusch. I have learned from each of them. I have developed an enormous appreciation for the power of applied operant behaviorism. I have used the setting of the department to explore the interrelationships and compatibilities of different research strategies and different theoretical orientations. I do not think the ideas developed in this book could have come to fruition anywhere but Kansas.

Fourth, just before I set out to write this book the fourth edition of the *Handbook of Child Psychology,* edited by Paul Mussen, was published. This four-volume compendium on the development of children was repeatedly a resource and its use is liberally acknowledged throughout. Its fortuitous appearance saved me from enormous amounts of literature reviewing in order to distill perspectives about areas relevant to the ideas I wanted to develop. To the authors of the chapters in the *Handbook* and to the comprehensive vision of the editors I owe many thanks.

Fifth, I carry, always, an enormous debt to those who have been my teachers and to my students for what each has helped me to learn. Some of my teachers provided direct instruction; others were mentors through their writing. Of the latter I want to mention Donald Hebb and Neal Miller. The model of their thinking, the thoughtful nature of their analyses, and their commitment to empiricism were always goals to be emulated. Of the former I had the good fortune to study under and be befriended by individuals who loved to learn and who were ever ready to think seriously about their subject. Madame de Staël, director of Cherry Lawn School, taught me history in my junior and senior year of secondary school. I learned from her the importance of historical perspective that was reinforced by Louis Filler at Antioch College. I studied philosophy as an undergraduate at Antioch with George Geiger and came to understand intellectual history and how systems of thought organize our precepts and our prejudices. As a graduate student in the legendary Iowa Child Welfare Research Station at the University of Iowa, Boyd McCandless was my mentor and friend and imparted a fascination for the question of how development happens that I have never lost. Kenneth Spence, Gustav Bergmann, Charles Spiker and Howard Meredith, teaching a variety of topics in relation to behavior and development, taught me about research, about framing research problems and about the importance of data for the formulation of theory.

Over the years, my students have become my colleagues in the study of infant behavior and development. Their energies and their enthusiasms have been infectious. They have constantly raised critical issues and asked important questions and have been a never-ending source of stimulation to my own thinking. Most recently, Marion O'Brien, John Colombo and Wayne Mitchell have taken particular interest in the model proposed in this book and they have helped me refine my thinking about it. John Colombo and Marion O'Brien, as well as John Wright and Gerald Siegel read the first draft of this manuscript and provided invaluable criticism. Lewis Lipsitt's comments on chapter 3 were also very helpful. John Wright, particularly, is responsible for some of the clarity that would otherwise have been missing. He and Marion O'Brien contributed importantly to the simplifying of complex sentences and to the presence of concrete examples to leaven the abstractions, although they did not entirely suceed in their goals. Charlie Greenbaum did yoeman service in his very thorough reading of the book.

For a number of years I have held administrative positions at the University of Kansas. University administration is a dangerous occupation for a scientist and scholar for it tends to swallow one's energies and time. I have been fortunate in being able to maintain a higher level of research and scholarship than is often possible in such positions. This has been due to the quality of the students with whom I have worked and the consequent motivation to keep up with their development. It has also been due to the support that the University of Kansas has provided me for my work and I am very appreciative of this. For the last 8 years I have been the Vice Chancellor for Research, Graduate Studies and Public Service and Dean of the Graduate School at the University of Kansas. My associates in this office have been exceptionally supportive of my insistence that we all maintain our own intellectual lives. Their competence and their concurrence with this goal enabled me to take my sabbatical year at the Center and to delegate and arrange responsibilities so that I could devote time to my own enterprises. This book could not have been written without such agreements and I am pleased to publicly acknowledge George Woodyard, Ed Meyen, Robert Bearse, Tom Patton, Carolyn Cross, Frank Starkey, and Marilyn Yarbrough for their colleagueship in this regard and to Cecil Miskel for his past association with the office. And, to Eveline Miller, my secretary and co-worker, I owe an enormous debt. Many of the individuals in my office worked on this manuscript at various times. I appreciate the efforts of Edith Hayes, Joanne Maxwell and the others who typed and proofed different versions.

Finally, my family has been an enduring source of satisfaction, learning, and encouragement. Living with my sons, Jason and Benjamin, I developed an appreciation of individual differences more than would otherwise have been the case. This book is dedicated to my husband, Floyd Horowitz. His partnership, friendship, and his belief in my abilities made it all possible.

Frances Degen Horowitz

1 Overture

Discussions of human behavior and aesthetic representations of the nature of human relationships are to be found in the earliest documents of recorded history and no doubt preceded them. In the time during which the human organism has inhabited this planet a certain amount of knowledge and wisdom have accumulated, much of it regulating our daily lives and codified into cultural values, legal systems, and everyday practices. Only recently, somewhat after the rise of the physical and biological sciences, has there been a large-scale systematic enterprise devoted to the scientific understanding of human behavior and development. Not everyone has welcomed this activity. Some consider that the folk wisdom about human behavior that each of us possesses and that has so affected the nature of the societies we have designed is sufficient for our needs. Others, mindful of the enormous problems our societies face, look expectantly and repeatedly for solutions based on knowledge that goes beyond the intuitive and the culturally transmitted. These people have been disappointed repeatedly both because we know too little to deal effectively with the most serious and complex problems in our world today, and because we often have promised solutions we could not possibly deliver given our knowledge base. Further, within the behavioral science community there has been a widespread lack of consensus about the theoretical orientation that will serve us best and even, sometimes, as regards what we will agree we know.

On the other hand, there has been an enormous explosion of information about human behavior and development in the last 30 years. Attempting to form a consensus and to consider adopting a kind of theoretical umbrella may be particularly timely. Even if the result is not fully acceptable to the broad range of opinions in developmental science, such an effort could be productive. These considerations and concerns gave rise to the ideas that shaped this book. The major focus revolves around the questions related to how we might best account for the development of human behavior in each individual person. The major conclusion involves the proposal of a model of human development that could represent the largest consensus given our current knowledge base. To arrive at this conclusion we must consider the basic concepts and issues that characterize current theories of development and we must also examine the concepts and issues in relation to the data available to us. In this book there is no attempt to represent, in text-like fashion, the full set of facts that populate university courses on human development; nor do we engage in a theory by theory analysis and critique. Rather, our journey through issues is a matter of theme and variations.[1]

A distinction or clarification needs to be made at the outset with respect to the use of the terms *development* and *behavior*. We attempt to consider which theoretical concepts apply to both terms and what is distinctive about each. In using the term *development*, reference is made to the events and processes that take the organism from conception to death, with particular emphasis in these discussions about development from the period of birth to the achievement of adult status. Within the focus upon development we are concerned with behavioral development both in terms of what develops and what processes can be invoked to understand behavioral development. The distinction in segregating out the term *behavior* is being made to indicate that the lawful relationships that apply to the performance of behavior may mirror those relationships that account for behavioral development. One of our goals is to ask questions that deal with the degree to which our present knowledge base illuminates developmental events and processes and/or explains how behavior functions. We try to understand the degree to which we can invoke the same variables and laws to explain the acquisition and evolution of a behavior within and across time periods (stages) and the performance and maintenance of that behavior in the individual's repertoire within and across time periods. In discussions of theories of development these distinctions have not always been made, but it does become clear that phrasing our questions with the possibility of such distinctions could provide for the synthetic bridges between seemingly quite opposing viewpoints and lead us toward a theoretical integration that would be useful. It is clear, however, that in discussing the corpus

---

[1]For systematic accounts of developmental theories the reader is referred to Baldwin (1980), Miller (1983), Lerner (1976), and Thomas (1979). Additionally, the first volume of the Mussen Handbook on Child Psychology (1983) edited by Kessen (1983) contains a number of good discussions of theories in developmental psychology.

of theories and observations available to us, where the distinctions have not been made, the conjoint use of "human development and behavior" is needed and we do so without comment until we reach the point in our discussions where it becomes important to consider what is to be gained by making the distinctions.

THEORETICAL ISSUES IN THE HISTORY OF DEVELOPMENTAL PSYCHOLOGY

The earliest systematic observations of human development available to us appear to be the result of the direct recording of the behaviors of one's own child. Almost 200 years ago Tiedemann published observations of his son from birth to 2½ years of age. In commenting upon Tiedemann's book, published in 1787, Borstelmann (1983) noted that

> Many aspects of early child behavior presented by Tiedemann are familiar to present day researchers: common sequences and differential rates of behavioral development, the effect of experience on feeding, transition of the grasp reflex into precise and intentional prehension, the significance of stimuli variability and novelty, the increase of crying by reinforcement, the animistic and anthropomorphic nature of the child's thoughts, and a range of behaviors that have become standard items in infant developmental scales. (p. 34)

Almost 100 years later Wilhelm Preyer (1881–1882/1909a, 1909b) published his landmark study on the *Mind of the Child,* again focusing upon observations of his own child, but now having not only the theoretical benefit of Darwin's theory of evolution but the outpouring of comparative analyses across the species, the integration of phylogenetic concepts and, as Borstelmann suggests, a new and growing perspective in which humans were viewed as understandable in terms of "their origins in nature and in the child" (p. 34). Cairns (1983) found reason to interpret this perspective as evidence that developmental psychology became the essential natural focus of the attempt to understand human functioning.

The ideas and goals that Cairns (1983) described as the themes that emerged in developmental psychology in the late 19th and early 20th centuries are still, remarkably, with us today: "(1) the ontogeny of consciousness and intelligence; (2) intentionality and how it arises; (3) moral development; (4) relations between evolution and development; (5) the relative contributions of nature and nurture; (6) the effects of early experience; and (7) how science may contribute to society" (p. 62). Over the years, some of the terminology has changed. There is obviously a considerably larger data base on children's behavior and development now as compared to 80 and 90 years ago, and we have reason to think our understanding of development has grown considerably. Present methodological approaches are more varied and infinitely more sophisticated than when developmental investigations began. Topics such as cognition and information processing and socialization have had extensive elaborations into subspecialties of investigation. Still, it is interesting and significant to note that the basic theoretical formulations concerning development which are currently of central influence were already developed by 1930 and several had been well articulated by 1920. Each of these major positions had its intellectual and scientific roots in the late 1800s.

Sigmund Freud's monumental theory concerning psycho-sexual development was available in his essays on the theory of sexuality in 1905 (Freud, 1905/1953); Watson had proffered his basic tenets of behaviorism by 1914 and had published his initial studies of conditioning in infants and young children by 1920 (Watson, 1914; Watson & Morgan, 1917; Watson & Rayner, 1920); Jean Piaget's early observations were published in French in 1923 and were available in English in 1926 (Piaget, 1926); and Arnold Gesell's *Mental Growth of the Preschool Child* appeared in 1925 to be followed by his influential book on infancy in 1928 (Gesell, 1925, 1928). Most of the other major attempts at theoretical accounts of behavioral development can be thought of as elaborations upon or variants of the ideas inherent in Gesell, Piaget, Freud, and behaviorism, although some points of view like that of James Mark Baldwin were antecedent and anticipatory of later conceptualizations (Broughton & Freeman-Moir, 1982). Piaget's work, available and contemporaneous with Gesell and Freud and Watson, did not become part of the major themes in American developmental psychology until Flavell's and Hunt's explications in the early 1960s (Flavell, 1963; Hunt, 1961). Similarly, two other non-Americans were also to have a delayed impact: Lev Vygotsky and Z.-Y. Kuo.

Vygotsky lived and worked in Russia in the 1920s. His death at the age of 38 in 1934 and prevailing world conditions contributed to a general ignorance of his highly original ideas concerning language, thought, and culture in relation to developmental processes. The work was largely unknown until relatively recently. Translations into English of his papers and monographs (Vygotsky, 1962, 1978) and of the work of his student and collaborator, Alexander Luria (1976, 1981) introduced important ideas that are now entering the mainstream of developmental theory (Laboratory of Comparative Human Cognition, 1983; Wertsch, 1979). Similarly, although longer lived and more in contact with American psychology, Kuo's very provocative challenge of traditional ideas concerning instinct and his innovative animal experiments demonstrating the violate nature of instincts began in the 1920s and continued through the turbulent years of upheaval in China in the 1930s. It was not until the appearance of his book (Kuo, 1967) on *The*

Dynamics of Behavior Development and his association with Gilbert Gottlieb that his ideas began to be cited in developmental psychology (see Gottlieb, 1983).

The only exception in terms of the "era" of originating ideas is Donald Hebb. Hebb's basic contribution came in the publication of his book *The Organization of Behavior* (1949), introducing into the dialogues on development a neurobiological orientation with important implications for issues related to developmental plasticity and early experience. His impact has been steady and often understated, for many of his ideas have been absorbed into developmental analyses without becoming the focus of a specific school of thought or theoretical camp.

Two current sources of influence having a significant impact upon behavioral science are general systems theory and cognitive science. General systems theory involves a set of propositions about the nature of living systems and organizations that were described by Ludwig von Bertalanffy (1968, 1975). The ideas related to organization have been taken up by those interested in business management and organizational and industrial psychology. The ideas related to development in living systems have long been compatible with developmental biology but only recently adopted as a potentially useful strategy for looking at behavioral development (Sameroff, 1983). The attraction of general systems theory to those interested in behavioral development involves concepts related to stages, multiple pathways to similar developmental outcome and the creative possibilities inherent in an "open system" as opposed to a "closed system" analysis of functioning.

Cognitive science represents a convergence of empirical and theoretical work related to neurobiology, artificial intelligence, information processing, structural linguistics, and systems theories. Considerable data are now available with regard to the manner in which humans use and organize information to analyze the stimulus world and to affect learning and thinking processes. Cognitive science is, in many ways, an emerging integrative new discipline which, oddly enough, has not had very much direct relationship to the knowledge development orientation inherent in Piaget's theory. It also has not been particularly developmental in its emphasis. Recent efforts by Sternberg and his colleagues (Sternberg & Powell, 1983) on the development of intelligence and Siegler (1983) on the development of information processing have involved some analysis from a developmental point of view and a concern for individual differences and how they function. These discussions are not psychometrically oriented and have important potential for providing significant theoretical qualifications related to prediction of developmental outcome.

In the range of ideas encompassed by Freud, Gesell, Piaget, the behaviorists, Vygotsky, Kuo, and Hebb and more recently von Bertalanffy and the cognitivists, we have most of the basic approaches to conceptualizing the development of human behavior and the issues that have become identified with child development, developmental psychology, and now life-span psychology. Parts of the issues find their way into every conceivable branch of behavioral science today, which is why the questions related to development, to the acquisition and maintenance of behavior, and to behavioral change invariably bring us back to questions concerning the processes of development. In turn, one finds the developmentalist capable of being interested in almost every behavioral area studied by psychologists, for one can invariably wonder—How did it happen? How did it come into the repertoire? Is there any connection between the manifestation and function of the behavior in an adult organism and the development of that organism?

CURRENT ISSUES IN THE
STUDY OF BEHAVIORAL DEVELOPMENT

In an attempt to frame a comprehensive explanation of development there has been, as Cairns noted, a core of questions that present themselves over again in the theoretical formulations related to understanding development. One of these involves the concept of periods or stages of development. Are stages merely convenient heuristics for chunking developmental time? Or, do stages have inherent properties that will reveal to us important aspects of development or developmental processes? A corollary set of issues concerns the relationships between periods or stages of development across time. What are the influences of events that occur in one period on what happens in another period? What predictive relationships can be found from one period to another? How should we think about continuity and discontinuity in development? And finally, what is the role of early experience on later functioning? Whether the concept of stage is important or relevant for the questions of early–late relationships and continuity–discontinuity issues has not been treated extensively yet comes within the arena of questions that are relevant to thinking about development and developmental processes.

When the discussion of early–late relationships expands to the issue of the relative developmental plasticity of the organism in relation to the roles of experience and biological factors, we arrive at what has perhaps been the most central question that has characterized theories of development— namely the "nature versus nurture controversy," or "heredity versus environment," or "maturation versus learning." Although not entirely synonymous, these various appositions frame poles of points of view even though hardly anyone now sits at one extreme or the other. On the other hand, it is possible to array the different traditional theories along the continuum between the poles with respect to the relative weights that have been given to the sets of variables associated with the factors represented by the ends of the continuum.

We can successively complicate the discussion of these issues by asking whether one would place different periods of development at different points along the continuum and/or different domains of development at various positions. For example, is it the case that the period of infancy is so "wired in" as to be relatively impervious to variations in environmental experience with the significant impact of environmental variations on development beginning only after the period of infancy (Kagan, 1978)? Conversely, are the first three years of life the maximally sensitive period for environmental impact with the basic developmental trajectory thereafter not easily affected by the variations in environment (White, 1975)? Or, does environmental experience cumulatively affect the individual's development across the life span with the weight of the history itself becoming a factor (Horowitz, 1969)? Is one domain of development more likely to be reflective of hereditary influences than another? Is motor development, for example, largely an expression of genetic characteristics and personality more a mixture of a gene-environment interaction? Is intelligence most strongly influenced by the environment? Could one claim an interaction between heredity and environment in every domain of development but with differential weights in different domains that change for different periods of development? Or, are heredity and environment each 100% in importance (Hebb, 1980)? Is it possible that the nature–nurture question is dispensable in favor of the notion that it is not possible to distinguish between the inherited and the acquired (Oyama, 1985)?

The nature–nurture controversy was most vigorously pursued in the 1920s and 1930s at a level somewhat less sophisticated than at present. The controversy then was focused mainly in the arguments between hereditarian Gesellians and environmentalist behaviorists—notably John B. Watson. The Gestaltists, taking a nativist position, also opposed the extreme environmentalism of the behaviorists. However, the Gestalt point of view was not used in a systematic way to address the matter from a developmental perspective. This left the argumentative field mainly to the Gesellians and the behaviorists. Piaget's theory, as has been noted, though in its early years contemporaneous with Gesell and behaviorism and perhaps more compatible with the "nature" side where Gesell fell (although open to various interpretations on this account), was not a serious contender in the argument as it was then dramatized in the American journals and in American research labs. The Freudian point of view, on the other hand, was very much relevant and is, in many ways, the most encompassing theoretical treatment of development of any of the theories. However, because its orthodox version did not make it amenable to objective verification, Freud's ideas concerning development entered the field of developmental psychology largely through behaviorist translations that formed the initial base of what came to be known as "social learning theory" (Miller, 1941; Miller & Dollard, 1941; Sears, 1975). Thus, Freud's ideas tended to be lined up with the behaviorists on the side of "nurture" and "environment" even though it could be argued that the Freudian account of development is supremely an account that involves the most complex interaction of nature and nurture.

Although nature–nurture issues have been raised with respect to all domains of development, the controversy has centered mainly on intelligence. This was true in the 1930s and it was true when the controversy was revived in the 1960s. More recently, advances in genetics, developments within the field of behavior genetics and extensive research have broadened the discussions considerably as investigators have studied topics related to personality, behavioral disorders, mental retardation as well as normal intelligence (see Scarr & Kidd, 1983). The traditional theories of development, however, having been formulated much earlier, are almost orthogonal to modern day discussions of nature–nurture issues, with a possible exception to be made in relation to the later writings of Jean Piaget (e.g., Piaget, 1971, 1980). Many of the directions in which current research has taken us— information processing, the development of high-risk infants, as well as advances in the neurosciences and developmental biology—have little direct relation to the large theories of development. The general theories often serve as umbrella references in introductions to research while more specific theoretical approaches within sub-fields such as cognition and linguistics serve to provide a particular focus for research.

ALTERNATIVE MODELS
FOR BEHAVIORAL DEVELOPMENT

Despite more than 60 years of research aimed at trying to understand development and developmental processes, and despite the waning of some theories and the ascendance of others, we are no nearer attempting a systematic account of development in the context of a theoretical perspective or with an agreed-upon paradigmatic approach than when the field first acquired a semblance of scientific and academic identity. We do have a much more extensive descriptive base telling us what children do and when they do it; we are assailed by vigorous partisans competing to explain how development happens. Although Piaget's ideas have only been incorporated into the intellectual ferment of developmental psychology in the last 25 years, Piaget's theory has not changed the questions or provided for a theoretical advance that somehow integrated previously diverse sets of data or created a new synthesis whereby previously discordant information would now fit with other existing facts. Further, it is not clear that there has been any recent structural synthesis that presents a model of development that more nearly approximates the complexity of developmental phenomena than do existing models of development and that might also serve as a more fruitful source of questions for developmental investigators. Such a state of affairs may reflect the fact that psychology and the social sciences are still in what Kuhn (1970) called a *preparadigmatic phase* although it has become popular of late to declare that mechanistic accounts of behaviorism have run their course and been replaced by a more valid "organismic" view (Mason, 1979; Sameroff, 1983; Stevenson, 1983). This replacement has been proclaimed a paradigmatic shift in the science of behavioral development even though it cannot be demonstrably shown that the criteria for paradigm shift are being met, such as, a higher level of actual data integration and the generation of new and different testable hypotheses.

Several factors have contributed to our failure to generate new theories or models beyond those formulated more than 50 years ago. First, many perceive that we have, in fact, adopted a new model of development in rejecting the supposed linear, mechanistic character of development espoused by the behaviorists and adopting a non-linear, organic model as suggested by Piaget's approach. Lending credence to this belief is the fact that Piaget's theory, although formulated not long after behaviorism came upon the scene, is a relatively recent entrant in American developmental psychology and has spawned an extensive amount of research. These efforts have given us a new perspective on the abilities in infants and children. Second, the Piagetian approach appears compatible with a general systems theory approach as described by von Bertalanffy (1968, 1975; Sameroff, 1983). In the general systems approach a mechanism–organism juxtaposition is explored extensively in service of the claim that machines are "closed systems" and organic phenomena are "open systems." According to von Bertalanffy, conventional physics deals with closed systems. In a closed system, conditions at $time_1$ inevitably lead to conditions at $time_n$ but in an open system the same final state may be reached from different initial conditions in different ways, a concept identified as equifinality. This closed–open analogy has been very appealing to developmental psychologists looking for models that might more successfully deal with the complexity of initial conditions and of developmental outcomes apparent in the human organism. von Bertalanffy's description of general systems theory as a theory dealing with wholeness and organization, which cannot be accounted for by linear causal chains or statistical outcome, meets some of the objections to the seemingly more simple characterization of behavior in terms of stimuli and responses. Historically, behaviorists did look to physics as a model of scientific endeavor. In doing so they adopted the philosophical propositions of the logical positivists with respect to the definition of concepts and the need to specify precisely the methods of measurement in order for a concept to be scientifically useful. The use of physics rather than biology as a model has been cited as a reason for criticizing behaviorism as relatively insensitive to developmental phenomena. As the philosophical vogue of logical positivism has weakened this has provided further justification for dismissing behaviorism and the methodological strategy with which it was identified as inappropriate for developmental theory. Notions of wholeness, complexity, and open-endedness have been welcomed as alternatives to stimuli and responses.

As is seen, there are important and useful perspectives in some of the concepts associated with general systems theory. Several attempts have been made to explicate the relationship of general systems theory to developmental theory (e.g., Sameroff, 1983). However, hailing the organismic point of view as a paradigm shift and implying that we are now on a more fruitful empirical and theoretical track because we have discarded the simplistic behavioristic analysis is symptomatic of the often muddled thinking that has tended to characterize theoretical discussions in developmental psychology. The notion of paradigm implies that at one point in time there is some basic agreement among investigators working in a field as to what constitutes an accepted body of facts and relationships. During the period that Kuhn (1970) describes as *normal science,* investigators are using a common set of investigative strategies to fill out the data base and there is a general agreement to ignore discordant information during this epoch. However, at some point in time, according to Kuhn, there is a "revolution" whereby information is reorganized, new methods of investigation are introduced, and there is a shift to a different predominant theory that succeeds because it integrates more data and relationships than a previous theory, and leads to new questions and hypotheses. A new paradigm has thus been adopted and another period of "normal science" sets in. The history of physics and chemistry and biology are replete with examples that more or less fit Kuhn's descriptions. Those who claim a revolution and a paradigm shift for developmental psychology see parallels.

Describing the current circumstances in developmental psychology in terms of a paradigm shift is attractive, puts psychology in the same tradition of some of the older or more "highly codified" sciences, and has some intellectual appeal. However, there are some questions that might be raised with respect to the appropriateness of the analogy. One might interpret Kuhn's descriptions of normal science and paradigms as requiring a body of fact that is generally accepted by all investigators in that field. Such fields as have bodies of accepted fact are characterized as being *codified* (Zuckerman & Merton, 1973). Physics and chemistry are considered as the most highly codified, the humanities the least, and the social sciences in between. Without a body of accepted fact there is some question as to whether one can talk about paradigms. Without a truly dominant organizing theory that attempts to account for that body of accepted fact a science may not be paradigmatic. According to Kuhn, the periods prior to the development of paradigmatic phases in a science are characterized by a number of different theoretical schools competing for acceptance. Then, there occurs a "notable scientific achievement" and "the number of schools is greatly reduced, ordinarily to one, and a more efficient mode of scientific practice begins" (Kuhn, 1970, p. 178). This initiates a period of normal science that typically involves a consensus as to (a) what is currently held to be true; (b) acceptable methodologies; and (c) acceptable scientific instruments and technologies. The lack of such a consensus tends to produce endless debate over fundamentals that are likely to be more philosophical and social instead of empirical and theoretical (Cole, Cole, & Dietrich, 1978). Periods of normal science, then, involve an expansion of facts that fit the paradigm. There is an increase in the codification. This is thought of as "the consolidation of empirical knowledge into succinct and interdependent theoretical formulations" (Zuckerman & Merton, 1973, p. 507). The less codified the science, the more it is characterized by a mass of descriptive facts and of low-level theories whose implications are not well understood.

An important corollary to discussions of paradigms and codification is the understanding that a paradigm shift does not mean one discards previously accepted basic facts. When von Bertalanffy talks about biological systems as being open rather than closed systems, of having "wholeness" and functioning according to principles different from those of a machine, he is not saying that the basic chemical laws that describe chemical reactions within the biological organism are invalidated or that the "mechanistic" laws of physics no longer hold true. When developmental psychologists adopt the notions of open systems as being more appropriate to the study of human development than using closed system models they are at once recognizing that many of the phenomena of interest are complex and require models of relationships that incorporate highly interactive systems and the need to search for complex patterns. But, such systems and patterns are not necessarily totally divorced from base phenomena that may be involved in the complex phenomena. An example here may be useful. In their chapter on "The School as a Context for Social Development" Minuchin and Shapiro (1983) take up the notion of the paradigm shift. They comment that traditional scientific paradigms have been linear, employing direct cause-and-effect relationships that can be tested and verified. However, they claim, there has been a movement away from such traditional approaches "toward new paradigms that challenge concepts of linear causality and discretely measureable units. . . . New paradigms stress the context of events and the organization of relationships within systems. From this point of view, the appropriate scientific search is for recurrent patterns that describe the characteristics of a system rather than for linear causal chains of events" (p. 199–200). It is claimed that this kind of thinking is "pervasive . . . in physics, biology, economics, ecology, and agriculture . . . (p. 199). True enough. However, in looking for recurrent patterns, in trying to understand the context of events and the organization of relationships, physicists do not discard their basic facts and biologists do not dismiss their accepted data base.

The use of Kuhn's analysis to describe the conflict between the mechanistic and organismic approach to behavioral development has been challenged recently with the introduction of alternative ways of characterizing scientific progress (Barker & Gholson, 1984; Overton, 1984). The ideas of Lakatos (1970, 1978) and Laudan (1977, 1981) have been suggested as being more appropriate to describing progress and the scientific enterprise. Rather than seeing science as periods of normality and revolution, science is described as involving different, but sometimes parallel research traditions wherein one tradition competes with the other, one overtakes the other, one may regain strength after a period of time. According to Laudan (1977), theories are eventually judged for their adequacy and effectiveness in terms of the significance of the problems they address and the nature and number of "anomalies and conceptual problems they generate" (p. 119). Whether this is a profound challenge to Kuhn's analysis remains an open question (Palermo, 1984).

In trying to reach for the very intuitively appealing concepts inherent in a systems theory approach it is not always easy to remain cognizant of the fact that such discussions and analyses must encompass microanalytical as well as macroanalytical levels of analysis if there is to be any consistency in the applicability of a theoretical model. Some integration of the facts of these different levels of analysis will need to be achieved to fully explain complex phenomena. This will require that the laws from one level of analysis be incorporated in and be compatible with or modified by the laws of functioning at a higher level of analysis. It may be true that biological systems involved in cancer require a different conceptualization than a simple linear model, but such a conceptualization does not nullify the functioning of linear mechanisms at certain levels of analysis of cancer-related phenomena. In building a useful model or theory of development one may forget that the complexity of the phenomena to be understood will likely involve many different levels of analysis and that different mechanisms will be implicated at different levels, but they will not invalidate one another unless the invalidation is part of a larger pattern of organization and qualification.

Basic mechanisms are still basic mechanisms when they are incorporated into larger systems though the context of the system may modify or qualify how the basic mechanisms operate and introduce different probabilistic valences for different outcomes. This is well accepted in developmental biology and other fields (Weiss, 1971). How far can this position be taken with respect to human development and behavior? Are there basic mechanisms about which there is now consensus? One of the problems in answering the first question about a position with respect to basic mechanisms is where to look for descriptions of the mechanisms. For the behaviorists the rat, the pigeon, the dog, and the non-human primate were equivalent to the child where language was not involved, and much of the basic data on the laws of response acquisition and learning cited in our textbooks were investigated in animal laboratories. Because it is obvious that the developing human organism is considerably more complex than any non-human animal and develops in a social context that has no parallel in the non-human world, some are ready to dismiss the laws derived from experiments with non-humans as irrelevant to human functioning or as being so limited in what they describe as to refer to essentially trivial phenomena.

It is true that there are no analogs in the animal world for much of what is interesting and central to human functioning. On the other hand, is it not possible that there are basic behavioral mechanisms that are imbedded within the complex context of the human organism's socializing milieu? If this were to be the case the challenge would be several-fold: To describe the basic mechanisms, to determine how much of the phenomena of interest they can encompass, to seek basic mechanisms at different levels of functions, and to discover how the various levels and mechanisms interact under different sets of conditions. It is quite conceivable that conditioning is a basic mechanism in human development that interacts with genetic phenomena and social contexts so that when a large enough picture of development is drawn we will understand how conditioning works, how it is qualified and how much of developmental phenomena can be accounted for in terms of conditioning. From such a perspective, conditioning will provide an adequate explanation for some phenomena at some levels of functioning, and an inadequate explanation for others. In other words, conditioning may well account for some very simple phenomena but not other simple phenomena, and for some very complex phenomena but not other complex phenomena. Rovee-Collier's (1986) recent discussion of the ubiquity of classical conditioning as a process accounting for the acquisition of important behaviors in all species is a case in point.

It is quite conceivable that animal analogs will unlock some lawful relationships that apply to the child but be totally inadequate and inappropriate for other lawful relationships. Vygotsky believed that the mechanisms of development are rooted in society and culture via the internalization of culturally produced sign systems that bring about behavioral transformations. He did not feel that animal analogs would have much applicability to illuminating the development of the child. On the other hand, there may be no essential incompatibility between basic laws of learning (derived from experiments with animals) and the processes that may be involved in some portion of the kinds of behavioral transformations that Vygotsky identified.

At the risk of reducing this discussion to a terribly simple level, it can be observed that when two parts of hydrogen combine with one part of oxygen the inevitable result on this planet is water. The splitting of the atom and whatever paradigm shifts have occurred in chemistry have not nullified that relationship. In the search for an understanding of developmental processes and in the frustrations that more than 60 years of research have produced there are now many small relationships in our scientific chest, but little consensus with respect to a dominant theory around which to organize and integrate the relationships. There has been a tendency to pronounce new paradigms and to dismiss demonstrated relationships as either trivial or not applicable to the complexity of development. A proliferation of new schemes appeals to ecology and ethology in an attempt to get at properties of systems that alternative schemes do not encompass. The inventors of the new schemes make little effort to determine how much of what they are dismissing could be incorporated in the new conceptualizations. Such behavior fits Kuhn's (1970) description of a science in its pre-paradigmatic phase or Laudan's (1977, 1981) ideas about competing research programs. Would it be worthwhile, however, to attempt to agree upon a set of facts and to examine theoretical constructions in a systematic manner so as to arrive at a model that incorporates existing facts? Might such a model of development serve for the derivation of testable hypotheses? Could efforts to expand the data base be made while ignoring, for the moment, discordant data—all in the interest of seeing how far a particular model might go? If such a set of propositions appears to be reasonable, it may be possible to enter a paradigmatic phase and carry out normal science until such time as an empirically verifiable "revolution" occurs. Then a paradigm shift will not have to be proclaimed. Instead there will be a recognition that it has occurred after it has happened. It is one of the central purposes of this book to explore these questions and to attempt the description of a model that incorporates ideas and data from a number of different sources.

COMPLEXITY, PREDICTION, AND
DEVELOPMENTAL HYPOTHESES

There is no question that the phenomena and processes of development are of a magnitude of complexity that has no parallel in any other science. The human organism likely encompasses the most complex phenomena on this planet and the behavioral system of the human organism is its most complex component. Additionally, it is likely that the behavioral system is an important modifier and generator of the chemical and physical functions within the organism. Thus, behavioral phenomena interact with chemical and physical phenomena and vice versa, amplifying the scientific challenge beyond the dimensions of the challenges already identified in the scientific world. It could be argued that such a challenge cannot be properly addressed given the present state of our knowledge and that any expectation that we might find a dominant theoretical formulation useful for developmental psychology is currently premature.

The failure to arrive at some semi-balance of a theoretical consensus that serves as a general guide to the research enterprise could be thought of as a presently healthy state of affairs. In place of such a dominant consensus related to an overarching, comprehensive developmental theory it might be better to proceed in terms of mini-theories formulated to account for limited behavioral phenomena, specific domains, and particular periods. Thus, the focus might best be oriented to specific question areas that are themselves characterized by more or less dominant theoretical orientations. This could be done without any necessary relationship between theories prevalent in one and another area except in a most loose sense. Investigations of language acquisition during the preschool period may be related to the studies of the acquisition of number concepts during this same period; studies of infant cognitive development may be theoretically related to studies of affective and emotional development during this same period or across adjacent periods. In other words, the islands of phenomena under investigation would be matched by the theoretical disconnectedness of the independent research efforts. True, the supposed "organismic" versus "mechanistic" theoretical dichotomy could serve to stereotype different investigatory lines but this is theory orientation in a most informal sense. In the state of affairs being described here theoretical strengths lie within specific behavioral areas. Little attempt is made to bridge across behavioral areas or developmental periods except in the marriage of mini-intersects such as is found in studies related to "social cognition" or in questions designed to determine the relationship between language acquisition and cognitive development. Under these circumstances, the theoretical excitement lies within the specific areas of investigation or at most in relation to the limited intersects.

A scan of the major developmental journals over the last 10 to 15 years or a review of the program content of the scientific meetings where developmentalists exchange information tends to support this description. It might be said that, in view of the enormous increase in our knowledge of children's behavior during the last 25 to 30 years, the strategy described has been a productive one and that there is no compelling reason to advocate a different approach at the present time. There is validity to such a position but there are consequences that affect both the kind of scientific progress that can be made and the kinds of questions that are likely to be asked. The consequences tend to push us in the direction of not asking strong developmental questions, of asking developmental questions that are specific to particular behavioral outcomes, and of ignoring the likely integrative nature of domain interactions that produce developmental outcome. The notion of "strong developmental questions" is a potentially important one. Strong developmental questions involve looking at a behavior or a behavioral system in terms of onset or initial appearance, describing the course of its development, determining the variables and parameters that come to play significant roles at different points in development, and attempting to provide a comprehensive account of what determines developmental outcome. Strong developmental questions involve not only normative questions over time but also, and most importantly, process questions. In the absence of a general theory of development or a generalizable theoretical model of development, it is difficult to formulate strong developmental questions. Instead, we ask a developmental question specific to particular behavioral outcomes and we ignore the complex interactions that are almost surely the norm and not the exception in behavioral development. Or, mistakenly, we use correlational data between two time periods as revealing something about processes.

Some examples may be useful to make these points concrete. Unless one takes an extreme hereditarian point of view, it is reasonable to assume that environmental experience has some impact on developmental outcomes. A strong developmental question with respect to environmental experience would involve asking how social and non-social stimulation, in what combinations of intensity, level, and variety, contribute to cognitive and personality functioning over time. Similarly, there has been an increased appreciation of the importance of individual difference parameters in how environmental stimulation is mediated and how they affect developmental outcome. A strong developmental question in this area might focus upon individual styles relating to social and non-social stimulation and the role of these individual differences in determining how particular experiences affect individual functioning situationally and over time. Finally, a last example: as a result of the intense research on cognitive development during the last 25 years we have an extensive data base that describes the general course of cognitive development in children. A strong developmental question would raise the issue of how affective and social factors interact to determine the circumstances that produce optimal cognitive functioning and whether or not the factors and circumstances change across the developmental span. There is no way that a correlation relating cognitive performance at 5 years of age and cognitive performance at 12 years of age can tell us anything about the processes involved, even though low correlations of this kind have led to pronouncements affirming basic "discontinuities" in development.

There are obvious problems in posing strong developmental questions. Some might assert that strong developmental questions are premature given our current understanding of development. Clearly, strong developmental questions are more likely to be stated in the context of research that is designed to gather data longitudinally or employing a developmental cross-sectional approach. Such research is not only expensive but, again, may be premature. On the other hand, if the theoretical or structural model that inspires and guides research is not sufficiently complex to accommodate the strong developmental questions, indeed to stimulate them, then they are not likely to be asked and our knowledge base will not be pushed to expand in the direction of approximating the complexity of the phenomena that are inherent in human development. Unnecessarily simplistic interpretations of data tend to be encouraged; correlational data become the basis for explanation of process. As has been noted, recent failures to predict later developmental outcome from early observations have produced declarations that there is no continuity in development from early to late. This reveals a lack of understanding that such data need to be understood in terms of the processes that are responsible for the facts. They cannot, by themselves, constitute evidence that enables us to declare the presence or absence of continuity.

Recent growing attention to life-span developmental analyses, to concepts related to transactional approaches (Sameroff, 1983) and formulations such as Lerner's (Lerner & Kaufman, 1985) discussion of contextualism reflect a groping toward posing the stronger developmental questions. A very thoughtful analysis of the early precursors of later depression by Cicchetti and Aber (1986) exemplifies the kind of movement toward asking the more structured developmental question. Cicchetti, like Patterson (1986), adds impact to the questions by focusing, as well, on the issue of the processes involved. Patterson's discussion of the development of antisocial behavior in boys looks to the mechanisms that underlie coercive family systems to produce antisocial patterns in an historical context.

A concern for process is of paramount importance. The term *process* is used here in a very particular manner. It involves the notion that developmental outcome must essentially and ultimately be describable in terms of an equation or groups of equations. When fully specified, the equations will contain the variables involved in development, the relative weighting of the variables, the combinatorial relationships among the variables, and the changing valences and elements that must be factored in over the developmental span. It is likely that the equation will be most useful if it yields outcome predictions stated in terms of a range of probabilities; the more that is known the higher the probability values. A useful theory or model of development will point investigators toward identifying all that must be entered into an equation to account for developmental outcome at any point in time. When an equation is fully specified and tested it will yield predictions because the variables that must be considered and the processes that involve the variables will be understood. The task, then, is to specify the variables and describe the processes.

At the present time there is a better catalog of potentially significant variables than a knowledge of how the variables function in processes, although few developmental scientists have analyzed the state of knowledge in this fashion. Such an analysis would prevent the issuing of simplistic statements that there is no continuity between early and later development. A relatively mundane example may be introduced here: At one point in time a cell is functioning normally; at a later point in time the cell is abnormal (e.g., cancerous). Is this reason to declare that there is discontinuity in cell development? Obviously not. Instead it would be assumed that at one point in time the cell functioned according to certain principles. Then, some factor or factors changed the normal processes into abnormal processes to produce cancer. The scientific challenge here is to understand the normal processes, to determine how normal processes change or are interrupted to produce abnormal processes, and to understand the abnormal processes. Similarly, even if abnormality is not involved but only the fact that basic changes occur in cell functioning, the questions will focus upon understanding the processes and how they change over time to produce the differences. Of such stuff is scientific prediction made. In behavioral science as well as cell biology scientific progress is made from such strategies. This does not obviate the possibility that some developmental changes are quantitative in nature and some qualitative; some gradually incremental and some quantum in character.

A reliance on prediction raises some issues that have been alluded to earlier. One of the concerns related to prediction has to do with the nature of biological systems as open systems in contrast to the mechanical closed systems. As described by von Bertalanffy, the open system is in dynamic development over time tending toward increased organization and stimulated in that organization by intrinsic aspects of the system as well as extrinsic elements. The closed system has all of its structural and process elements defined and determined at the outset; its developmental endpoint is determined by the initial condition. Additionally, the developmental endpoint is likely to be achieved via one or only a few alternative processes. The open system, in contrast, can arrive at the same endpoint via different processes and given different initial conditions, suggesting a much more complex and dynamic level of functioning. A process orientation to human development has been most closely associated with behaviorism and its heavy reliance upon learning and conditioning as the major, sometimes sole, process to account for development. The model of development presented by behaviorism has appeared to be more analogous to the closed system of the machine than to an open biological system that is dynamically affected by intrinsic and extrinsic elements. Behaviorism is said to rely upon the essentially linear model of the machine. The human organism is seen as clearly more complex, more dynamic. Machines are "closed systems"; organisms "open systems." Open systems, according to von Bertalanffy (1968, 1975), are dynamically changing as a function of their interaction with external stimuli. At the risk of some redundancy with earlier discussion, the open system thus appears a more appropriate analogy for human development. The closed system is inappropriate because it has a set of properties that cannot be changed by external stimulation if the system (i.e., machine) is not already programmed to respond to those external stimuli. Additionally, the closed system is finite in its characteristics and response capabilities, the open system theoretically infinite and capable of potentially unlimited combinations and permutations and creative evolution. If there are infinite and unlimited potential outcomes, is prediction possible? Thus, the question of prediction becomes a central one when the organismic model of the open system is adopted as a model appropriate to human development.

Obviously, completely accurate prediction is impossible under conditions of infinite potential outcomes. If it is granted that an open system model of human development is incompatible with complete predictability, and if it is believed that we have not made significant progress toward acquiring a systematic account of complex human behavior and behavioral systems, is it any wonder that some behavioral scientists have become discouraged and disenchanted with the prospects for a reliable scientific account of development or complex behavior? There are a variety of responses to be found in the behavioral science community given the acknowledged complexity of human behavior and its seemingly scientifically unyielding nature. One is to declare for phenomenology and the existential uniqueness of each individual. Psychological accounts, in this approach, become clinical insights supported by some very general principles that serve only as a beginning point for a completely individualistic analysis. Another is to relinquish the search for laws at the behavioral level and to seek to reduce behavior to biochemical and genetic phenomena.

The dramatic advances in the neurosciences and in genetics have made this a particularly attractive alternative for those engaged in some areas of inquiry, especially in the study of language and information processing; similarly this has appealed to some who are concerned with personality development and psychopathology. The third response is one already discussed—namely, to reject any supposed linear, mechanistic model as too simple, to flail at behaviorism as the epitomy of such a model and to aver that a paradigm shift has occurred with two implications. One implication is to dismiss as trivial whatever laws the simpler model described. The other implication is to claim that prediction and understanding of human behavior are, in principle, limited to those areas of behavioral functioning that are the least significant and meaningful for the human organism (e.g., Koch, 1981).

Several problems arise from each of these points of view. To adopt the phenomenological point of view is essentially to abandon science as a strategy for enlarging our systemic understanding of human development or behavior. However clinically useful for individual cases, and however personally satisfying the phenomenological approach, the knowledge gained remains always particularistic and never generalizable except as a starting tentative hypothesis for the next individual analysis. The second alternative, reductionism, always has been and will continue to be an attractive alternative. Because the human organism is a biological system that encompasses events described within the domains of physics and chemistry, and because dramatic advances have been made in the neurosciences and in genetics, it is ever tempting to think that the behavioral phenomena that seem so messy and complex might be more easily analyzed and explained by translating them and fitting them into more highly organized and replicable non-behavioral phenomena. Whenever evidence is reported that some language and information processing behaviors appear to be more easily understood in terms of neural biochemistry and neurophysiology and that some pathological behaviors appear to be understandable in terms of deviant biochemical phenomena or as having genetic markers, the impetus to entertain a reductionist model is strengthened. However, there is also increasing evidence for the complementary side of the coin: Behavior can alter biochemical phenomena and affect neurophysiological development and functioning. Thus, it is unlikely that a reductionist approach will succeed except for some particular behaviors.

Finally, we return to the third alternative—declaring behaviorism as obsolete and averring the supremacy of an open systems model. This often tends toward a kind of romanticism about an organismic approach as better capturing the essence of human functioning in its full flowered complexity. But this has also been accompanied by something of a retreat from the notion that what we are about as scientists studying development and developmental process is the rigorous pursuit of laws of development and that those laws will involve the description of basic processes that may well include the base elements of conditioning as they function in lower animals. If one does not retreat from a basic process orientation it does not mean that we cannot entertain the notion that other processes may have to be introduced to understand more complex and specifically human behavior; it does not mean that we must reject ideas related to biological reorganization and modification and qualification of basic processes, perhaps including the appearance of new processes at different points in development. All of these possibilities contain hypotheses that need to be entertained in a comprehensive account of human development and that are compatible with an open systems model. But such ideas do not obviate the basic scientific credo that there are processes, that there are laws, and that the scientific challenge is to discover and illuminate these. Further, the question of how fully we can predict human behavior and development is an empirical one and not a philosophical one. There may well be limitations on the extent of prediction and on the level of complexity that can be accounted for in a predictive model. But this is not reason to declare the entire enterprise of understanding development as outside the realm of science. Nor is it reason to abandon the search for a theory or structural model that is based upon the premise that there are processes and lawful relationships to be described.

THE PURPOSES AND PLAN OF THE BOOK

There is, now, a full circle to noting the purposes of this book. One is to examine questions of method and strategy in developmental research and to discuss models of development. Another is to try to estimate the degree to which there is an existing knowledge base that stands as replicated fact and constitutes what can be claimed as knowledge about human development. Still another purpose is to consider the standard current theories that vie, more or less, for the allegiance of developmentalists. In this regard there is a discussion of the issues that have been introduced into the discourse concerning theories of development but that have been outside of the traditional theoretical approaches. An exploration of the relevance of various methodological approaches to the different accounts of development is also made. Finally, there is an attempt to develop a line of argument that culminates in the proposition that a different synthesis and a more complex structural/behavioral model of development is needed. It is argued that such a model will prove useful as a basic guiding approach to formulating specific research questions and strong developmental questions. Such a model, even if not representative of a true paradigm in the Kuhnian sense, could perhaps lead us to a more fully paradigmatic phase of behavioral science. Inherent in this argument are claims that more consensus exists than is often acknowledged and that the current theoretical morass that characterizes approaches to the study of behavioral development is not necessary.

A set of basic themes have characterized developmental theories: growth, structure, systems, response acquisition, mechanisms, environment, culture. Over the course of this book these themes are considered as they have been expressed by Gesell, Piaget, Freud, and the behaviorists although a systematic account of each of these major theories is not presented (see footnote 1). There are also the themes and their variations as they have appeared in the writings of Kuo, Vygotsky, and Hebb. Development is discussed in terms of roots in the ecological, ethological, neurological, neuroscience, and developmental biology literatures. Throughout, a set of issues that needs to be addressed in the context of any developmental theory that purports to guide us toward an adequate account of development is entertained: Are there stages/sequences that can be used to describe development and what functions do they play in developmental processes; how can we account for the different domains of development (i.e., cognition, motor development, social, emotional, language development, etc.), and what interaction between them is posited; in what manner is the matter of continuity–discontinuity handled, and what is the relation of process to this topic; how is the topography of development and the level of quality of developmental functioning considered and/or differentiated; how is developmental process described, and what changes or evolution of processes over time must be considered; how is the environment conceptualized in relation to biological structure and genetics; what is the functional role of individual difference parameters? The evidential base concerning development that has emerged from the research traditions that have evolved under the general umbrella of different theoretical orientations is also discussed and an attempt is made to try to assay the extent to which that knowledge base is supportive of the theory that generated the research.

Chapter 2 is devoted to the concepts of growth, structure, and system. Although a somewhat arbitrary grouping of notions, they tend to dominate the theories of Gesell, Piaget, and the cognitivists. We concentrate our most intensive discussion of the ideas of Gesell and Piaget in this chapter. Chapter 3 involves consideration of questions related to processes and mechanisms as they have been treated by Gesell and Piaget but particularly as they have played central roles in behavioristic accounts of development. In chapter 4, the larger conceptualizations of environment and culture as they relate to development are discussed. In chapter 5, an integration and a synthesis is attempted with respect to data and with respect to the major theoretical themes in terms of a particular structural/behavioral model of development.

A very brief presentation of this model is provided here because it may help the reader obtain a better picture of where the arguments being made in the chapters that follow will lead. The model has evolved since it was first presented in the context of a Presidential Address to the Division of Developmental Psychology of the American Psychological Association in 1978 (Horowitz, 1978). It has been published at various times in the context of other discussions (e.g., Horowitz, 1984; Horowitz & O'Brien, 1985). In its form it is an adaptation of a model originally proposed by Gowen (1952, 1962). Gowen used it to analyze the relationship of the resiliency and susceptibility of an organism to bacterial infection. The Horowitz adaptation of the model is shown in Fig. 1.1.

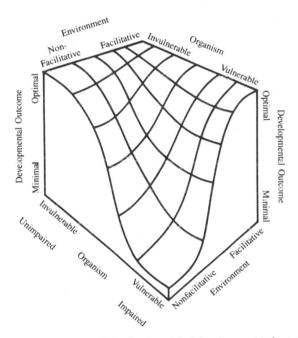

FIG. 1.1. The Structural/Behavioral model of development (adapted from Gowen, 1952.)

The dimensions of the model involve the organism and the environment and developmental outcome or status. The organism in this model can be characterized along two independent continua: impairment and resiliency. The organism, at any point in time, can be said to range along the continuum of being unimpaired to impaired. Impairment is domain specific in the

sense that an organism can be impaired, for example, in the motoric
domain but not in the cognitive domain; the organism could be impaired in
more than one or in all developmental domains. Similarly, the organism, at
any point in time, can be said to range along the continuum of vulnerability
or resiliency; individuals can be characterized as highly invulnerable or
resilient, or efficient and effective in the use of environmental experience
all the way to being quite vulnerable (i.e., not resilient and not making or
perhaps not being able to make good and effective use of environmental
experience).

The organismic dimension of invulnerability–vulnerability can be domain
specific and an individual's place on that continuum can change over time.
The organismic dimension is not, as some have wished to interpret it,
analogous to genetic endowment because it reflects both the genetic and
the cumulative biological and environmental impact of experience that
determines organismic impairment and vulnerability over the course of
development.

The environmental dimension is labeled as ranging on a continuum of
being facilitative of development to being non-facilitative of development.
As with the organismic dimension, this dimension is domain specific. For
example, an environment may be very facilitative of motor development
but not of cognitive development. Similarly, the role of the environment in
each domain may differ over time. The environment may be highly facilitative
of language development during the period of infancy but not at later
stages of development.

The surface of the model represents the adequacy of developmental
outcome or status at any point in time. The lower, near quadrant depicts
poor developmental outcome; the far high quadrant of the surface represents optimal or good developmental status. The adequacy of developmental outcome is also conceived as being domain specific, permitting the
obvious outcome profile of differential levels of developmental status in
different domains at any given point in time. Over the course of development the adequacy of developmental status in given domains may move
across the surface to reflect continuities and discontinuities of development.

The model shown in Fig. 1.1 represents an attempt to focus on a
theoretical strategy that permits an incorporation of the data base that now
appears to exist so that testable hypotheses about development and developmental outcome can be generated. Consideration is given as to how the
model can aid us in dealing with questions of useful levels of analysis for
understanding complex variables such as socioeconomic status; how it can
help to describe universal laws, while at the same time delineating the
cultural variabilities that must be taken into account; and how it is possible
to entertain a sensible set of alternatives to the questions of genetic deter-
minism and the nature–nurture continuum.

It has been traditional to oppose theoretical orientations with phrases like "nature–nurture," "active–passive," "mechanistic–organismic" and to claim that one or the other term in the phrase connotes a world view about human development and involves diametrically different philosophical ideas about the very essential nature of the human organism. There has been a tendency to cast orientations into the good–bad, or nice–harsh dimensions as when behaviorism is labeled *the mechanical mirror* and Piagetian ideas *the organic lamp* (Langer, 1969). Such strategies have not been productive and it is likely that the implicit and explicit characterizations have encouraged a mistakenly dichotomous approach to conceptualizing development. Geneticists no longer consider the heredity–environment discussion a meaningful way in which to organize theory or data and this has been true for developmental biologists already for many years. Oyama's (1985) analysis of this issue makes it clear that psychologists must follow suit. Behavioral scientists would also be advised to abandon the active–passive, mechanistic–organismic appositions. They neither provide for a coherent organization of existing data nor lead to the formulation of useful questions. Further, as is discussed, it is possible to consider the so-called mechanistic and organismic orientations as both useful for different kinds of phenomena and at different levels of analysis.

This book concludes with some restatement of the basic themes and a consideration of the implications of the new synthesis for the science of human development and its current and potential applications. Each chapter may be thought of as an essay on the concepts, ideas, and theoretical orientations that currently permeate our thinking about behavioral development. These essays are characterized by "theme and variation." This theme and variation strategy involves some redundancy and repetition as ideas and concepts are reintroduced, played out in a different key and reanalyzed. Hopefully, as in a good symphony, the final synthesis will give rise to an integrated statement that contains the elements that make for the aesthetic unities that are to be found in both art and science.

REFERENCES

Baldwin, A. (1980) *Theories of child development.* New York: Wiley.

Barker, P., & Gholson, B. (1984). The history of the psychology of learning as a rational process: Lakatos versus Kuhn. In H. W. Reese (Ed.), *Advances in child development and behavior* (Vol. 18, pp. 227–244). New York: Academic Press.

Borstelmann, L. J. (1983). Children before psychology. In P. H. Mussen (Ed.), *Handbook of child psychology* (4th Ed., Vol. 1, pp. 1–140). W. Kessen (Ed.), *History, theory, and methods.* New York: Wiley.

Broughton, J. M., & Freeman-Moir, D. J. (1982). *The cognitive developmental psychology of*

James Mark Baldwin: Current theory and research on genetic epistemology. Norwood, NJ: Ablex.

Cairns, R. B. (1983). The emergence of developmental psychology. In P. H. Mussen (Ed.), *Handbook of child psychology* (4th Ed., Vol. 1, pp. 41–102). W. Kessen (Ed.), *History, theory and methods.* New York: Wiley.

Cicchetti, D., & Aber, J. L. (1986). Early precursors of later depression: An organizational perspective. In L. P. Lipsitt & C. Rovee-Collier (Eds.), *Advances in infancy research* (Vol. 4, pp. 87–137). Norwood, NJ: Ablex.

Cole, S., Cole, J., & Dietrich, L. (1978). Measuring the cognitive state of scientific disciplines. In Y. Elkana, J. Lederberg, R. Merton, A. Thackray, & H. Zuckerman (Eds.), *Toward a metric of science: The advent of science indicators* (pp. 209–251). New York: Wiley.

Flavell, J. (1963). *The developmental psychology of Jean Piaget.* Princeton, NJ: Van Nostrand.

Freud, S. (1953). Three essays on the theory of sexuality. In J. Strachey (Ed.), Freud, S. *The Standard Edition of the Complete Psychological Works.* Vol. XVII. London: Hogarth Press. (Originally published 1905)

Gesell, A. (1925). *The mental growth of the preschool child.* New York: Macmillan.

Gesell, A. (1928). *Infancy and human growth.* New York: Macmillan.

Gottlieb, G. (1983). The psychobiological approach to developmental issues. In P.H. Mussen (Ed.), *Handbook of child psychology* (4th Ed., Vol. II, pp. 1–26). M.M. Haith & J.J. Campos (Ed.), *Infancy and developmental psychobiology.* New York: Wiley.

Gowen, J. W. (1952). Humoral and cellular elements in natural and acquired resistance to typhoid. *American Journal of Human Genetics, 4,* 285–301.

Gowen, J. W. (1962). Genetic patterns in senescence and infection. *Journal of American Geriatrics Society, 10,* 107–124.

Hebb, D. O. (1949). *The organization of behavior.* New York: Wiley.

Hebb, D. O. (1980). *Essay on mind.* Hillsdale, NJ: Lawrence Erlbaum Associates.

Horowitz, F. D. (1969). Learning, developmental research, and individual differences. In L. P. Lipsitt & H. W. Reese (Eds.), *Advances in child development and behavior* (Vol. IV, pp. 84–126). New York: Academic Press.

Horowitz, F. D. (1978). *Toward a functional analysis of individual differences.* Presidential address to the Division of Developmental Psychology, American Psychological Association meetings, Toronto, Canada.

Horowitz, F. D. (1984). The psychobiology of parent–offspring relations in high-risk situations. In L. P. Lipsitt & C. Rovee-Collier (Eds.), *Advances in infancy research* (Vol. 3, pp. 1–22). Norwood, NJ: Ablex.

Horowitz, F. D., & O'Brien, M. (1985). Epilogue: Research and developmental perspectives. In F. D. Horowitz & M. O'Brien (Eds.), *The gifted and the talented: Developmental perspectives* (pp. 437–454). Washington, DC: American Psychological Association.

Hunt, J. McV. (1961). *Intelligence and experience.* New York: Ronald Press.

Kagan, J. (1978). *Infancy.* Cambridge, MA: Harvard University Press.

Kessen, W. (Ed.). (1983). *History, theory and methods* (Vol. 1). In P. H. Mussen (Eds.), *Handbook of child psychology* (4th Ed.). New York: Wiley.

Koch, S. (1981). The nature and limits of psychological knowledge. *American Psychologist, 36,* 257–269.

Kuo, Z.-Y. (1967). *The dynamics of behavior development.* New York: Random House.

Kuhn, T. (1970), *The structure of scientific revolutions.* Chicago: University of Chicago Press.

Laboratory of Comparative Human Cognition. (1983). Culture and cognitive development. In P.H. Mussen (Ed.), *Handbook of child psychology* (4th Ed., Vol. I, pp. 295–356). W. Kessen (Ed.), *History, theory and methods.* New York: Wiley.

Lakatos, I. (1970). Falsification and the methodology of scientific research programs. In

I. Lakatos & A. Musgrave (Eds.). *Criticism and the growth of knowledge* (pp. 91-196). London & New York: Cambridge University Press.

Lakatos, I. (1978). *The methodology of scientific research programs.* London & New York: Cambridge University Press.

Langer, J. (1969). *Theories of development.* New York: Holt, Rinehart & Winston.

Laudan, L. (1977). *Progress and its problems.* Berkeley: University of California Press.

Laudan, L. (1981). *Science and hypothesis.* Boston: D. Reidel.

Lerner, R. M. (1976). *Concepts and theories of human development.* Reading, MA: Addison-Wesley.

Lerner, R. M., & Kaufman, M. B. (1985). The concept of development in contextualism. *Developmental Review, 5,* 309-333.

Luria, A. R. (1976). *Cognitive development. Its cultural and social foundations.* Cambridge, MA: Harvard University Press.

Luria, A. R. (1981). *Language and cognition.* New York: Wiley.

Mason, W. (1979). Ontogeny of social behavior. In P. Marler & J. G. Vandenbergh (Eds.), *Handbook of behavioral neurobiology* (pp. 1-28). New York: Plenum Press.

Miller, N. E. (1941). The frustration–aggression hypothesis. *Psychological Review, 48,* 337-342.

Miller, N. E., & Dollard, J. (1941). *Social learning and imitation.* New Haven, CT: Yale University Press.

Miller, P. H. (1983). *Theories of developmental psychology.* San Francisco: Freeman.

Minuchin, P. P., & Shapiro, E. K. (1983). The school as a context for social development. In P.H. Mussen (Ed.), *Handbook of child psychology* (Vol. IV, pp. 197-274). E. M. Hetherington (Ed.), *Socialization, personality, and social development.* New York: Wiley.

Mussen, P. H. (Ed.). (1983). *Handbook of child psychology.* New York: Wiley.

Overton, W. F. (1984). World views and their influence on psychological theory and research: Kuhn-Lakatos-Laudan. In H. W. Reese (Ed.), *Advances in child development and behavior* (Vol. 18, pp. 191-226). New York: Academic Press.

Oyama, S. (1985). *The ontogeny of information.* Cambridge: Cambridge University Press.

Palermo, D. S. (1984). In defense of Kuhn: A discussion of his detractors. In H. W. Reese (Ed.), *Advances in child development and behavior* (Vol. 18, pp. 259-272). New York. Academic Press.

Patterson, G. (1986). Performance models for antisocial boys. *American Psychologist, 41,* 432-444.

Piaget, J. (1926). *The language and thought of the child.* New York: Harcourt, Brace.

Piaget, J. (1971). *Biology and knowledge.* Chicago: University of Chicago Press.

Piaget, J. (1980). *Adaptation and intelligence.* Chicago: University of Chicago Press.

Preyer, W. (1909a). *The mind of the child. Part I: The senses and the will.* New York: D. Appleton. (Originally published in German, 1881-82)

Preyer, W. (1909b). *The mind of the child. Part II: The development of the intellect.* New York: D. Appleton. (Originally published in German, 1881-82)

Rovee-Collier, C. (1986). The rise and fall of infant classical conditioning research: Its promise for the study of early infant development. In L. P. Lipsitt & C. Rovee-Collier (Eds.), *Advances in infancy research* (Vol. 4, pp. 139-159). Norwood, NJ: Ablex.

Sameroff, A. J. (1983). Developmental systems: Contexts and evolution. In P.H. Mussen (Ed.), *Handbook of child psychology* (Vol. I, pp. 237-294). W. Kessen (Ed.), *History, theory and methods.* New York: Wiley.

Scarr, S., & Kidd, K. (1983). Developmental behavior genetics. In P.H. Mussen (Ed.), *Handbook of child psychology* (Vol. II, pp. 345-433). M.M. Haith & J.J. Campos (Eds.), *Infancy and developmental psychobiology.* New York: Wiley.

Sears, R. R. (1975). Your ancients revisited: A history of child development. In E.M. Hetherington

(Ed.), *Review of child development research.* (Vol. 5, pp. 1-73). Chicago: University of Chicago Press.

Siegler, R. S. (1983). Information processing approaches to development. In P.H. Mussen (Ed.), *Handbook of child psychology* (Vol. 1, pp. 129-211). W. Kessen (Ed.), *History, theory and methods.* New York: Wiley.

Sternberg, R. J., & Powell, J. S. (1983). The development of intelligence. In P.H. Mussen (Ed.), *Handbook of child psychology* (Vol. III, pp. 341-419). J. H. Flavell & E. M. Markman (Eds.), *Cognitive development.* New York: Wiley.

Stevenson, H. (1983). How children learn—the quest for a theory. In P.H. Mussen (Ed.), *Handbook of child psychology* (Vol. I, pp. 213-236). W. Kessen (Ed.), *History, theory and methods.* New York: Wiley.

Thomas, R. M. (1979). *Comparing theories of child development.* Belmont, CA: Wadsworth.

von Bertalanffy, L. (1968). *General system theory.* New York: George Braziller. (Rev. Ed.).

von Bertalanffy, L. (1975). *Perspectives on general system theory.* New York: George Braziller.

Vygotsky, L. S. (1962). *Thought and language.* Cambridge, MA: MIT Press.

Vygotsky, L. S. (1978). *Mind in society.* Cambridge, MA: Harvard University Press.

Watson, J. B. (1914). *Behavior: An introduction to comparative psychology.* New York: Holt.

Watson, J. B., & Morgan, J. J. B. (1917). Emotional reactions and psychological experimentation. *American Journal of Psychology, 28,* 163-174.

Watson, J. B., & Rayner, R. (1920). Conditioned emotional reactions. *Journal of Experimental Psychology, 3,* 1-14.

Weiss, P. A. (1971). *Hierarchically organized systems in theory and practice.* New York: Hafner.

Wertsch, J. V. (1979). From social interaction to higher psychological processes. A clarification and application of Vygotsky's theory. *Human Development, 22,* 1-22.

White, B. L. (1975). *The first three years of life.* Englewood Cliffs, NJ: Prentice-Hall.

Zuckerman, H., & Merton, R. (1973). Age, aging and age structure in science. In R. K. Merton, *The sociology of science* (pp. 497-559). Chicago: University of Chicago Press.

2

Organismic Theory: Stage, Structure, and System

Systematic observers of children have typically commented upon three characteristics of development: (a) there is a remarkable correspondence among normal children with respect to the general behaviors and capabilities that develop; (b) the appearance and transformation of those abilities tend to occur along a quite similar timetable and sequence in most children; and (c) there is a tendency for deviations and deflections from the normal course of development to be short-lived and of temporary influence with respect to a developmental trajectory. All of this appears to occur despite seemingly wide variations in the environments in which children grow and develop. The facts of such universalities have greatly informed and helped shape the major theoretical efforts of James Mark Baldwin, Arnold Gesell, Jean Piaget, and Heinz Werner. Each sought to understand human development in the context of inherent biological characteristics that provide a basic template for forming and guiding the behavioral development of the child—albeit searching as well for some of the psychological properties and principles unique to the human organism. The assumptions that underlie such conceptualizations, the phenomena for which these theorists tried to account, the data bases that contributed to them, and the manner in which these viewpoints were applied to questions of stages, continuities, and domains, require analysis in order to evaluate the contributions they can make to a productive modern developmental model or theory. The basic approach embodied in these theories has been compelling and dominant in American developmental psychology for almost 30 years. They have, however, some serious limitations and these need to be considered along with other viewpoints and other facts.

29

Baldwin, Gesell, Werner, and Piaget, spanning collectively almost 100 years of scientific activity, are tied together by two basic emphases. One involves an intellectual and scientific commitment to the central relevance of evolution and the need to place the human in a context of evolutionary history in order to understand human ontogenetic development. From this perspective the second emphasis follows. Human behavior is organized across a continuum of time in which structural development and transformation occur in a cyclic fashion to foster and make development possible. The specific mechanisms proposed by each of the theorists differed or were variants. As well, there is a difference in the degree to which a comparative developmental approach is featured. However, each viewed human behavioral development as being at the apex of the evolutionary course. Many of the behavioral characteristics and some of the mechanisms were viewed as having come into existence along various points in the evolutionary stream, observable in more primitive forms among other members of the animal kingdom. The human behavioral repertoire and its development were seen as incorporating those evolutionarily surviving aspects and building and elaborating upon them to form the creative edge of evolutionary history.

The perspective that derives from this basic orientation shapes the entire manner in which the development of the child is seen. That shaping involves, at its core, the notion of structure. *Structure* has been variously defined by different theorists. For Gesell it was a physical entity that permitted behavioral function; for Piaget it was a system of rules and transformations that governed thought processes at a particular point in time. In its most generic sense, structure is used to refer to a unit of organization that, by its existence, exerts functional control over behavior. Particularly in relation to cognitive and mental development, but applied to social and moral and language development as well, the ontogenetic evolution and transformation of structural characteristics defines the progress of development from infancy to adulthood. This builds upon the embryological structural course prior to birth and mirrors, partially, the phylogenetic history of the organism. However, the degree to which biological structures are models for behavioral or psychological structures varies considerably in the different theories.

Structure can serve as an organizing principle. It can also be the vehicle for development, with different emphases given to mechanisms and descriptors, depending on whether the theorist is Baldwin or Gesell or Piaget or Werner. What is shared in this perspective is a way of looking at facts of development and of organizing those facts so as to arrive at universal principles of development. In contrast to the cumulative analysis of development espoused by some behaviorists, the structuralist approach posits developmental periods or stages that embody a set of organizing characteristics that govern behavior during each developmental epoch. These organizing principles are considered to permeate the behavioral functioning of the child at any particular point in time, leading to the characterization of the point of view as "organic" in its emphasis. Further, growth and development are typically viewed as an outcome of adaptive, transactional processes that involve the organism in an interaction with the environment. This leads to the further characterization of this general approach as one that claims for the organism an "active" as opposed to a "passive" role in its own development. Finally, recognition of the regularity and universality of the developmental course, despite environmental variations, produced the belief that there is an inevitability to developmental progress laid down by the biological nature of the organism. This involves a structural progression of development that is innate or innately predispositioned.

Speaking of development from a *comparative and organismic point of view* (Werner, 1957a) or in terms of *genetic epistemology* (Baldwin, 1906; Piaget, 1952) or as *developmental patterning* (Gesell, 1954) and use of terms such as *reciprocal interweaving* (Gesell, 1954), *assimilation and accommodation* (Baldwin, 1906; Piaget, 1952), *equilibration* (Piaget, 1952), and *hierarchic integration* (Werner, 1957a, 1957b), have all involved presuppositions that the course of development is not linear. The processes of development in these theories are described as something of a see-saw interaction between the organism and the environment whereby the response repertoire evolves and sometimes regresses in successive passes at approximating an understanding of and an ability to correctly negotiate the real world.

In illustrating and discussing what is involved in this general approach to development and to evaluate the knowledge base in terms of this central point of view, the focus will be on the work of Arnold Gesell and of Jean Piaget, bringing in some of Werner's ideas more tangentially. James Mark Baldwin predated and influenced Piaget (Piaget, 1982), and Werner's developmental theory and work cut a broader path than any other developmental theory (with the possible exception of Freud) in relation to life-span concepts and the phenomena he considered. However, Baldwin's influence on contemporary developmental theory has been largely indirect and Werner's was rather restricted even though some recent publications have tried to focus more attention on the work of Baldwin and on Werner (see Barten & Franklin, 1978; Broughton & Freeman-Moir, 1982).

The concepts of "stage" and "structure" have been work-horse ideas in developmental psychology. They also have served developmental biology but in a larger context of system organization (Weiss, 1971). More recently, as noted in chapter 1, developmental psychologists have taken up the concept of "system," with considerable attention being given to general systems theory. A consideration of systems, therefore, follows the discussion of stages and structures. The concepts within general systems theory that have been most appealing to developmental psychologists and other developmentalists are discussed. The basic purpose of our consideration of stage, structure, and system is to undertake a critical analysis of these concepts toward the goal of incorporating some of their dimensions into the proposed model of development that could serve a productive developmental research agenda. In order to set the base understanding for what is discussed there is some rather elementary explication of the concepts involved and how they have been used by different theorists but a systematic presentation of each theory in its full form is not attempted.

GESELL'S STRUCTURES AND STAGES

For Arnold Gesell, steeped as he was in the traditions of evolutionary history and comparative biology, and influenced significantly by his teachers, G. E. Coghill and G. Stanley Hall, the task in understanding development was to describe the form and patterning of behavioral development, to elucidate the principles by which the form and patterning occurred and thus to understand not individual behaviors but the operation of the child's "total action system." Behavior was to be seen in the context of a system that had structure and that evolved in terms of what he called principles of developmental morphology applied to behavior. His strongest observations and his most intense theoretical analyses were focused upon the first two years of life, although he believed the basic principles extended across the period from conception to adulthood. His summative statement, almost at the end of his career, was "The Ontogenesis of Infant Behavior" (Gesell, 1954), and it is a grand presentation of a quite consistent point of view that had a profound impact upon how Americans thought about children for many years. Cairns (1983) regrets that few currently include Gesell as a developmental theorist. Indeed, Alfred Baldwin in his *Theories of Child Development* (1967, 1980) omits any reference to Gesell and two other texts on developmental theory give him only scant mention (Lerner, 1976; Miller, 1983). Yet in his very thoughtful discussion of developmental stages, Wohlwill (1973) clearly recognizes the importance of Gesell and his contributions and it is useful to review Gesell's principles and his data base for their influence on how we think about development and for the contribution they make to the discussion of the major issues and questions.

Principles of Developmental Morphology

Gesell proposed five principles of developmental morphology: The Principle of Developmental Direction, the Principle of Functional Asymmetry, the Principle of Reciprocal Interweaving, the Principle of Individuating Maturation, and the Principle of Self-Regulatory Fluctuation. All were in service of trying to understand the organizing principles that determine the growth of the organism both physiologically and behaviorally. Gesell took the point of view that physiological concepts related to morphology could be applied to behavior: "Psychological growth, like somatic growth, is a morphogenetic process" (Gesell, 1954, p. 338). Structural development underlay functional behavior and the principles Gesell proposed would, he believed, account for the expression of function as reflective of the development of structure. In this analysis, behavior cannot appear unless the physiological structure has "matured" but the appearance and development of the behavioral repertoire could be described by the five principles. The Principle of Developmental Direction was clearly close to the facts of physical growth and development: Behavioral development tends to occur in "successive sweeps" from head to foot and from "central to peripheral segments." Although exceptions are to be found, the general principle holds—especially in the early years of life. Except for the structure–function relationship, which is present in the other principles as well, this principle does not bear directly upon the issues central to our discussion at this point. The Principle of Functional Asymmetry is somewhat of a corollary to the Principle of Reciprocal Interweaving and also does not figure prominently in our concerns.

The Principle of Reciprocal Interweaving, the Principle of Individuating Maturation, and the Principle of Self-Regulatory Fluctuation are very germaine to the larger issues of developmental mechanisms. Each reflects processes and mechanisms that have been suggested (in variant forms) to explain the patterning of the growth of behavior in all of the structurally oriented theories. Gesell makes quite clear that these principles were proposed almost as metaphors to extract the patterned aspects of the processes thought to underlie the development of behavior. However, the metaphorical nature was intended to imply guiding neurological operations characteristic of the species. For example, the Principle of Reciprocal Interweaving refers to complementary elements of what Sherrington (1906) called the "law of reciprocal innervation" in which there is action and counter-action that each time takes the organism to a slightly higher level of organized activity. Gesell characterized the process: "neurologically, this process implies an intricate cross-stitching or involuted interlacing which organizes opposing muscle systems into reciprocal and increasingly mature relationships. Functionally, such a process results in a progressive spiral kind of reincorporation of sequential forms of behavior" (Gesell, 1954, p. 342). The qualification for this Principle was the Principle of Functional Asymmetry that recognized the presence of some asymmetric elements in development. These were considered important because they helped to focus the child directionally toward certain functional dominances such as handedness and eye dominance. Evolutionarily, functional asymmetries had survival value—the prime example being the tonic neck reflex (TNR) in infants. The asymmetrical orientation that typifies the TNR interferes with any tendency to proneness that would result in suffocation. It was also thought to facilitate an angular approach to the world. The duality of symmetry and asymmetry was considered by Gesell as insuring the organism a higher probability of access to information about the environment than if only one form of orientation were involved.

The Principle of Individuating Maturation and the Principle of Self-Regulatory Fluctuation together represent the core zeitgeist view of behavioral development that is characteristic of the structural–organic approach. In the Principle of Individuating Maturation, Gesell stated the primacy of maturational mechanisms as in basic control of the development of behavior. Specific training and environmental experience cannot be prime influences on development: "The maturational mechanisms are so firmly entrenched that they are not readily transcended by training . . . " (Gesell, 1954, p. 356); and the environmental factors can only "support, inflect, and specify . . . they do not engender the basic forms and sequences of ontogenesis." Gesell regarded the child's activities as making learning possible but only after the maturational structures had come into existence. His data for this position were to be found in the frequently cited identical twin training studies where, controlling for genetic differences, only one twin was trained, and development of the two compared. The stair-climbing study serves as a useful illustration. Twin T received early training in stair climbing before the structures necessary to perform the behavior were thought to have developed. Twin C did not receive the early training but when the structures were thought to be mature some specific direct instruction was provided for a short period of time. At the end of the experiment, when both twins were the same age, no difference in stair-climbing behavior was in evidence. This was proof for Gesell that the maturational element was most important and that early experience and special environmental manipulation could not affect the eventual competence of the behavior. Maturational forces are in control and training will not override those forces. Figure 2.1 illustrates the general form of findings that come from the co-twin control studies with respect to verbal and other behaviors. Typically, the training prior to maturation produces some behavioral performance but some direct teaching when maturation is thought to have set the proper structures in place is much more efficient and the resultant level of performance for the two children no different.

This is an important demonstration for several reasons. It is interesting to consider that during early training, supposedly prior to structural maturation, some behavioral performance does occur. One will note the general form of response on the curve for Twin T as evidencing some response acquisition. However, at the point where it was assumed that the relevant structures have matured, acquisition occurs much more efficiently. At the end of the experiment, the two children are performing at the same level. If, however, Gesell's point of view is to be taken very seriously, one should not see any acquisition of the behavior prior to the maturation of the structural basis for learning. In this sense, Gesell's theory permitted him and his colleagues to ignore a potential inconsistency—an inconsistency with which Piaget dealt more successfully (Piaget's assimilation–accommodation model acounts for initial performance of new behaviors in terms of existing structures with successive modification and accommodation until a new response has formed). To some extent, one might counter that Gesell's Principle of Self-Regulatory Fluctuation takes care of the problem.

The Principle of Self-Regulatory Fluctuation is invoked to reflect the supposedly inherent spiral nature of development with advances, regressions, consolidations, and new advances. It is akin to some aspects of Piaget's notion of assimilation–accommodation. Similar ideas also play an important role in Werner's developmental conceptualizations (Werner, 1958). In some ways the assimilation–accommodation dimension of Piaget covers both the Principle of Individuating Maturation and the Principle of Self-Regulating Fluctuation. In that sense, Piaget's proposal (like J.M. Baldwin who anticipated him on this matter) is more sophisticated than Gesell's. Although Gesell overlapped both Baldwin and Piaget professionally, there is no indication that Gesell was influenced by either of them even though the three share a common reference literature in some of their citations. Gesell saw the Principle of Self-Regulatory Fluctuation as accounting for the developmental advancement of the organism:

> The course of development, however, being spiral, turns back toward the point of departure; and it does not return precisely to this point. It returns to the same region but at a higher level. The neurological result is an interwoven texture which expresses itself in progressive patterns of behavior. The unity of the ground plan of the organism is preserved. It is a process of reincorporation and consolidation, rather than one of hierarchical stratification. (Gesell, 1954, p. 358-359)

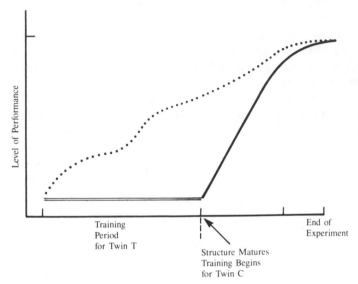

FIG. 2.1. Prototype of co-twin control experimental studies.

Structure

Gesell and Piaget both gave immense importance to the presence and role of structure in behavioral development; each saw structure in relation to a unified ground plan. Piaget stressed the active construction of the structures by the child in interaction with the environment. Gesell's child was more structurally passive though obviously concourse with the environment was necessary for development to occur. Gesell's notion of structure, tied as it was to the concept of maturation, was also more physiologically and neurologically based than Piaget's concept of structure.

The unity of the ground plan for both Gesell and Piaget refers more to the topography of the behavior than to individual differences in competence in a given behavioral domain. Gesell assumed individual differences were largely the result of hereditary characteristics. He did distinguish between maturation and acculturation with the latter representing the cumulative characteristics of environments that can be taken on by the child if the maturational structure permits. What is not made clear is the degree to which the environmental experience determines the level of eventual competence, although one gets the distinct impression that environmental variations of the normal sort have little to do with the competence level the child achieves in the intellectual domain. The emphasis, however, is on the development of the form of the behavior, the importance of the presence of structure for function, and the organizing element of sequential growth. For Gesell, it was sufficient to demonstrate that the form of the behavior was not influenced by training and that the eventual level of competence was the same with and without early special experience.

Gesell's data and his interpretation of them had an enormous influence on the popular conceptualization of the child in terms of "ages and stages" and with respect to supporting a general belief that there was no reason to make any special effort to provide early training experiences. When the child was "ready," the child would learn what had to be learned. Special environmental manipulations, particularly in the first 2 years of life, would have little ultimate influence on the child's eventual development, especially in the intellectual domain. It is interesting to note that the behaviors Gesell chose for experimental analysis were often limited, quite discrete, and not of central importance for long-term development. In the case of stair climbing one can ask what is the possible asymptotic level of stair-climbing behavior. Or, more colloquially, how well can one ever learn to climb stairs? Are different levels of final competence in this behavior of any importance in the behavioral systems of the child? Obviously, even if one is highly competent in stair climbing, its importance is of limited value. Additionally, stair climbing is not part of a behavioral system whose ultimate level of complexity is centrally important to the dimensions of human functioning we are most interested in understanding.

The implications of this analysis may not seem entirely fair to Gesell. After all, in the context of his time, his research was of the highest quality and the data were clear. (Some of the data he and his colleagues generated stand today.) His longitudinal studies of children revealed remarkable relative individual consistency in developmental rates. Children who were adopted were shown to have IQs that correlated more closely with their biological mothers than their adoptive mothers. There was thus a concordance between diverse kinds of information across a variety of behavioral domains. Although stair-climbing behavior is a discrete and perhaps not important behavior, similar studies on vocabulary were obviously aimed at the centrally important system of language acquisition. The critique therefore should not be aimed at Gesell's work and his interpretations so much as at the relative simplicity–complexity of the developmental model he had formulated (quite reasonable in his time) and which served as the guide for both the kinds of research he attempted and the interpretations he applied to his data. His theory, although impressively grounded in an evolutionary context, and sophisticated in those terms, now appears quite unsophisticated with respect to the potential complexity of the factors that would need to be taken into account in understanding development and developmental processes.

Interestingly, structure for Gesell became a delimiting developmental element. Although he recognized that the organization of behavior had to be seen in the context of what he called a "total action pattern," the final form and level of that total action pattern was fixed. In contrast, Piaget assigned to the child a much more active role of concourse with the environment so that the child constructed the structures and the patterns of behavior. This tends to emphasize what Feldman (1980) has called the "modal tendency" of a behavioral pattern at any given developmental stage. But this pulls the reader ahead of the structure of our analysis. Lest it get too far beyond the developmental level of the discussion here, it is necessary to turn attention more specifically and systematically to Piaget's model and conceptualizations.

PIAGET'S STRUCTURES AND STAGES

No one has had more impact upon mainstream developmental psychology in the last 30 years than Jean Piaget. From the perspective of the discussions of developmental theory to the dominance of studies on cognitive development, the literature reflects his extensive and profound influence. Numerous commentators have attempted to assess why this has been the case and no effort is made here to repeat those considerations except to note that many of the discussions perpetuate, unproductively, the active–passive, mechanistic–organismic dichotomies (caricatures? See Brown, Bransford, Ferrara, & Campione, 1983 for a notable exception). The central and most attractive feature of Piaget's model was his conceptualization of development as a creative product of the child's interaction or transactions with the environment. The model was made compelling by the behavioral demonstrations that supported it. As Gelman and Baillargeon (1983) observe, one has only to carry out a conservation task showing that children of certain ages will act in seemingly illogical ways, even after direct demonstrations of the logical approach, to become convinced that Piaget has tapped a behavioral system that bears further investigation and that may provide important clues to understanding development.

Structure

One of the most critical elements in Piaget's theory is his notion of structure. Like Gesell, Piaget saw the structural aspect of behavior as its organizational key. However, Piaget's notion of structure and its role in the development of the child is considerably more sophisticated and abstract than Gesell's. Whereas, for Gesell, maturation in the physiological sense provides a concrete structural underpinning that permits behavioral acquisition and organization, for Piaget, structure is not only something the child creates in transaction with the environment, but structure does not have a physicalistic basis except as it might be reflected in neurological functioning. Rather, in Piaget's system, structures are basically systems of transformations (Piaget, 1970). Structures are not physical entities. They are behavioral systems that are isomorphic with laws of transformations whereby the child interacts with the environment in an organized manner at any particular point in time. Like Gesell, Piaget saw the child's behavior as a total action pattern with emphasis upon "pattern"—or structure as reflected in the laws by which the child operated upon and interacted with the environment. Structure is first and foremost a system of transformation rules, that are further characterized as having "wholeness" and self-regulation. Wholeness for Piaget is not entirely analogous to the Gestalt concept that "the whole is more than the sum of its parts." Wholeness is comprised of elements that act in relation to one another and as a function of the laws that govern the structure.

   A child considers two rows of beads. One has nine beads, the other six, but the row with six beads is stretched out so that it is perceptually longer than the row with nine beads. In answer to the question, "Which has more beads?" a 5-year-old child, who has counted the beads in each row and knows that nine is more than six, will choose the row with six as having more beads because the transform law (i.e., cognitive structure) under which the child is operating considers the whole percept as being dominated by the contrast on extension (one is longer than the other) rather than by the unit count in each row. The transform law has been constructed by the child on the basis of the child's experience with the environment. It cannot be induced cumulatively from a "one-by-one association of its elements." In that sense the whole is more than the sum of its parts, but the whole comes about from the creatively evolved laws in which the elements operate—not from the laws that might be described for the individual relationships among the elements. This relational wholeness depends on, for its character, the laws of structuring or the laws of transformations. "A structure's laws of composition are defined 'implicitly,' i.e., as governing the transformations of the system which they structure" (Piaget, 1970, p. 10).

Now this may appear somewhat tautological. However, if transformation laws are thought of as being rules and structures constituted in terms of a set of related behaviors that are rule governed for their occurrence, then the concern for tautology diminishes. Structures are closed systems characterized by self-regulation and self-maintenance achieved through the operation of cybernetic-type regulations that depend on feedback and self-correction. A structure is a closed system and an internally consistent system of transformation laws but structures evolve through the course of development. The entire course of structural development takes from 12 to 15 years until the structures for interacting with the world (i.e., the transformation rules that organize experiential concourse with the environment) approximate those that characterize the adult of our species.

For Piaget, structure is a systematic whole of self-regulating transformations; it is inseparable from performance. At birth, the infant has an initial structure that is a "general coordination of actions" or what Piaget characterized as connections common to all sensori-motor coordinations that are part of the evolutionary inheritance of the human organism. Another way of stating this is that the infant is born with a general wiring for a set of actions. From then on, those coordinated actions undergo development as sets of structures or transformation rules are created by the child out of interaction with the environment. The mechanisms for creation and for change are assimilation, accommodation, and equilibration.

There have been thousands of statements trying to convey how Piaget defined his "mechanisms." Gesell's mechanisms were thought of as metaphors, although Gesell insisted repeatedly that there was nothing mystical about them and that eventually their neurological bases would be identified. Piaget could also be thought of as using the mechanisms as metaphors although he speaks of them as concrete processes. The definitions and descriptions are intuitively meaningful; yet, because there is almost no behavior that is a pure example of either assimilation or accommodation, an objective verification of the mechanisms does not seem possible without some operational translation. Most investigators have been content to leave it at the metaphorical level and even in the case where the data are not supportive of many aspects of Piaget's theory a general faith has been expressed that assimilation and accommodation are central developmental mechanisms (see Gelman & Baillargeon, 1983). Assimilation and accommodation are represented as follows: The child interprets (assimilates) experience with the environment in terms of his or her existing set of transformation rules; accommodation involves behavior that reflects an alteration of structure (or the transformation rules) to better account for the interaction with the environment. There is a constant see-sawing of assimilation and accommodation until sufficient evidence must be accounted for that requires the child to make a more permanent shift in structural organization or in the transformation rules being used. At this point, a stability of functioning occurs (equilibrium); this lasts for varying amounts of time, depending on the relative robustness of the equilibration. But, until adult structures have been created, assimilatory and accommodative functions set in again.

There is a continual interplay between assimilation and accommodation that defines the dialectic of Piagetian equilibrium. The balance of assimilation/accommodation is a teetering one that is guaranteed to create the next constructive disequilibrium out of its striving for the last equilibrium. Thus, each achievement contains the seeds of the next disequilibrium due to functional assimilation followed by generalizing assimilation. This inevitably assures an accommodation, followed by recognitory assimilation that regularizes and normalizes the modified schemes. With equal inevitability, this is followed by functional and generalizing assimilation of the new scheme until an overgeneralization requires new accommodation. This continues successively, each time a structure is created that represents a higher, more general, more flexible level of organization. This successive creation of structures via assimilative and accommodative behavior occurs in a fixed sequence. Piaget proposed that a given form of a structure characterizes functioning across cognitive domains in a somewhat unitary manner at any given point in development, thus representing a "stage" in development. The fixed sequence of these structures constitutes the stages of development.

Structure is a central concept for Piaget but its essence has been challenged by neo-Piagetians and related cognitivists. As Beilin (1983) has noted, many Piagetian cognitivists are closer in their actions to a neo-functionalist position than to a strict Piagetian structuralist stance.

Stages

Gesell considered development as occurring in a fixed sequence, although he tended to use sequence and stage interchangeably and the concept of stage was not particularly elaborated. Piaget, on the other hand, considered the fixed sequence as one of the criteria for designating stages. It is interesting to note that Gesell, and Werner as well, believed stages characterized all aspects and domains of development. Piaget, however, was inclined only to grant stages to the domain of cognitive development (Piaget, 1977b). This is an important point because the Piagetian model has been claimed to epitomize an evolving, comprehensive organismic approach to the development of the child—indeed, as representing a major paradigm shift in developmental psychology. Piaget's notions of stages and structures have been generalized to characterize all domains of development. Piaget himself, however, was much more circumspect. First, he believed stages were devised as an "instrument of analysis," as a form of classification. In that sense, he did not reify stage in the manner that Gesell did. Second, he believed stages were most particularly useful for an analysis of cognitive development and not necessarily other areas. He did not believe there was structural unity in individuals across all domains of functioning. "And, if there is no structural unity, there are not general stages that permit fixed and verifiable correspondences in all domains among all functions" (Piaget, 1977c, p. 818). In contrast, Werner believed stages were applicable to all domains of development, but he felt that an individual could be at one level or stage in a given domain and at a different developmental level in another area in what he called developmental stratification (Werner, 1957b).

Piaget believed that different stage approaches were invented to make different kinds of analyses in varying domains. He therefore resisted attempts of others to show that his stages in development were analogous to other stage systems. The most notable contemporaneous stage analysis was to be found in Freudian theory. Freud was not a structuralist in the sense that Piaget was. Stages, however, played a central conceptual role in Freudian developmental theory and Freud's use of stage forms a useful comparison to highlight Piaget's particularization of the stage concept. Freudian stages involve a chunking of behavioral organization to deal with personality development, whereas Piaget's stages were devised to make an analysis of cognitive development. Although most Piagetians would not agree, it is possible to think of Piaget's use of stage as a heuristic and thus not require that it exist as a verifiable entity.

On the other hand, Piaget did give criteria for stages (Piaget, 1977c): (a) a constant order of succession with the timing dependent on both maturational and social milieu factors; (b) successive integration so that structures at one age become an "integral part of structures at the following age"; (c) the existence of a structural whole so that a reduction of seemingly unrelated operations to a "higher unity" was possible; (d) periods of preparation and completion for the stages occur; and (e) there are processes of formation and forms of final equilibrium that are the whole. The first three criteria are pretty standard kinds of criteria for stage-like analyses. A fixed order of succession is an obvious criterion and common to all stage theories although the question of factors related to timing will differ from theory to theory. For example, Piaget probably gave slightly more weight to social milieu factors than Gesell, particularly for his last stage of development (Piaget, 1972), whereas the social environment was especially critical for affecting the timing of stages in the Freudian analysis.

The criterion of successive integration is a stalwart of developmental approaches. It has strong roots in evolutionary and developmental biology. Of the third criterion, the presence of a "higher unity," it can probably be said that its value is both heuristic and an exemplar of the scientific ideal whereby diverse phenomena are organized into one or a few single explanatory concepts or laws. Being able to characterize as "oral" or "anal," as sensori-motor or formal operations, or more colloquially as one finds in the Gesellian approach—"the terrible twos and the trusting threes"—not only communicates the unifying principle for a stage but provides a principle against which to test the data base to validate whether a stage exists. It is this criterion against which the notion of stages is most frequently examined. The fourth and fifth criteria are more particular to Piaget, although Gesell's principles of reciprocal interweaving and self-regulation have bearing upon them and one can find within Freudian mechanism analogous elements.

The question of whether stages really exist or are simply an organizing framework for us to think about development is an important one. The alternative to a stage conceptualization of development is to think of development as a process of continuous change. Behaviorists sometimes are thought of as eschewing stage concepts entirely and opting for continuous change making corrolary assumptions of linearity in development. This is sometimes seen as a simple approach. However, positing a continuous process rather than a set of "stages" is not necessarily simpler. In fact, the difficulty of dealing intellectually with continuous change may make stage theories particularly attractive because stages give the appearance of organizing behavioral progress. In that sense, stages are a theoretically simplifying device. Nevertheless, there are no universally agreed upon criteria for a stage in behavioral development. Gesell's theory, for example, is stronger in relation to the notion of fixed sequences than in relation to the concept of stage in development even though in his popular books he reified age as stage. He talked about ages as nouns (e.g., 4 was discussed as having particular behaviors and characteristics).

The clearest evidence for sequence is in the domain of motor development. The belief in a relatively stable sequence of other behaviors is evident in the large number of child-development assessments related to intelligence and language development. Although sequence is a necessary criterion for stage, sequence is not a sufficient criterion. For stages to be validated, one must demonstrate the unity of function within a period of time. Gesell's theory was never specific enough to have been tested against this criterion. The stages proposed by Freud have had wide clinical appeal within the community of practicing psychoanalysts and therapists but the theory has not lent itself to an objective verification of the stages. In contrast, Piaget's theory has had the most explicit and testable stage implications.

The four basic broad stages Piaget originally posited devolved in Piaget's last years toward three stages with one of the stages divided into two subperiods (Piaget, 1970). The first stage, sensorimotor development, was particularly elaborated into six sub-stages and has been the most intensely investigated of Piaget's developmental periods.

As a result of this level of scrutiny it was possible to conclude, in a recent major review, that the sub-stages in the sensori-motor period and indeed the existence of infancy as a stage according to Piaget's criteria, have not received strong validation if all of Piaget's own criteria for the presence of stage are invoked (Harris, 1983). What is clear is that the ordinal sequence that Piaget described with respect to cognitive achievements during the infancy period is roughly substantiated. (This same ordinal sequence, in less detail and with less emphasis on cognitive structural processes, can also be found in Gesell's descriptions of infant development.) There is much less evidence for the proposition that the same specific structures function at a given time across a range of tasks dealing with different cognitive phenomena. Performance in one sensori-motor domain has not always been found to correlate with performance in another sensori-motor domain at the same age. This raises serious questions concerning the presence of structural unity during the sensori-motor period, an important criterion for Piaget in designating a period as a developmental stage.

The evidence for the next two stages posited by Piaget, pre-operational and concrete-operational, is also weak. In a recent major review Gelman and Baillargeon (1983) came to conclusions about pre-operational and concrete-operational "stages" not very different from those that Harris (1983) drew with respect to the sensori-motor period:

> In our opinion there is little evidence to support the idea of major stages in cognitive development of the type described by Piaget. Over and over again, the evidence is that the pre-operational child has more competence than expected. Further, the evidence is that the concrete-operational child works out concepts in separate domains without using the kind of integrative structures that would be required by a general stage theory. In addition, there is evidence in some cases that the structure underlying the way a preschooler reasons about a problem is much like that used by older children and even adults, for example, the principles of causal reasoning. In other cases, the evidence is that there is structural change reflected in the development of a concept. The case of number concepts is one clear example of the latter. (Gelman & Baillargeon, 1983, p. 214)

These authors suggest that it may turn out that stages will be shown to exist in some cognitive domains but not in others. This would mean basically that the stage concept proposed by Piaget is a more limited feature of cognitive development than he originally thought.

Early attempts to validate the existence of the last developmental stage, the period of formal operations, were not always successful, especially in environments and with populations different from those with which Piaget and his colleagues had worked in Geneva. In one of Piaget's first full discussions of the role of different kinds of environments for fostering cognitive development he acknowledged that some social contexts may not be conducive to the full flowering of formal operational thought (Piaget, 1972). Although there has been less work done on formal operational thought than on earlier periods of cognitive development, the evidence is not unlike that which pertains to other periods of development. Piaget proposed that formal operations are achieved in early to middle adolescence but investigators have not always been able to demonstrate that college students could succeed at the problems designed to test formal operational thought (Siegler & Richards, 1982).

There has been extensive discussion as to the validity and usefulness of postulating stages in development. Piaget's proposals were clear and specific on this account. He not only defined particular stages but indicated the behaviors to be expected, the sequences that would occur and the criteria against which the evidence needed to be judged. This has permitted a test of his ideas—and has afforded developmental investigators real opportunities to make progress in trying to understand how fully Piaget's theory would account for the facts. It is now clear that with respect to a general concept of stages in cognitive development the facts are equivocal. Over 10 years ago, Wohlwill (1973) suggested that the evidence was pointing in the direction of the conclusion that "the scope and applicability of a stage will be more narrowly circumscribed than Piaget's theory suggests" (Wohlwill, 1973, p. 238). Similarly, Flavell, who has been extremely thoughtful in his consideration of the issue of stage, suggested even before the weight of evidence against stages as Piaget had proposed was as extensive as it now appears to be, that the all-or-none stage descriptions were not appropriate. He postulated that there was a much more gradual evolving of stages with considerably more overlap than Piaget's theory originally permitted (Flavell, 1971). Feldman (1980), in his attempt to extend cognitive developmental theory to cover non-universal and discipline-related cognitive development, has found Flavell's gradual evolving and overlapping of stages a useful strategy, although others have been much less tolerant of retaining Piagetian stages as representative of cognitive functioning (e.g., Brainerd, 1973). Another formulation is to be found in Fischer's (1980) skill theory dealing with the construction of developmental sequences by the child in the context of specific tasks and specific environments. As a rapproachment between cognitive and behavioral psychology, with an appeal to an operant analysis, it is particularly attractive and promising.

In many ways, the research on cognition and intelligence has moved on beyond stage concepts. The literature on children's learning and on cognition and intelligence appears to be more heavily dominated with discussions of learning strategies (Brown et al., 1983), information processing characteristics as applied to different tasks and at different ages (Siegler, 1983), and the parsing out of intelligence in terms of global or executive processing systems and local processing systems (Sternberg & Powell, 1982, 1983). Although sequence, order, and hierarchical integration are still topics of investigation, they tend to be tied more closely to particular tasks and domains rather than as inherent developmental properties of the organism (e.g., Feldman, 1980; Fischer, 1980).

So, where does this leave the issue of stages and development? It is clear that the most direct test of an overall stage concept as descriptive of different unified developmental levels yields equivocal results at best and disconfirming results at worst, depending on the theoretical predilections of the individuals interpreting the data. That there is a rough order and that sequential phenomena exist is not questioned. However, it is doubtful whether anything can be said about the nature of the constraints on the behavioral development of the human organism in terms of broad generalizations using stage as an organizing concept. Can developmental stage serve as a guide for educational and environmental arrangements for children? Brainerd (1983) has concluded that there is no support for the notion that children's learning is constrained by stages of cognitive development as a broadly applicable description of the child at a given point in time. Feldman (1980) has suggested a shift of the idea of stages from a child characteristic to a domain characteristic, wherein the development of competence with respect to particular tasks has stage-like characteristics. Such a suggestion is, interestingly, entirely compatible with notions of programmed learning so strongly espoused by behaviorists. And, as Beilin (1983) notes, it is characteristic of a neofunctionalist approach that has moved Piagetians and cognitivists away from structuralism.

If in the one domain where Piaget considered stages most appropriate as an organizing concept there is reason to use the concept loosely, if at all, of what relevance is stage to developmental analyses? It is interesting to speculate that stage as an organizing principle of human development may exist only in terms of being an evolutionary vestige, seen incompletely in some domains of functioning and not at all in other domains. It is quite possible that stages of development are part of our evolutionary heritage, seen more clearly in lower organisms, reflected to some extent, although less clearly, in our own embryological development. However, evolutionarily, the greater flexibility that characterizes the functioning of the human organism may run counter to a more rigid stage organization, particularly in the behavioral realm. What may characterize human behavioral development are elements of stage organization from an evolutionary history that have gotten broken down and apart and scattered in the behavioral repertoire in the course of evolution, leaving as dominant a greater behavioral plasticity that is advantageous for human survival. Thus, there may be nodes of stages in some areas, as several have suggested, but overall it may well be that for the human organism stage qua stage does not exist as a pervasive organizing principle in human behavioral development.

The notions just described are not typically invoked by developmental psychologists, although analogous ideas have been common in developmental biology. For example, Weiss (1941), in discussing basic patterns of motor coordination in amphibians and mammals, describes the fact that amphibian motor differentiation reflects a relatively heavy contribution of preformation with motoric behavior able to be conditioned by the environment but only within a relatively narrow range because of the strong structural constraints. Mammals, on the other hand, standing at a higher evolutionary level, show a decreasing influence of structural constraints and a correspondingly greater proportion of patterns of coordinated behavior controlled by environmental exigencies until, at the level of the human organism, the "non-preformed, 'invented' coordination patterns become so prominent that they obscure the more ancient stereotyped patterns with which they coexist and overlap" (Weiss, 1941, p. 88).

The conclusion that Gelman and Baillargeon (1983) came to with respect to the possibility that stages may exist in some cognitive domains but not others may be compatible with such notions although we would have to add that stages may be more obvious in cognitive domains that are later in their evolutionary appearance in the human repertoire. In this regard, it may be possible to marry some of Feldman's notions about the incorporation of initially novel cognitive achievements into the area of universal achievements as novel behaviors become available for learning and modeling to all members of a population (Feldman, 1980). In discussing this progression from novel to universal, Feldman suggested that at some point in human history number was invented as a novel tool activity and eventually, through wide use and effective cultural transmission, moved over into a category of universal achievement. A further step can be added. In the relatively early period of its existence as a universal phenomenon, individuals should acquire the concept in accordance with a more rigid stage progression model; later, when it becomes an older universal achievement (in an evolutionary context)[1] the stage progression dimension should weaken.

For developmental psychologists such as Werner, the concept of stage was discussed in terms of successive and hierarchic integrations of abilities and microgenetic processes of progression. As we have noted, Werner was comfortable with a non-unitary approach to stages, using the concept of "developmental stratification" wherein individuals could operate at one level in one domain and at a different level in another domain. But a larger principle was operating for Werner that he called an "orthogenetic principle": "whenever development occurs it proceeds from a state of relative globality and lack of differentiation to a stage of increasing differentiation, articulation, and hierarchic integration" (Werner, 1957b, pp. 108–109). Werner used the notion of differentiation much more generally than it has typically been used in developmental biology (e.g., Waddington, 1966). For Werner, differentiation was a heuristic principle, not easily subjected to empirical test. But it was a central heuristic, particularly with respect to the notion of a hierarchic integration into increasingly complex systems whereby the same achievement could be reached through different routes within a system that was operating as a whole.

The concept of stages and stage organization for behavioral development has not lost its intuitive appeal despite the growing evidence that formal stages of cognitive development as posited by Piaget probably do not exist. If one wanted to rescue the concept for its heuristic value, stages could be seen as a construct that helps us describe the different characteristics of child behavior that tend to cluster together at a given point in time. Other disciplines have found such a strategy useful. For example, plant ecologists use the construct of plant communities at different altitudes even though if you walk up a mountain you will not find a clear dividing line between them. Using stage as a loose descriptive principle may be useful, but employing it as a heavy duty theoretical concept has not yet

---

[1]This leads to the interesting proposition that those domains of cognitive development that are now acquired in a stage progression are more recent human acquisitions. This proposition is not meant to endorse Piaget's controversial theory about behavior as the "motor of evolution" (Piaget, 1978) in which he postulates modification of the genotype as a function of phenotypical behavior without including a mechanism for reproductive advantage. Rather, one would assume the process of genetic assimilation (Waddington, 1975) whereby the genotypical element of stage progression initially could have occurred by giving organisms who had acquired certain cognitive skills a reproductive advantage. As those cognitive skills became evolutionarily older in the human behavioral repertoire, the stage structure would become less dominant. To determine whether the notion of the presence of stages in the acquisition of cognitive skills might reflect a more recent evolutionary history, we would have to review those cognitive skills where a stage sequence is in evidence, compare them with those where there is less evidence for stages, and consider whether such an ordering made the proposition logically defensible.

been fruitful nor, given the evidence, is it likely to be fruitful. Another example from plant ecology is relevant here. Plant ecologists used to describe plants in terms of stages of succession in temperate climates. They then proceeded to try to determine how the community of plants in one stage resisted the approach of plants of another stage. Finally, it was proposed that the process of succession was continuous and driven by an overall goal: the search for light. The switch from viewing succession as a stage-to-stage jump to a process of continuous change not only made a big difference in the kind of questions that were asked but in the meaningful organization of evidence.[2] If behavioral development is seen as a process of continuous change, the questions we pose to understand behavioral development are different than if we posit stages as describing behavioral development and then look for the mechanisms that take the organism from one stage to another. Fischer's (1980) skill theory straddles these alternatives by positing sequences and developmental tiers wherein movement is continuous and gradual and where there is no necessary synchrony across skill domains. Because skill theory also posits operationally defined mechanisms for change it is testable and subject to verification. This is a very promising advance.

SYSTEMS

An approach to development that involves systems acting as wholes has been emphasized in developmental biology (e.g., Weiss, 1971) and more recently in developmental psychology under the rubric of "organismic" as contrasted with "mechanistic." Piaget, of course, had consistently juxtaposed his organismic approach with the Watsonian–Hullian–Skinnerian "mechanistic" approach but it was Reese and Overton (1970) who provided an overview perspective of this dichotomy and its implications for developmental psychology. In trying to take the Reese and Overton analysis a bit further, Kitchener (1982) has made several distinctions that will be useful in our consideration of the issues. Instead of using "mechanistic–organismic," he chose to cast the analysis in terms of elementarism and holism. And this distinction is parsed out as methodological holism, methodological elementarism, metaphysical holism, and metaphysical elementarism. The methodological level involves the question of whether behavior of the whole system can best be investigated by analyzing the whole into its basic parts and studying them in isolation, or whether the whole must be studied "qua whole." At the metaphysical level, one addresses the essential nature of

---

[2]I am pleased to acknowledge Marion O'Brien's suggestion of the examples from plant ecology as having relevance to this discussion.

complex entities. Kitchener characterizes the metaphysical elementarist as one who believes the complex whole is constituted from the sum of its parts plus their relations. The metaphysical holist is said to hold three beliefs: (a) the whole cannot be defined in terms of an additive linear model involving only the sum of the isolated parts and their external relations; (b) the nature of the parts of the whole and their typical ways of behaving are determined by the whole; and (c) a whole is defined in terms of parts that are internally related to each other. The internal relations define the system; the system is identified as a unit, not in terms of its elements. The elements do not make up the whole but they are constrained by the whole. The whole is usually characterized as not analyzable into linear, cause–effect sequences.

In this view the whole is an organized system that cannot retain its identity as a unit without what Weiss has called the "coordination of the collective behavior of its parts" (Weiss, 1971, p. 13). Yet, sophisticated discussions of such metaphysical holism do not involve a denial of the utility of so-called mechanistic analyses that define methodological elementarism. Such strategies are considered important, perhaps necessary, for understanding some aspects of the functioning of complex entities. In discussing the behavior of the cell, of development, and of nervous functions, Weiss (1971) notes that "we find that they are neither entirely in the class of unbroken linear 'cause–effect' sequences, nor wholly the kind of self-adjusting operations denoting systems character. They are both partly chains, partly networks at one and the same time" (p. 20). However, the presence of this duality of function does not mean that the whole can be synthesized merely by knowing how isolated elements of the whole operate. Weiss and other developmental biologists commonly regard cells and other organismic units as exhibiting higher and higher degrees of organization that emerge from lower levels of organization but are not the additive result of their constituents. Further, from a developmental point of view, once the higher level of organization has come into existence it is not possible to return to a lower level of organization by reduction to component elements or processes. Polanyi (1958) expressed this idea as follows: "Lower levels do not lack a bearing on higher levels; they define the conditions of their success and account for their failures, but they cannot account for their success, for they cannot even define it" (p. 382).

These conceptualizations are not foreign to the developmental theories we have been discussing. Piaget clearly regarded higher levels of cognitive functioning as irreducible to elements at lower levels once the higher levels had come into existence. Gesell's patterns of developmental direction also reflect this notion as does Werner's idea of hierarchic integration. An essential element to the attractiveness of this point of view is recognition that in both behavioral and physical development there appear to be emergent characteristics that involve not only a reorganization from one level of functioning to another but new levels of complexity that defy description simply as the cumulative result of earlier levels of behavior or physical development. Each emergent level is represented as a system of organization that has a unity of its own. It is easy to see how a stage theory of development is compatible with such a systems approach although positing stages within levels is not necessary to thinking of development in a systems framework. However, when emergent levels are proposed there is an implicit and often explicit commitment to the idea of stages.

Open and Closed Systems

Concepts related to hierarchic ordering, progressive differentiation, feedback, and levels of organization characterize what is known as *general system theory,* the most elaborated discussions of which have been undertaken by von Bertalanffy (1968, 1975). An application of general system theory to behavioral development has been made by Sameroff (1983). He tried to suggest that general system theory could be used as a more specific theoretical organizing principle than the somewhat general notion of "organismic." Part of the attraction to general system theory is that it does not involve negating linear cause-effect relationships as they might characterize components of a larger system, thus incorporating mechanistic sub-systems within organic systems whose growth and development involve hierarchic ordering, progressive differentiation, feedback mechanisms, and overall systems characteristics. Further, general system theory recognizes that at different levels of organization in a developmental system there will be emergent organizations that are qualitatively different from organizations that preceded them.

The most central aspect of general system theory as applied to biological organisms and units is the characterization of the organism as an open system, in contrast to a closed system. As we have already indicated, in a closed system such as a machine all the elements and their interactions are specified and do not change as a result of stimulation external to the machine. A closed system has a finite set of cause-effect event sequences that can be entirely specified in advance if one knows all the elements and their relations. An automobile engine, a computer, and others are closed systems. Although input–output arrangements can be highly complex, they are essentially defined by the initial design of the system. Closed systems are not able to maintain themselves, and cannot engage in self-restoration or in reproduction. In contrast, open systems are characterized as self-maintaining, self-restoring, and self-reproducing. Biological organisms are open systems. Therefore, accounting fully for the functioning of biological organisms will require laws that apply to open systems even while sub-systems within biological systems may operate as closed systems. Cybernetic feedback loop systems such as information processing are closed systems and may characterize some aspects (perhaps large amounts) of human information processing capacities and strategies. On the other hand, cognitive development, according to a system theory approach, can never be completely accounted for by understanding information processing because cognitive development, according to this view, is part of the open system functioning of the human organism.

Advances in machine design may eventually blur the open–closed system contrast—or, highly complex machines may be designed with features that make them more analogous to open systems. For this reason, one can retain some skepticism concerning whether the open–closed system contrast will forever remain an entirely rigid dichotomy. Still, it is clear that the open system analysis of biological organisms is relevant for looking at aspects of behavioral development. This is said with an important caveat. The scientific understanding of behavioral development will only be aided by considering the implications of an open system analysis if we keep in mind what Weiss and von Bertalanffy so clearly recognized: There is, in living organisms, a duality of systems—both open and closed. Failure to remain fully cognizant of this is to risk obviating such understandings as we have concerning the linear cause-effect laws that do govern aspects of human behavior (and they are considerable both in number and significance) and therefore to negate what has been well established and upon which we need to build if the scientific understanding of behavioral development is to progress. The recent popularity of proclaiming paradigm shifts and flailing at cause-effect behaviorism as inappropriate for understanding human development is evidence that many fail to understand that significant portions of functioning of open systems may be explained by laws that are more characteristic of closed systems and that our goal is to build upon what we know, not discard our data base.

Equifinality

One of the characteristics of an open system is that from different initial conditions and through different paths, similar end-points can be reached. Any hope of specifying the set of initial conditions and the path of events that produces a given outcome is likely to remain unfulfilled. Intuitively and colloquially, this makes a great deal of sense. Much of the recent evidence on progressions in children's cognitive development and learning points clearly to the fact that different children reach the same end point via different sequences in concept acquisition. Further, it has long been clear that a variety of programmed sequences can produce the same final level or scope of performance. To what extent deliberately planned programmed learning sequences match or are similar to those multiple pro-grams of acquisition that occur without direct intervention is not known. But the data are obviously compatible with the notion of equifinality: Multiple circumstances will tend to produce similar outcomes in both natural developmental progressions and in learning environments that have been deliberately manipulated.

A serious understanding of the existence of equifinality in human behavioral development must affect how questions are posed and the kinds of interpretations brought to data. An example is used to illustrate this implication. The history of the study of infant intelligence as a predictor of later intelligence begins with tests of infant intelligence. They were origi-nally developed with the anticipation that a reliable measure of infant performance on items considered to reflect intellectual potential would enable prediction of intellectual status in later years. The evidence was not supportive, and it was finally concluded that such infant evaluations were not predictive of later intelligence (Bayley, 1955; Stott & Ball, 1965). Discussions of these results have ranged from analyses of task requirements in infant intelligence tests and later intelligence tests to proposals that there was an essential discontinuity in intellectual development from infancy to later years. Recently, however, later intelligence has been predicted from evaluation of infant performance in sensory processing tasks. There is now some converging evidence with respect to both infant auditory dis-crimination (O'Connor, Cohen, & Parmelee, 1984) and visual novelty preference (Fagan & Singer, 1983) that performance on these sensory processing tasks does significantly predict later measures of intelligence with Pearson r correlations ranging from .31 to .66. Fagan and Singer have chosen to interpret the results as pointing toward the kind of information processing characteristics that can be identified in early infancy that under-lie or are similar to the processes being tapped by later intelligence tests, suggesting a "continuity in kind" or continuity in process across time.

Earlier correlational studies of intelligence test performance did not permit a process analysis, whereas the recent experimental studies of sensory discrimination and novelty response do. However, a developmental model that includes the principle of equifinality would require an under-standing that identification of different initial sensory processing character-istics does not mean that the path and the explanation of the outcome, even given significant predictions, are thereby specified. Obviously, no one interprets significant correlations on the order of .31 or even .66 as account-ing for all of the variance in a set of relationships. On the other hand, it is easy to slip into discussions of significant early–late relationships as if they did, without searching for those variable paths that will enable us to understand the totality of the processes involved in developmental outcome. Even qualifications such as offered by O'Connor, Cohen, and Parmelee

(1984), when evaluated from the point of view of the principle of equifinality, must be accepted with reservations. O'Connor et al. found that when they factored in maternal education along with auditory processing performance as measured at 4 months of age the prediction of IQ at 5 years of age increased from .60 to .65. They concluded that "intelligence-test performance is influenced by early information processing abilities of the infant that are facilitated by as yet undefined maternal characteristics" (p. 164). The next obvious step is to try to understand the nature of that facilitation. However, if the model of development from which one is operating includes the principle of equifinality, then one of the possibilities that needs to be retained with respect to lining out the next steps in research is that for some infants maternal characteristics may be unrelated to any facilitative processes and that other variables are involved. Further, for some infants their own sensory processing characteristics may well suffice to explain the outcome. In other words, variables external to the infant may be critical for some infants, irrelevant for others. A model of development fully sensitive to the equifinality principle is not only built differently but affects the set of alternatives that one will entertain in formulating research questions.

Of course, one could raise the question as to whether it is realistic to suppose that it will be possible to delineate the many different process pathways involved in the development of particular behavioral systems. Perhaps all we can hope to specify are the controlling variables that appear to be functioning along the pathways and assume that the range of individual differences in pathways is potentially as large as the number of individuals. Such a position would mean that each person's developmental course is unique. It is difficult to answer this on a priori grounds. It is possible that at some level of variation uniqueness prevails. The challenge is to try to determine how much of the path and how many different paths can be specified that will encompass significant portions of the variance so as to give us useful laws. If the principle of indeterminacy operates in the behavioral realm as it does in the physical sciences then there is every reason to expect that prediction down to the minutest level of behavioral elements is in principle unlikely. However, it is also likely that there is much to be understood about lawfulness before we get to that point and that we are nowhere near approaching it at the present time.

Organization and Reorganization

General system theory puts great emphasis on the idea that at certain points in the course of the development of organisms there are reorganizations of systems and emergent levels of functioning that are not linearly related to prior levels. This raises several very important issues with respect to behavioral development. Piaget's stage theory, particularly the division of cognitive development into three or four major epochs, embodies an emergent levels notion. There is an element of emergent levels in Freudian stages although it is not as clear as it is for Piaget. Werner's hierarchic integration also includes the concept of emergently reorganized system functioning. More recently, Emde proposed bio-behavioral shifts at certain ages (Emde, Gaensbauer, & Harmon, 1976) and White (1965) applied the notion of hierarchical arrangements to learning processes that incorporated notions of emergence. One of the most dramatic examples of system reorganization and emergent newness is, of course, the metamorphosis of the caterpillar to the butterfly. The human organism does not, obviously, undergo such dramatic changes in form. However, is there in the development of the behavioral system a similar dramatic aspect in the changes that occur? Stages are the most convenient rubric for considering system reorganization and notions of emergent new levels of functioning. Yet, it seems clear that a discrete step-like stage organization has not been validated for the area where it has been thought most likely to exist—in cognitive development. On the other hand, there are some aspects of cognitive development that have stage-like progressions. The notion of stages, however, is not a concept entirely synonymous with levels of hierarchic integration and system organization.

There are a number of characteristics that are implied with respect to system reorganization and levels. The first is that although there may be quantitative elements that can be identified in comparing one level to another, the primary dimension of change is qualitative in nature. Second, elements that operate at one level of a system may or may not be present at other levels. Third, the principles or composition laws that describe the interrelationships among elements at different levels may or may not be the same—more likely they will be different. Fourth, successive levels involve a hierarchical incorporation of elements and laws from earlier levels that operate differently, usually in a more advanced manner at the new level. Fifth, the relationship between the system at one point in time and the different system at another point in time is not linear. And finally, the contextual relationships of the unit—that is, the system and its surroundings (environment, context)—are qualitatively different at different levels.

One of the problems in applying these characteristics to an analysis of behavioral development is that it is not clear what strategy would be the most productive. Obviously, the infant is very different from the 10-year-old and a system of analysis of the differences would verify the characteristics we have just listed. But such a gross differentiation is not likely to be terribly useful. How finely should we make our differentiations for purposes of analysis? And should it be whole system, à la "child," or might we best consider behavioral systems individually such as cognition, emotion, language? As "whole child practitioners" are fond of noting, one must consider the entire organism acting as a unit for many purposes. On the other hand, general system theory countenances isolation of system parts. Intensive study of those system parts, however, will not permit one to achieve an understanding of how the whole operates even though within increasingly complex system organizations there is also increasing mechanization of sub-systems. The question that must be addressed, then, is what are the practical, scientific consequences of adopting a general system theory approach to the understanding of human behavioral development.

When general system theory characterizes biological organisms as evidencing in their development increasingly complex levels of system organization, four related concepts are considered inherently important: Hierarchic integration, internal relationships as defining the whole, increased differentiation, and mechanization. How are these to be seriously applied in choosing research questions and in pursuing investigations? Obviously, hierarchic integration requires looking for patterns of sequences that involve incorporation of lower orders of functioning into higher orders. One of the problems in specifying some aspects of hierarchic integration is that some lower order elements are lost, some are submerged within higher order functioning, and some are transformed. It is not difficult to note the absence of elements or processes at a higher level, but tracking submergence and transformation can be more difficult at the behavioral level. Submergence can be identified with sub-routines and with elements moving from dominant to minor components of processes; transformation at the behavioral level can present problems. Piaget tried to deal concretely with hierarchic integration in his use of the concept of decalage whereby vertical decalage describes the presence at a higher level, in a more sophisticated form, structures from a lower level. The concept has not been widely applied, has been considered more descriptive than explanatory, and has not been particularly prominent in the general use of Piagetian theory. Werner considered hierarchic integration as not directly verifiable and kept the notion largely as a heuristic device for theoretical purposes. In the long run, however, if hierarchic integration is to play an important role in our understanding of behavioral development we will need to specify the elements and processes and their interrelationships. Some of this is occurring in studies of information processing and intelligence (Siegler, 1983; Sternberg & Powell, 1982), and there has been a growing recognition that the developmental study of learning needs to be influenced by similar notions (Brown, 1982; Brown et al., 1983). It may not be possible to consider hierarchic integration until a better understanding of sub-systems at different levels of functioning exists. One of the reasons why phenomena related to hierarchic integration may be more evident in the cognitive-learning areas is that we have a better data base in this area than, for example, in the area of emotional development. The most extensive evidence for hierarchic integration probably exists with respect to language development, particularly in the period of early acquisition.

Progressive Mechanization

The notion of internal relationships as defining the whole, and the corollary that the whole cannot be synthesized from its parts, is, as we have already noted, at the heart of the mechanistic–organismic or elementarism–holism discussion. Translating this aspect of general system theory into its practical scientific implications for studying behavioral development cannot be done without also considering the notions of increased differentiation and mechanization. At any given point in time the whole being defined by the set of its internal relations obviously means that cognitive functioning is not entirely independent from emotional functioning, etc. This is not difficult to understand, although operationalizing it for the purposes of research is not easy. Freudian theory, more than any other developmental theory, recognized the importance of the set of relationships at a given time but it provides no particularly useful key for the scientific strategy that would be dictated by the idea. The most obvious implication is that multiple measurements are always needed in order to understand the operation of a complex whole and that the functioning of one component of the whole cannot be entirely understood without recognizing the pull of other components and relationships. On the other hand, as one gets to higher and higher levels of organization there is increased differentiation and mechanization. This implies that sub-units and components become more identifiable and more machinelike. von Bertalanffy's (1968) discussion of this is particularly cogent:

> Organisms *are* not machines; but they can to a certain extent *become* machines, congeal into machines. Never completely, however, for a thoroughly mechanized organism would be incapable of reacting to the incessantly changing conditions of the outside world ... The *principle of progressive mechanization* expresses the transition from undifferentiated wholeness to higher function, made possible by specialization and "division of labor;" this principle implies also loss of potentialities in the components and of regulability in the whole. (p. 213)

The scientific implications for the study of behavioral development, given the dual principles of increased differentiation and mechanization, are that the study of component systems, often machine-like in their functioning, is not only legitimized but necessary. However, the ultimate question for understanding the organismic operation as a whole cannot be answered via the study of its sub-parts. And, indeed, one of the implications of this way of looking at behavioral functioning and development is that there will always be some circumstances of environmental surround that will disturb the laws that have been identified for the sub-systems because the organism, as a living organism, retains the capability of responding to novel and rare events in ways that are adaptive and not entirely encoded in the existing laws that govern its functioning. This might be thought of as a capability for emergent responsiveness. Often, this aspect of human behavior becomes so impressive and thought of as so significant that it obscures the fact that most of human functioning, particularly as development progresses, is highly codified, routine, and machine-like. In that sense, the bulk of human behavior may not always appear to be among the most interesting aspects of human behavior.

On the other hand, if an understanding of significant portions of human behavior at the adult level is ever going to be achieved, it is very important to try to understand how behavioral characteristics come into the repertoire and become regularized parts of the functioning of the whole. Additionally, if the goal is to understand enough so as to enable intervention that facilitates development when it is not progressing at a proper or at a healthy rate, there is a need to know enough about the system and its sub-parts to do intervention effectively and wisely. For all these reasons, and likely more, the acquisition and development of behaviors that ultimately become codified, routine, machine-like must remain among the core questions addressed by developmentalists, even as there are efforts to understand the creative, novel, and different dimensions that contribute to the rich variety of developmental outcomes.

RECAPITULATION

Although the data base with respect to overall stages in development is equivocal in the cognitive domain, it is likely that the basic notion of stage-like progressions will be retained both for heuristic purposes and because there are promising developments with respect to domain-specific uses of stage concepts. Also, as some of the current work in emotional development proceeds, there may be some support for the utility of stage-related analyses in this area of functioning. It is not as clear that structure will have a similar fate, partly because the empirical utility of structure as a concept is not as immediately obvious and partly because the direct evidence for structure as Piaget defined it has not been supportive. In some ways, the direct support of the utility of the concept of system is the weakest; yet discussions of development in terms of systems approaches have strong intuitive appeal. What is not obvious is how a systems approach affects the science that is done, except to broaden the context of the consideration of variables and their interrelationships. Equifinality may be among the most important of the systems concepts in affecting strategies for understanding behavioral development. Taking the concepts of differentiation and mechanization seriously can make important contributions to phrasing strong developmental questions.

The discussion of stages, structure, and system has involved a journey through a number of the major issues that have typified developmental psychology and developmental theory. Stage and structure have had particularly long histories in the field of developmental biology and developmental psychology; system is of somewhat more recent origin in both these fields. The model of development that might best serve the research agenda in the coming era of developmental research will need to incorporate the most productive elements of the stage, structure, and system approaches into its framework.

There are several questions often introduced in the discussion of these issues that have not been addressed here. One involves matters related to continuity and discontinuity in development. This is discussed subsequently. Another revolves around genetic–environmental variables. Omission of that issue here has been deliberate. When juxtaposing stage–structure notions and gene–environment considerations it is difficult not to become polemical. The concern in this book is to parcel out the issues in such a manner as to make the most constructive use of concepts and approaches for the purpose of defining productive research strategies and to do so in the light of a model of development that now appears most consonant with what we know. As a result, there should emerge clearer indications of the research strategies and directions that might be most useful. These issues are considered in due course.

REFERENCES

Baldwin, A. (1967). *Theories of child development.* New York: Wiley (Rev. ed., 1980).

Baldwin, J. M. (1906). *Mental development in the child and the race.* New York: Macmillan.

Barten, S. S., & Franklin, M. B. (1978). *Developmental processes* (Vols. 1 & 2). New York: International Universities Press.

Bayley, N. (1955). On the growth of intelligence. *American Psychologist, 10,* 805.

Beilin, H. (1983). The new functionalism and Piaget's program. In E. K. Scholnick (Ed.), *New trends in conceptual representation* (pp. 3–40). Hillsdale, NJ: Lawrence Erlbaum Associates.

Brainerd, C. J. (1973). Neo-Piagetian training experiments. Is there any support for the cognitive-developmental stage hypothesis? *Cognition, 2,* 349–370.

Brainerd, C. J. (1983). Modifiability of cognitive development. In S. Meadows (Ed.), *Developing thinking* (pp. 26–66). London: Methuen.

Broughton, J. M., & Freeman-Moir, D. J. (1982). *The cognitive developmental psychology of James Mark Baldwin: Current theory and research on genetic epistemology.* Norwood, NJ: Ablex.

Brown, A. L. (1982). Learning and development: The problems of compatibility, access, and induction. *Human Development, 25,* 89–115.

Brown, A. L., Bransford, J. D., Ferrara, R. A., & Campione, J. C. (1983). Learning, remembering and understanding. In P.H. Mussen (Ed.), *Handbook of child psychology* (Vol. III, pp. 77–166). J. H. Flavell & E. M. Markman (Eds.), *Cognitive development.* New York: Wiley.

Cairns, R. B. (1983). The emergence of developmental psychology. In P. H. Mussen (Ed.), *Handbook of child psychology* (4th ed., pp. 41–102). W. Kessen (Ed.), *History, theory, and methods* (Vol. 1). New York: Wiley.

Emde, R. N., Gaensbauer, T. J., & Harmon, R. J. (1976). Emotional expression in infancy. A biobehavioral study. *Psychological issues, a monograph series,* (Vol. 10). New York: International Universities Press.

Fagan, J. F., & Singer, L. T. (1983). Infant recognition memory as a measure of intelligence. In L. P. Lipsitt & C. K. Rovee-Collier. (Eds.), *Advances in infancy research* (Vol. 2, pp. 31–78). Norwood, NJ: Ablex.

Feldman, D. H. (1980). *Beyond universals in cognitive development.* New York: Ablex.

Fischer, K. W. (1980). A theory of cognitive development: The control and construction of hierarchies of skills. *Psychological Review, 87,* 477–531.

Flavell, J. (1971). Stage-related properties of cognitive development. *Cognitive Psychology, 2,* 421–453.

Gelman, R., & Baillargeon, R. (1983). A review of some Piagetian concepts. In P.H. Mussen (Ed.), *Handbook of child development* (Vol. III, pp. 167–230). J.H. Flavell & E.M. Markman (Eds.), *Cognitive development.* New York: Wiley.

Gesell, A. (1954). The ontogenesis of infant behavior. In L. Carmichael (Ed.), *Manual of child psychology* (2nd ed.). New York: Wiley.

Harris, P. L. (1983). Infant cognition. In P.H. Mussen (Ed.), *Handbook of child psychology* (Vol. II, pp. 689–782). M.M. Haith & J.J. Campos (Eds.), *Infancy and developmental psychbiology.* New York: Wiley.

Kitchener, R. F. (1982). Holism and the organismic model in developmental psychology. *Human Development, 25,* 233–249.

Lerner, R. M. (1976). *Concepts and theories of human development.* Reading, MA: Addison-Wesley.

Miller, P. H. (1983). *Theories of developmental psychology.* San Francisco: W.H. Freeman.

O'Connor, M. J., Cohen, S., & Parmelee, A. H. (1984). Infant auditory discrimination in pre-term and full-term infants as a predictor of 5-year intelligence. *Developmental Psychology, 20,* 159–165.

Piaget, J. (1952). *The origins of intelligence in children.* New York: International Universities Press.

Piaget, J. (1970). *Structuralism.* New York: Basic Books.

Piaget, J. (1972). Intellectual evolution from adolescence to adulthood. *Human Development, 15,* 1–12.

Piaget, J. (1977a). The multiplicity of forms of psychological explanations. In H. E. Gruber & J.J. Vonèche (Eds.), *The essential Piaget* (pp. 746–766). New York: Basic Books.

Piaget, J. (1977b). Structuralism: Introduction and location of problems. In H.E. Gruber & J.J. Vonèche (Eds.), *The essential Piaget* (pp. 767–774). New York: Basic Books.

Piaget, J. (1977c). The stages of intellectual development in childhood and adolescence. In H.E. Gruber & J.J. Vonèche (Eds.), *The essential Piaget* (pp. 814–819). New York: Basic Books.

Piaget, J. (1982). Reflections on Baldwin. In J.M. Broughton & D.J. Freeman-Moir (Eds.), *The cognitive developmental psychology of James Mark Baldwin* (pp. 80–86). Norwood, NJ: Ablex.

Piaget, J. (1983). Piaget's theory. In P.H. Mussen (Ed.), *Handbook of child psychology* (Vol. I, pp. 101–128). W. Kessen (Ed.), *History, theory, and methods*. New York: Wiley.

Polanyi, M. (1958). *Personal knowledge*. Chicago, IL: The University of Chicago Press.

Reese, H. W., & Overton, W. F. (1970). Models of development and theories of development. In L.R. Goulet & P.B. Baltes (Eds.), *Life-span developmental psychology* (pp. 115–145). New York: Academic Press.

Sameroff, A. J. (1983). Developmental systems: Contents and evolution. In P.H. Mussen (Ed.), *Handbook of child psychology* (Vol. 1, pp. 237–294). W. Kessen (Ed.), *History, theory and methods*. New York: Wiley.

Sherrington, C. S. (1906). *The integrative action of the nervous system*. New York: Scribners.

Siegler, R. S. (1983). Information processing approaches to development. In P.H. Mussen (Ed.), *Handbook of child psychology* (Vol. I, pp. 129–211). W. Kessen (Ed.), *History, theory, and methods*. New York: Wiley.

Siegler, R. S., & Richards, D. D. (1982). The development of intelligence. In R.J. Sternberg (Ed.), *Handbook of human intelligence* (pp. 897–971). Cambridge, MA: Cambridge University Press.

Sternberg, R. J., & Powell, J. S. (1982). Theories of intelligence. In R.J. Sternberg (Ed.), *Handbook of human intelligence* (pp. 975–1005). Cambridge, MA: Cambridge University Press.

Sternberg, R. J., & Powell, J. S. (1983). The development of intelligence. In P.H. Mussen (Ed.), *Handbook of child psychology* (Vol. III, pp. 341–419). J.H. Flavell & E.M. Markman (Eds.), *Cognitive development*. New York: Wiley.

Stott, L. H., & Ball, R. S. (1965). Infant and preschool mental tests: Review and evaluation. *Monographs of the Society for Research in Child Development, 30,* (Serial No. 101).

von Bertalanffy, L. (1968). *General system theory*. New York: George Braziller. (Rev. Ed.).

von Bertalanffy, L. (1975). *Perspectives on general system theory*. New York: George Braziller.

Waddington, C. H. (1966). *Principles of development and differentiation*. New York: Macmillan.

Weiss, P. A. (1941). Self-differentiation of the basic patterns of coordination. *Comparative Psychology Monographs, 17,* 1–96.

Weiss, P. A. (1971). *Hierarchically organized systems in theory and practice*. New York: Hafner.

Werner, H. (1957a). *Comparative psychology of mental development* (3rd ed.). New York: International Universities Press.

Werner, H. (1957b). The concept of development from a comparative and organismic point of view. In D.B. Harris (Ed.), *The concept of development: An issue in the study of human behavior* (pp. 125–148). Minneapolis, MN: University of Minnesota Press.

White, S. H. (1965). Evidence for a hierarchical arrangement of learning processes. In L.P. Lipsitt & C.C. Spiker (Eds.), *Advances in child development and behavior* (Vol. 2, pp. 187–220). New York: Academic Press.

Wohlwill, J. F. (1973). *The study of behavioral development*. New York: Academic Press.

3

Behaviorism: Processes of Acquisition and Organization of Mechanisms

It has been referred to as *the mechanical mirror* (Langer, 1969), *black box psychology,* and many other names, some of which are even less complimentary. It has been declared obsolete, overthrown, and outmoded. Yet, paradoxically, this object of derision, behaviorism, has given us our most unassailable behavioral laws and has provided the underlying principles from which our most powerful behavioral technologies have been derived to help the retarded, the handicapped, the dependent, and the ill. To understand the intellectual contradictions inherent in this paradox it is important to briefly reflect on the orientations that stand in opposition to behaviorism and to consider the kinds of questions about development that can be posed from a behavioristic framework. Some of the early history of behaviorism is then reviewed in order to get at the source of the caricatures that have come to be associated with stimulus-response ("S–R") psychology. The essential scientific power inherent in the behavioristic approach is also discussed. This leads to a consideration of the relationship between learning and development and, finally, a discussion of processes and mechanisms to account for behavioral development.

The overarching scientific question about behavioral development is: "How is the behavioral repertoire of the human organism acquired?" The answers provided by Gesell, Piaget, and the structuralists have focused much more on the issue of "what" is acquired during development than on "how" behavior is acquired. "How" ultimately leads one to the mechanisms and processes of acquisition. To the extent that Gesell invoked mechanisms they are contained in his principles of developmental morphology undergirded by the organismic impetus to grow and mature. Piaget's "how" is to be found in the processes of assimilation, accommodation, and equilibration. Gesell's principles are largely descriptive, whereas Piaget's mechanisms are largely metaphorical. Learning is definitely not considered the prime mechanism driving development. Those holding to a strong structuralist position typically acknowledge that learning is not irrelevant to the acquisition of behavior. However, learning is made possible by development; development and learning are not synonymous nor is learning the mechanism considered to be driving development. Behavioral development is described by the succession of structures. In Piagetian terms, this refers to transform rules that each child invents for operating in the world.

One explanation for the development of structure could involve the hypothesis that the basic mechanisms of learning are intimately involved in the creation of these structures. Successive structures would then be analyzed as learned behaviors that form and dissipate, to be replaced by or shaped into more sophisticated behaviors and behavioral classes (structures?). However, there has been considerable reluctance to invoke such an explanation. Rather, the structures are said to evolve out of the child's concourse with the world. The existence of the structure then makes learning of specific content possible. For example, the development of classification structures permits the child to learn to manipulate numbers. Classification structures enable the teaching of arithmetic. Learning arithmetic is not possible if the classification structures have not developed to a certain point. Obviously, the child who does not receive formal instruction in arithmetic will not spontaneously add, divide, subtract, and multiply numbers. However, given the existence of classification as a general structure, the latent possibility of learning arithmetic is present. If and when effective instruction is provided, arithmetic skills will be learned. Another way of saying this is that structure gives possibility to learning while learning gives substance to behavioral structure.

THE BEHAVIORIST'S PERSPECTIVE ON DEVELOPMENT

From the point of view of behaviorism, nothing is gained by positing, on the one hand, the development of structures as an evolving process fueled by assimilation, accommodation, and equilibration and then, on the other hand, acknowledging that the substantive behavioral acquisitions are accounted for by learning. Cognitivists give the more important role to the structures, but the mechanisms for structural development are at best fuzzy metaphors; learning is acknowledged but given a secondary, somewhat trivial role even though the mechanisms of learning are clearly defined and behaviors that must be learned constitute large and important portions of the behavioral repertoire of the child and the adult. The trivialization of learning and its subordination to structure turns the story the wrong side out for many behaviorists.

It is assumed by most behaviorists that the larger portion of behavioral acquisition will eventually be understood by the application of the basic principles of learning as they have been demonstrated in laboratory studies of animals and humans. The extensive data base that has been accumulated with respect to the newborn infant's conditionability (Lipsitt, 1979; Rovee-Collier, 1986) gives reason to claim that learning mechanisms are "in place" at birth. Indeed, Neal Miller (1959) believed that it was possible to load the mechanisms of learning with the larger share of responsibility for behavioral acquisition precisely because the human organism was born so well equipped to learn. From the data gathered subsequent to Miller's assertion, it is now known that in addition to conditionability, the newborn and young infant is not, as William James claimed, confronted with a big, buzzing, confusing array of environmental stimuli. Rather, the human infant either has or quickly develops an impressive array of behavioral competence in discriminating environmental stimulation in all sensory modalities and in recognizing instances of stimulus repetition. The initial or early developing ability to respond discriminatively to a broad range of environmental stimuli makes even more plausible the invocation of learning mechanisms to account for behavioral acquisition because a discriminative stimulus is a key component in the basic conditioning paradigms.

There are, to be sure, variations within behaviorism that reflect strong theoretical disagreements. The continuum of differences ranges from what is thought of currently as "radical" behaviorism to a more mellow form. This continuum involves the degree of tolerance for inferred variables such as mental operations to account for behavioral acquisition. Corollary issues relate to how much is granted or denied with respect to the role of genetic endowment, evolutionary factors, and individual difference determinants as given starting points for behavioral acquisition. With respect to the basic mechanisms that are invoked to account for the acquisition of behavior, however, there is no disagreement. They involve the paradigms of classical and operant conditioning and all the variables and laws that have been found to determine whether or not a response is acquired, maintained, elaborated, or extinguished in the behavioral repertoire of an individual.

Behaviorists have focused almost exclusively on trying to understand the laws that govern the learning and unlearning of responses. They have not paid particular attention to questions that are framed in terms of "development" except to make age comparisons and to try to specify the degree to which different variables might function differently at different ages. Are behavioral acquisition and development synonymous? Are they co-existing phenomena or complementary aspects of the organism's growth? Most behaviorists consider that behavioral laws are the mechanisms for developmental change. If so, are they the only or the major mechanisms? Are the facts of developmental change in any way relevant to how behavioral laws function? The structuralist clearly views learning as a nested element in development. Behaviorists have been less theoretically consistent in discussions of *learning* and *development,* sometimes using the terms interchangeably, sometimes using *development* as a metaphor. Do the models of developmental systems have any impact on a behavioral analysis of response acquisition? Is there any power to marrying structural and behavioral perspectives in our effort to understand behavioral development?

From the sheer point of view of power of scientific explanation the advantage clearly lies with the behaviorist account of response acquisition. It is useful to examine the roots of that power in the early formulations of the behaviorist doctrine. These are to be found in the work of Pavlov and Watson. Watson, as the formal founder of behaviorism, made the outright assumption that learning accounted for all of developmental outcome. Therefore, in setting a full discussion of the questions related to behaviorism and its processes and mechanisms, Watsonian behaviorism serves as the starting point for making a distinction between methodological behaviorism and theoretical behaviorism. This requires a consideration of the implications that resulted from the philosophical constellation that formed around behaviorism, logical positivism, and physics, and from whence came the characterization of behaviorism as "mechanistic." The behaviorist tradition must also be viewed as it developed from Watson to Hull and Skinner and the variants of behaviorism as they have been reflected in attempts to translate Freudian theory. Freud's influence on the formulation of social learning theory and recent rapprochements with cognitive psychology are also considered. Also of interest is the growth of applied behaviorism and the kinds of conclusions that need to be drawn from the many demonstrations of the utility of behavioral principles in intervention programs in natural and semi-natural settings. A relevant set of issues is found in the processes and mechanisms that have come to the fore in those theories of learning that Bower and Hilgard (1981) classify as "cognitive-organization" that have generated a considerable amount of recent developmental research related to intelligence, information processing, memory, and understanding. Finally, attention is given to the issue of processes of acquisition and the organization of mechanisms from the perspective of proposed sources of constraints on human development such as genetic factors, organismic specialization, and biological boundaries of learning as seen in the context of evolutionary processes.

The purpose of this historical and theoretical odyssey is to try to determine if out of the cumulative history of research on behavioral processes, especially as it has focused upon learning, there is a corpus of mechanisms and a data base that might serve as one set of foundation stones for structuring a model or theory of human development. In doing this, it is important to try to evaluate the utility of the apposition of "mechanistic" and "organismic" views of development. Are the processes, the data base, behavioristic viewpoints, and the so-called mechanistic orientation relevant to an attempt to account for human behavioral development? Or, can they be dismissed as essentially trivial, inappropriate, and unrelated to development? If the current system theory approach has contributed a useful dimension to the understanding of human development, might the "mechanistic" sub-systems that are thought to be part of complex open systems be governed in the behavioral domain by the processes described by behaviorists? What portion of human functioning might be accounted for by these laws and are such laws equally or differentially applicable to the functioning of a sub-system as well as to the development of that sub-system? Are there behavioral principles and laws that can be considered the sole mechanisms of development, or might these principles, in some combination with structural ideas, provide a better account of human development than is now available? In the haste to declare behaviorism an obsolete model there has been a tendency to ignore the empirical base that has resulted from research in the various behaviorist traditions. Science, however, is not ever advanced by dismissing knowledge as obsolete; progress is only made if one builds systematically upon what is known, even if such knowledge must be reinterpreted as new theoretical models are entertained. This point of view informs the historical survey as well as the synthesis that will ultimately be attempted.

ISSUES RAISED IN EARLY BEHAVIORISM:
METHOD, THEORY, PHILOSOPHY

When John B. Watson rejected introspection as a method appropriate to behavioral science, he declared that psychology was, in kind, no different from any other science. An objective methodology, preferably experimental, would provide sufficient access to the laws that govern behavior; subjectivism and postulations of any entities that could not be directly observed and measured were to have no place in a modern behavioral science. As every undergraduate student of psychology learns, this meant that the psychologist need not have any recourse to concepts like mind or consciousness, but only to behaviors that were defined in terms of how they were measured. In addition to authoring an essentially methodological manifesto, Watson also placed a theoretical bet with respect to behavioral development, adopting the Lockian position that at the beginning there is nothing more than a "white paper, void of characters and without ideas," and that human attributes are acquired solely from experience (Locke, 1690/1936). Watson was much more sensitive to the evolutionary legacy that the human organism brings into the world than many of his critics grant. He did not deny that some behavioral changes occur as the result of growth and change in biological structures (Watson, 1924/1970). His emphasis, however, was on environmental experiences and on learning as accounting for developmental outcome through the mechanisms of conditioning.

It has been noted that Watson was ever the scientist, guided by facts, and that his position with respect to mind and the nervous system in relation to the behavioral system was not, for his time, an unreasonable one (Hebb, 1980). Nothing was known then about neural circuits, about the coding of stimulus information, or about inhibitory mechanisms. And, it might be added, little was known about the nature and extent of the behavioral repertoire of the newborn infant except for the presence of reflexive behavior. William James is often quoted for his characterization of the human infant as coming into a world that was essentially a big, buzzing, blooming confusion because the newly born was presumed to lack any ability to make discriminate sense of the environment. Both Gesell and Piaget assumed the initial behavioral repertoire was almost entirely made up of reflexes. It has only been in the last 25 years that the normal newborn infant has been known to, in fact, possess a behavioral repertoire that is not entirely reflexive (Lipsitt, 1979; Self & Horowitz, 1979). As has been noted, the normal newborn human infant exhibits a behavioral repertoire that involves stimulus discrimination and habituation and that appears subject to simple laws of conditioning (Horowitz, 1984; Lipsitt, 1979; Rovee-Collier, 1986); but this was not known in 1910, 1920, or even in 1950. So Watson, in his time, could justifiably take the demonstration of conditioning and extinction of the fear response as a prototype of behavioral acquisition in the young infant (Watson & Rayner, 1920). This resulted in Watson and the early behaviorists being squarely in the nurture camp of the nature–nurture controversy.

Methodological Behaviorism

The distinction between methodological behaviorism and theoretical behaviorism in relation to developmental research is an important one. Watson's emphatic rejection of introspection and his insistence upon objective, reliable observations was further codified and broadened by the alliances formed by behaviorists. They made connection with logical positivism; they adopted as the model for scientific inquiry propositions articulated by the physicist, Percy Bridgman (1927), in his book, *The Logic of Modern Physics;* they eventually relied heavily upon one particular approach within the philosophy of science (Bergmann, 1957). Behaviorism has been assailed for using physics (mechanistic) rather than biology (organismic) as its model. There is no evidence, however, that a large number of the elements that characterize the basic tenets (although not necessarily the extreme dogmatism) of the logical positivist approach to the philosophy of science are not equally applicable, and indeed, used in everyday science in both the physical and biological sciences. The issue may not be physics versus biology per se but the range and complexity of elements that enter into a theoretical model. In this regard it is useful to make explicit some aspects of methodological issues.

It is elementary to note that the key criterion for a scientific definition is the ability to make an accurate and independently verifiable measurement or observation. This, of course, introduces immediate problems with respect to qualitative variables, although ratings, categorical assignments, and the like, if they meet the independently verifiable criterion, can be used to handle qualitative distinctions, up to a point. The early behaviorists adopted a scheme to distinguish two levels of scientific meaning: "Meaning I and Meaning II" (Bergmann, 1957). Meaning I is achieved if a concept or term can be defined by the operations required to make measurements and can be shown to yield essentially the same results if carried out by at least two independent observers. Meaning I is equivalent to the phrase "an operational definition." Meaning II is achieved if it can be shown that a term or concept with Meaning I relates in some predictable way with one or more other phenomena that have Meaning I. Meaning II is equivalent to a low-level law.

Reliable measurement is, obviously, the basic requirement for concepts used by *any* working scientist. Empirical investigations are thus restricted to phenomena that yield themselves to meeting Meaning I criteria. Some complex phenomena and some of the more interesting and intuitively significant phenomena may not seem amenable to being formulated in terms of Meaning I. This has had consequences for the behavior of scientists. Critics who consider that logical positivism has been an inappropriate philosophical basis for behavioral science often are really objecting to these consequences. For example, investigating only variables that are reliably measurable leads to the accusation that the variables chosen for study are often trivial. Some behaviorists will not even speculate about behaviors they feel they cannot measure. Critics claim this produces paucitous theory and shallow speculation. Still another consequence may involve taking a complex and seemingly "rich" variable and defining it in a manner that yields to meeting the criteria for Meaning I, but doing so at a cost that essentially robs the variable of its complexity or intuitively attractive elements, resulting in a kind of trivialization of non-trivial variables.

There is however, considerable evidence that many of the behavioral concepts that do meet Meaning I criteria (used both by behaviorists and nonbehaviorists) do tap into important phenomena in a manner that appears to be useful and conducive to increasing our scientific accounts. In fact, almost all research carried out by behavioral scientists involves measurement procedures that fulfill Meaning I criteria. It is hard to imagine how any science can advance without an initial adherence to a simple principle that involves objective and reliable criteria for observation and measurement of phenomena.

Meaning II criteria should provide a natural corrective for some of the problems related to triviality. A scientific concept is said to have Meaning II if it can be shown to enter into one or more relationships with other concepts, all initially having met the criteria for Meaning I. Bergmann's example was the C-coefficient: C-coefficient = the white blood count of an individual multiplied by the person's weight in ounces and divided by the number of hairs on the person's legs (Bergmann, 1957, p. 50). However reliable the measurement of this coefficient, it is likely a scientifically useless concept because of its low probability (zero?) of being related to any other phenomenon. It is clearly a terribly trivial concept which, although having Meaning I, could hardly be thought to have any Meaning II. Thus, triviality should be a self-correcting problem, as investigators fail to find relationships. But this is not necessarily the case. It is quite possible to devise concepts that meet Meaning I and Meaning II but the realm of Meaning II relationships could, itself, be quite circumscribed and thought trivial, resulting in a science of trivial events.

The Mechanistic Model and Methodological Behaviorism

Although the terms *Meaning I* and *Meaning II* are not in current vogue, the ideas they represent have exerted a powerful influence on the definition of proper research and theory building in experimental psychology and particularly within behaviorism. It is this powerful influence that has been the object of recent and vociferous criticism focusing especially on experimental research with children. The study of factors determining response acquisition in controlled environments (i.e., laboratories) has been cited as producing a science of trivial and arbitrary behaviors that is unlikely to shed any light on how children learn in the complex, noisy natural environment. Such research, it is said, lacks ecological validity (Bronfenbrenner, 1979), is characterized as being too mechanistic and thus having no relevance to development because development is an "open" system. This criticism arises from reasoning that views the child as a biological organism whose growth and development occur in a complex social milieu. The "mechanistic" model (i.e., the model based upon physics) is thought to be inappropriate to the scientific study of human development.

However, as Rovee-Collier (1986) has recently observed, the basic mechanisms of classical conditioning can be studied in an experimental paradigm fitted to ecologically valid conditions. The early work of Papoušek (1967) and Rovee-Collier's own work on infant learning and memory (Rovee-Collier, 1984) are excellent examples of such a strategy.

Because the criteria for defining scientific concepts within psychology were so strongly emphasized by the early behaviorists and because behaviorism has been so fully associated with investigations of learning, there has been a tendency to classify controlled analyses of children's learning as trivial and unlikely to lead to an understanding of the complex phenomena involved in behavioral development. This criticism involves a dangerous over-generalization borne of an "either-or" mentality about the theory that will most successfully account for behavioral development. Complex organisms typically contain sub-systems that may be highly machine-like in their functioning. Thus, a physics-based model such as the behaviorists adopted could well illuminate important and central mechanisms involved in large chunks of human behavior. Learning processes may well characterize some of the fully functioning behavioral sub-systems. The extent to which they are also responsible for those sub-systems has important implications for our discussion of the relationship between learning and development.

Most current experimental and observational research, whether undertaken by behaviorists, by those interested in cognition, or by those who espouse organismic approaches will choose variables that meet the criteria for both Meaning I and Meaning II and thus exemplify methodological behaviorism. A possible exception is to be found in the Piagetian type of clinical experiment where children are "probed" for descriptions of reasoning. These may then be used to illuminate theory, or sometimes as the source of qualifying children's responses in order to arrive at a categorization of groups. In this latter instance we are right back to Meaning I criteria. If the operations for arriving at the categorization scheme can be specified and shown to result in agreement between different individuals who read the protocols and make the classifications, then Meaning I criteria will have been met.

To state all of this more succinctly: Methodological behaviorism itself is not at issue in the current debate concerning appropriate models and theories of development. Some investigators heavily influenced by methodological behaviorism (many of whom also happen to be theoretical behaviorists) do choose to constrain their interpretations of data and their speculations about development quite narrowly with respect to limiting themselves to the use of terms that meet Meaning I criteria. Thus, methodological behaviorism appears to spill over into theoretical behaviorism. The more narrowing these constraints, the farther the discussions and interpretations appear to be from some of the core developmental issues that characterize an organismic approach to development. This contributes significantly to the wide gap that appears to separate so-called organismic and mechanistic analyses.

Theoretical Behaviorism and Developmental Outcome

Sometimes it is claimed that behaviorism is not, per se, a theory of development and there is some justification for such a point of view. Watson's initial formulation of behaviorism involved a theoretical commitment to the proposition that developmental outcome was a function of the opportunities for a child to learn. His claim that he could fashion any developmental outcome for any healthy infant by manipulating the environment in which the infant would grow has become legendary. Thus, he was a protagonist for the "nurture" side in the nature–nurture controversy, taking a stand against the "nature" position held by Gesellians.

The Watsonian belief that developmental outcome is the result of the history of the child's opportunities to learn formed the basis for some important research efforts in the 1920s and 1930s. First, there was the attempt to demonstrate that the newborn infant could be conditioned. If the newborn infant could be conditioned then the proposition that development was shaped by learning would appear reasonable. The early attempts at newborn infant conditioning ultimately were inconclusive, partly because the technology for doing the experiments properly had not yet been developed then. It would be some 30 years until such demonstrations were made (Lipsitt, 1979; Papoušek, 1967; Rovee-Collier, 1986).

A second major effort born of the belief in environmental influence on developmental outcome is to be found in the empirical attempts to show that intellectual functioning could be influenced by environmental manipulations. Similar to the fate of the infant conditioning research, the results of the famous Iowa studies carried out by Skeels and his colleagues (Skeels & Dye, 1939) were declared as uncertain. Methodological flaws and inadequate statistical treatment of data were cited to raise questions concerning the seemingly enormous effects on IQ scores in children brought about by changes in environmental circumstances. More than 25 years would pass before a longitudinal follow-up resulted in evidence showing that the effects of the experimental manipulations were subsequently compounded by different life histories to produce major differences in adult status (Skeels, 1966). It is interesting to observe that this intervention research that was so admittedly methodologically vulnerable did produce information that ultimately proved to be more valid than originally believed. This was true, as well, for the infant conditioning research.

Behaviorism was early on theoretically allied with the environmental position in the nature–nurture controversy. However, the theoretical developments within behaviorism tended to be more focused upon theories related to response acquisition than to the developmental course of response acquistion. The article of faith laid down by Watson, supported to some extent by the infant conditioning data, was rooted in the belief that investigation into the laws of learning would ultimately lead to an understanding of human behavioral development. The laws were thought to have cross-species validity so that whether the subject was a child or rat did not seem to be terribly important. It was thought that especially in the early phases of behavioral research the laws being discovered would be the more simple and the most fundamental laws. Later elaborations would take cognizance of specific organismic characteristics that might modify the laws and/or require extensions and elaborations. The elaborations that were developed were thought of as generic even as they involved attempts to encompass increasingly complex aspects of behavioral acquisition.

The most extensive elaborated theoretical model to explain response acquisition was proposed by Hull and his colleagues. This approach, built in logical parallel with theories in physics, involved a set of basic propositions and mathematically described equations that were used to derive testable hypotheses concerning the variables that control response acquisition (Hull, 1943; Spence, 1956). Rats were convenient subjects for testing the hypotheses about how different variables would affect curves of learning. The elements identified in the theory, also included by Watson and Pavlov, became stalwart variables in later approaches to learning, whether or not formal Hullian theory was of central interest: the influence of such stimulus characteristics as discriminability, duration, timing of appearance, conditions of presentation, or response acquisition, and the characteristics of responses that influence behavioral change. A special class of stimuli received particular theoretical attention: reinforcing stimuli. B. F. Skinner, although eschewing theory development, elaborated the notion of reinforcers, giving them almost sole power in the controlling conditions responsible for the acquisition of responses. Both Hullian theory and Skinnerian psychology have figured prominently in the application of behaviorism to child development research, to discussions of the relationship between learning and development, and to the topic of developmental outcome.

LEARNING AND DEVELOPMENT

Watson assumed that developmental outcome for normal healthy organisms was shaped largely by the forces of the individual's environment, and specifically via the operation of the principles of conditioning. Subsequently, behaviorists ranged on a continuum with respect to the degree to which they assigned to principles of conditioning and therefore environmental variables, the responsibility for developmental outcomes. Watson and then Skinner represented that end where a very large (almost total) effect of conditioning is assumed. Others, including Pavlov, gave different amounts of recognition to the role of structural and organismic variables. At some point on this continuum we pass what behaviorists will tolerate. The continuum then shades over into the position of the structuralists who assign minimal responsibility for developmental outcome to environmental factors except as they provide the necessary milieu in which development takes place. White (1970) stated one of the basic tenets of learning theory as: "Unless there is definite evidence to the contrary, classes of behavior may be assumed to be learned, manipulable by the environment, extinguishable, and trainable" (pp. 666–670). Structuralists believe learning is made possible by the organization and evolution of structures. Behaviorists believe structural elements, if they exist, are derived from the cumulative effects of learning. These, ultimately, are expected to account for both qualitative behavioral changes and long-term developmental outcome (Gagne, 1968).

The issues and debate are clouded, often by imprecise use of terms. For example, *learning* and *conditioning* are sometimes used interchangeably. Actually, learning should be reserved for referencing the notion that behavior is aquired as the result of experience. Conditioning is a specific reference to the processes thought to account for acquired behavior. Pavlov (1927) described the procedures for classical conditioning; Miller and Konorski (1928) are credited with the first report on conditioning experiments that became the prototype for instrumental or operant conditioning. The two paradigms are well known to every introductory psychology student, and a further description of them is not needed here. It is interesting to note that considerably more research emphasis has been placed upon instrumental and operant conditioning in relation to development than upon classical conditioning. Skinnerians, particularly, believe the operant paradigm to be the more pervasive process in behavioral development. (Rovee-Collier, 1986, however, suggests that there has been some blurring of the distinctions in actual laboratory experimental procedures.)

The ubiquity of operant conditioning to account for behavioral development is open to question especially when it comes to the role that emotions play in the acquisition of behavior. There is ample evidence, going back to Watson's demonstration of the conditioning of the fear response in little Albert (Watson & Rayner, 1920) that emotional reactions to stimuli can be acquired through classical conditioning. For example, the hungry baby learns to associate the relief of hunger distress and the accompanying feelings of pleasure with presence of the mother. The mother then takes on the ability to reinforce a wide range of the child's behaviors through operant conditioning. But, the initial, and perhaps necessary component for what ultimately involves the entire process of early socialization rests in a classically conditioned association of pleasure with the stimulus of the mother. The recent observational experimental work by the Papoušeks on "intuitive parenting" makes liberal use of these paradigms as they are embedded in the natural environment (Papoušek & Papoušek, 1983, 1984, 1985). In fact, the natural environment may offer a more efficient setting for conditioning than the laboratory (Horowitz, 1968).

The recently renewed interest in early emotional development has been largely descriptive in nature and not undertaken in the context of learning paradigms. How emotional responses function in the transactional relationship between the young child and his environment will likely require an analysis involving classical conditioning and operant conditioning.

Hullian Theory and Child Development

One of the most systematic applications of learning theory to child behavior and, by implication, to developmental theory, occured in relation to Hullian theory. Kenneth Spence, among Hull's foremost students/colleagues, moved to the University of Iowa where, in the Iowa Child Welfare Research Station, Skeels and his associates were attempting to demonstrate the impact of environmental factors on IQ. Here, behaviorism with its emphasis on learning and the environment would receive a sympathetic hearing. Eventually, scores of obvious experiments using children suggested themselves as tests of Hullian theory. Children were considered good subjects to test the generality of Hullian theory. With seemingly minimal histories of environmental experience (compared to adults), they were considered relatively naive learners. They thus provided a nearer test of extension to human behavior from animal behavior for Hull's theory of learning (McCandless & Spiker, 1956). If the theory enabled predictions about learning in children then the animal behavior models on which the theory was built could be seen as providing data for a general theory to account for behavioral development.

In the mid-1940s and on through the next 2 decades, experimental child psychology based on Hullian theory flourished. Many of the studies were specifically designed to replicate findings with rats. A 1972 review of research on children's learning (Stevenson, 1972) listed more than 500 references, more than half of which might be claimed to have been influenced by Hullian theory and its derivatives. In all the studies, the variables and phenomena of interest were typically those specified by the theory: different kinds of stimulus presentations (e.g., simultaneous vs. successive) and their effect on discrimination learning; the role of partial as opposed to continuous reinforcement; the influence of reinforcement delay and magnitude; stimulus and response generalization; the effect of motivational variables such as anxiety or stress on response acquisition. Many of the studies were designed to test specific theoretical predictions, especially with respect to discrimination learning, and also in relation to the issue of whether or not "drive" was multiplicative or additive with habit in the equation predicting the form of the learning curve and response strength.

Some of the questions were directed at developmental phenomena, comparing the learning of younger and older children. Here, it soon became clear, the theory would require some elaboration if it were to account for developmental events. The earliest indication of this came from Kuenne's (1946) classic study on the role of verbal labels in learning about relations that exist between stimuli: Spence (1937) proposed a theory that accounted for "transposition," relational learning in animals involving choosing stimuli on a size dimension. An animal trained to choose the larger of two stimuli will, when presented with another pair of stimuli, also choose the larger of the two. However, the tendency to choose the larger of the two (i.e., transpose) will decrease as the absolute difference between the stimulus sizes of the second pair (test pair) increases when compared to the first pair (training pair). Kuenne reasoned that older children would be more likely to use verbal mediational responses such as "pick the big one" than younger children. The result would be an increased tendency to transpose with age, even to pairs quite dissimilar in absolute size. Here prediction proved correct in an experiment with children at mental ages of 3, 4, 5, and 6. Children at the higher mental ages tended to transpose even to stimulus test pairs relatively far from the stimulus training pair.

If Hullian theory was to predict learning in children and to provide the prototypical model of behavioral development, then additional variables and processes would need to be introduced. Some phenomena described at a relatively simple level for infra-human organisms would require extension and reformulation—a not surprising perspective, and one fully recognized by Hullians. Unlike radical Watsonian and Skinnerian behaviorism, Hullian theory tolerated speculation regarding events and variables intervening between stimulus or task presentation and the occurrence of the response. In this case S-R theory really became S-O-R theory where "O" is represented by postulation of internal variables and processes with various experiments designed to test differential predictions from the postulates. And so, the Hullian variety of theory and research on learning in children began to be elaborated and augmented to include such factors as linguistic variables, imagery, memory, verbal rehearsal, and learning set, including intervening variables already posited for infra-humans and extending that list.[1] Sometimes experiments could be designed using animals as well as humans, but

---

[1]Beilin (1983) regards these developments as movement toward functionalism within behaviorism and, ultimately, as a source of weakening the force of behaviorism.

for such abilities as language and imagery, only children and adults would serve. For many developmental questions children were seen as the ideal subjects.

The behavioristic study of learning in children has occasioned significant comment with respect to the supposed "passive" nature of the child in behaviorism as opposed to the "active" child of the organismic view. Because the experimenter set the task and the theory set the variables, the specific nature of the child, qua child, appeared to be ignored. In the enthusiasm for the child qua child that appears to be inherent in the organismic view, behaviorism has come in for considerable criticism, shading almost into caricature. Hebb (1980) has noted that in some circles behaviorism has become a term of "abuse," and the object of "contemptuous comment" rather than the subject of reasoned analysis by appeal to facts and evidence. Part of this stems from the seeming contrast between the organismic and mechanistic world views (e.g., Overton & Reese, 1972) wherein the organismic approach appears to capture the child's behavior in richer and more complex dimensions than the S–R approach. This gives rise to the implication that behaviorism produced a terribly simplistic analysis of child behavior that is now practically obsolete.

Another element contributing to the critique/caricature of behaviorism involves the fact that Piaget's observations of children and the strategy he employed revealed phenomena that were surprising in their complexity, structure, and dynamic progression. Everyone who now looks at child behavior can readily see these behaviors. In all the child watching by behaviorists they were never discerned. Behaviorists have insisted upon bringing every behavioral sequence into an analysis that admitted only of stimuli and responses. They have assumed that current behavior reflects a history of stimulus-response pairings. For all the complexity of the historical response chain and for all the theoretical niceties of intervening variables and the resulting operational elegance to be found in theoretical behaviorism, in the face of Piagetian behavioral descriptions, the S–R analyses have appeared to fall woefully short of the complex, structural, organizational, and dynamic dimensions that are considered inherent characteristics of behavioral development by organismic developmentalists. Learning theory was thereby declared "wrong" in its conceptualization of development and developmental processes. As a result, the knowledge base that has been accumulated has been all but ignored as irrelevant to the organismic point of view. Only recently has there been an effort at rapprochement between the traditional experimental child-learning literature of theoretical behaviorism and the cognitive development literature (e.g., Gholson & Beilin, 1979).

Skinnerian Psychology and Child Development

Although Skinner's manifesto declaring operant conditioning primal for the acquisition of the behavioral repertoire was written in 1938 (Skinner, 1938), it was not until the late 1960s that his position began fully to impact child development. Gewirtz (1967), Bijou and Baer (1961), Etzel (Etzel & Gewirtz, 1967), and others focused on the investigation of child behavior using the Skinnerian model or what came to be called *behavior analysis techniques.* This model contained several elements that resulted in an almost total segregation of operantly oriented child development research from Hull–Spence S–R research on children's learning. Foremost among these was the use of single-subject design and the rejection of inferential statistics as a valid path to scientific truth. Instead, in agreement with Skinner, the validity of experimental results was to be found when single subjects were studied and there was replication across subjects. As a consequence, when main line developmental journal reviewers, more often than not drawn from the ranks of traditional investigators, rejected manuscripts that did not contain statistical analyses, new journals whose editorial boards shared the single-subject design bias were formed. Thus, a distinct and for the most part non-interacting or intersecting child development literature evolved. The *Journal of Experimental Child Psychology* has been a notable exception and publishes operant as well as other experimental studies of children's learning. However, one looks in vain for a chapter in the 1983 *Mussen Handbook of Child Psychology* devoted to the considerable and impressive data base amassed by operantly oriented investigators. (An exception is Alexander and Malouf's, 1983, discussion of problems in personality and social development and intervention.) Bronfenbrenner (1979) totally ignored this literature even though some of what he called for with respect to natural environment analyses characterizes much of the work in applied behavior analysis (e.g., the *Journal of Applied Behavior Analysis*). A heartening exception, however, is to be found in Fischer's (1980) proposal of skill theory that builds in operant mechanisms to account for cognitive behavior and development.

The narrow, radical behaviorism espoused by Skinner rejected theory building or recourse to any intervening variables. It championed a strict and extreme environmentalism that gave to reinforcing consequences the full causal responsibility for response acquisition. Development, according to this point of view, involves nothing more than a series of "changes in operant behaviors" resulting from the processes of conditioning and extinction. "Nothing more" should not be taken as synonymous with simple. Inherent in these processes are not only discrimination and generalization of responses that are shaped from approximations to full behavioral form, but there is also included the acquisition of long and complex chains of behaviors that are organized into response classes and that function under the control of an elaborate network of stimulus cues. Painstaking efforts have gone into specifying the operational definitions of responses, response classes, and discriminative stimuli. Extensive descriptions of procedures designed to achieve control of behavior change involving shaping, fading, and prompting have been developed. Reese (1980) has characterized the operant account of development as referring "fundamentally to the procedures of conditioning and extinction . . . but . . . also . . . to certain stimulus and response constructs, most notably reinforcers of various kinds, response classes, and imitation" (p. 369).

The most fundamental aspect of disagreement that exists between operant developmentalists and structuralists as to the root account of developmental change is the insistence of the Skinnerians that all behavioral (i.e., developmental) change can be attributed to the successive effect of reinforcing consequences without any reference to structural, or neurological events and/or organismic organization and reorganization. Eschewing almost all notions of any behavioral "givens" with respect to behavioral organization Baer (1976) has asserted: "There is no *integral* constraint on separate responses to organize themselves into groups. Each will do what *its* environment programs for it according to the rules of conditioning" (p. 89). According to this view, the organism is a structure but it is a given and it does not control the responses that will be acquired by the organism nor determine how they will change—the environment does that. The title of the paper from which the previous quote was taken is "The Organism as Host," in which the claim is made that what changes are the responses of the organism, not the organism itself. Environmental control via a broad array of reinforcing agents, including those that occur as automatic consequences or as ecological reinforcers (Bijou & Baer, 1978), and those that function as conditioned and generalized reinforcers, are assumed to be responsible for all behavioral change. The program of developmental research that is recommended therefore involves identifying reinforcing agents and specifying the conditions and variables that affect their operation. This appears to the structuralist not only as extreme but as actually an incorrect placement of the locus of control for development. And, for the theoretical behaviorist who is willing to posit intervening variables or who may view behavior as a window to neural events and neural organization, the operant analysis fails on theoretical grounds as too narrow and incomplete.

The final element that may be cited as contributing to the parting of theoretical and Skinnerian behaviorism is the growth of applied behavior analysis wherein principles developed in the context of the laboratory were applied to real behavioral problems of real children in both laboratory and natural settings. In some ways, the emphasis and successes of application drew operant behaviorists further and further from the issues central to theoretical behaviorism. The fact that many of the basic principles were developed with rats and pigeons involving particular responses and then applied to humans of varying ages without any theoretical concern for organismic differences or for the vastly different response topographies involved has led to the charge that S–R psychology, the Skinnerian brand particularly, is both "subjectless" and "contentless" in its approach.

In contrast, theoretical behaviorism addressed developmental issues early on and came to terms with trying to account for human-type developmental phenomena in relation to learning, thinking, imaging, planning, and problem solving. These issues continue to be the focus of current experimental work on children's learning (e.g., Gholson & McConville, 1974; Kendler, 1979; Spiker & Cantor, 1977). Skinnerians have been much slower to take up peculiarly developmental issues. Possibly, the important successes of applied behavior analysis have served to reinforce the belief that creating theoretical constructs beyond those already specified by operant analysis is not necessary. Baer (1973), in fact, described the ideal program for developmental research as beginning with laboratory analyses showing that behavioral changes obey operant principles, observing analogous phenomena in the natural environment to ascertain if the same functions apply, and intervening in the natural environment to validate the hypotheses in experimental manipulations and/or to remediate problem behavior and delayed development. Contrary to Reese's (1980) claim that such a program of research has not really been undertaken, the applied behavior analysis literature abounds with examples of just such a strategy although not necessarily in as lock-step a fashion as suggested. However, it is fair to say that the most dramatic demonstrations of effective intervention have occurred in what might be called semi-natural controlled environments such as institutions with populations of subjects who are dependent and developmentally impaired by mentally or physically handicapping conditions. The behavioral technologies derived from Skinnerian principles and single-subject design research strategy today enjoy growing application in medicine, education, and a variety of behavioral therapies. These accomplishments no doubt prompted Hebb to observe that Skinnerian behaviorism has probably contributed more and more directly to human welfare than almost any other approach within the social sciences (Hebb, 1980).

It is interesting to consider that the supposedly subjectless and contentless S–R analyses should have had such wide application to so many different subject populations and content areas. Not only is there evidence for successful engineering of behavioral change with retarded children and handicapped children, but one can readily find evidence for increasing school achievement, (Hall, Lund, & Jackson, 1968; O'Leary, Becker, Evans, & Saudargas, 1969; Sulzer & Mayer, 1972), for altering social behaviors of normal children (Patterson & Gullion, 1968), for enhancing language development in low-income children (Hart & Risley, 1980), for affecting some of the behaviors in the repertoire of delinquent youths (Kirigen, Wolf, Braukmann, Fixsen, & Phillips, 1979), and for modifying aggressive and disruptive behaviors in children of varying ages. So much for one aspect of the subjectless and contentless issue. However, there is another, more profoundly developmental aspect that must eventually be resolved. It is embodied in the somewhat simple question of whether demonstrating that one can make something happen in a particular way necessarily implies that the same processes are responsible for development in the natural environment. Or, put another way—are demonstrations of learning as synonymous with behavioral change the complete and sufficient analog for developmental changes in the normal organism in the natural environment? Before these issues can be addressed it is necessary to consider several other approaches to developmental questions within the behaviorist tradition and with respect to processes and mechanisms.

Translating Freud and Social Learning Theory

One of the most, if not the most complete theory of human development is the one proposed and elaborated upon by Freud. Orthodox psychoanalytic theory was not meant to nor is it easily amenable to verification strategies that meet the criteria of methodological behaviorism, although in recent years a more empirical tradition has evolved within psychoanalytic circles (Masling, 1983). Nevertheless, the influence of Freudian theory on mainstream developmental psychology and its empirical traditions has been considerable.[2] Many of the early investigations of the effect of early experience on development were stimulated as much by Freudian theory as by the behavioristic commitment to the influence of environment on development. Many of the topics that have been the mainstay of psychological interest have their roots in Freudian theory, mother–infant attachment and temperament to name two, affective development, dependency, aggression among others. Some of this influence can be very directly traced to Freudian theory (as in the work of Emde, 1980, and his colleagues). In other instances Freud's influence is less directly acknowledged both in relation to topic and paradigmatic approach. Recently, a reverse course of influence is to be observed. In light of the explosion of empirical information concerning early infant behavior and development, psychoanalysts have been re-evaluating the early Freudian stages with respect to the now established facts about infant behavior that were not available in the era when psychoanalytic

---

[2]I acknowledge Robert Emde for his prod in stimulating me to be more explicit on this point and what follows.

characterizations of infants were first formulated (Lichtenberg, 1983; Stern, 1985).

Freudian theory, in its completeness and in its intuitive appeal, provided a challenge to behaviorists. The faith that S–R analyses would and could account for even the most complex of human behaviors was thus to be tested in attempts to translate aspects of Freudian theory into learning theory. One of the first significant efforts in this regard was made by Dollard, Doob, Miller, Mowrer, and Sears (1939). They took up Freud's hypothesis that aggression is always the consequence of frustration. They subjected it to extensive analysis in stimulus–response terms. The evidence for its validity was searched out in diverse research literatures on socialization practices directed at children, development during adolescence, deviant behavior, and finally, complex social systems. A similar but more delimited and more experimentally based analysis was applied to social learning and imitation (Miller & Dollard, 1941) and finally to personality and psychotherapy (Dollard & Miller, 1950) in a book dedicated jointly to Pavlov and to Freud. Dollard and Miller's (1950) book on personality and psychotherapy represented the most explicit attempt to integrate ideas from quite different realms—psychology, psychoanalysis, anthropology— and to integrate them in an analysis based upon the assumption that "neurosis and psychotherapy obey the laws of learning" (Dollard & Miller, 1950, p. 8). This and the other two publications cited here formed the basis of what ultimately developed into social learning theory—an attempt to take basic learning principles and elaborate them as needed to account for complex social behavior and development with perhaps more emphasis upon complex social behavior than upon developmental issues (e.g., Miller, 1959).

Social learning theory is today perhaps the most viable and vigorous descendant of Hullian theory, shorn of a mathematico–deductive strategy and the insistence upon drive reduction as a major variable. It is also a considerably elaborated theory with the introduction of processes other than reinforcing consequences to account for response acquisition. In the most recent systematic presentation of social learning theory, Bandura (1977) places the traditional strong emphasis upon the importance of reinforcing consequences although vicarious reinforcement and observational learning strategies extend the armamentarium of available sources of reinforced learning. Quite significantly, the theory now includes an important role for cognition. Bandura (1977) introduced his discussion of cognitive control as follows:

> If human behavior could be fully explained in terms of antecedent inducements and response consequences, there would be no need to postulate any additional regulatory mechanisms. However, most external influences affect

> behavior through intermediary cognitive processes. Cognitive factors partly
> determine which external events will be observed, how they will be perceived,
> whether they leave any lasting effects, what valence and efficacy they have,
> and how the information they convey will be organized for future use. (p. 160)

Included in cognitive events are imagery, representation of experience in
symbolic form, and thought processes. These variables are not new to
learning theory (e.g., Kendler & Spence, 1971), but their treatment within
current social learning theory involves an attempt to make a direct connection with modern cognitive psychology (e.g., Rosenthal & Zimmerman,
1978) and in some instances explicitly with Piagetian theory (e.g., Gholson
& Beilin, 1979).

In the current theoretical expansions of learning theory there has not
been any abandonment of an essentially process orientation. In other
words, the incorporation of cognition into accounts of learning does not
involve relinquishing the idea that development is essentially the result of
the cumulative effect of learned behavior. Understanding learned behavior
and development may require extension of principles, introduction of new
principles, and inclusion of variables associated with mental processes. But
there is a distinction to be made between the expansion of learning theory
and the incorporation of the basic assumptions of the structuralist point of
view. Bandura's social learning theory analysis stops short of the structuralist
position with regard to developmental reorganization. Similarly, Rosenthal
and Zimmerman (1978) in their discussion of cognition and social learning,
accept Bandura's notion that the individual's interaction with the environment involves three components: stimulus controls, reinforcement controls,
and cognitive controls. The cognitive controls are, however, acquired
through experience:

> Although recognizing that typical structural frameworks might be useful in
> describing the modal changes in thought and language, a social learning view
> suggests that the organizing structures can usefully be examined in terms of
> component rules and operating assumptions. Since these rules can be learned
> through experience, no assumptions of fixed maturation or innate sequences
> of development need be made. This formulation enables both short- and
> long-term changes in behavior to be explained by the same principles. (p. 30)

Thus, the account of development has been expanded in terms of processes,
variables, and place in a socio-cultural context, but the base nature of
development as the result of the cumulative effects of learning is not
relinquished. This is true, as well, for those working within the Skinnerian
framework who have incorporated cognitive concepts into their work and

who have utilized variables associated with cognition in operant analyses (e.g., Meichenbaum, 1977).

The strength of what might be called a *learning* view of development has been its emphasis upon process and upon validating the variables involved in process. As has been suggested, an enormous and important data base on learning has been amassed within this orientation. From one subset of efforts within this general point of view, a behavioral technology has been developed that has had wide and successful application. One of the strengths of behaviorism has been in the attention given to processes and mechanisms that have been applied to learning, information processing, memory, and the operation of intelligence. They also have been discussed in the context of the evolutionary history of the human organism.

PROCESSES AND MECHANISMS

Miller's (1959) observation that it was not unreasonable to load upon the mechanisms of learning the major responsibility for human response acquisition already has been noted. The evolutionary history of the human organism was such as to have resulted in there being, at birth, a capability to attend selectively to stimuli and to form simple associations. More recently, Siegler (1983), in setting the base for his review of the information-processing literature and development, observed that the normal human newborn is already behaviorally equipped with a set of basic information-processing and representational skills: recognition, visual scanning, categorical perception, associational learning, and intersensory integration. In many ways, the human organism shares a number of these characteristics with animals of other species, but for the human they are destined, under normal circumstances, to be elaborated into a behavioral repertoire that is unparalleled in the animal kingdom. How this happens and what the peculiarly human aspects of this developmental course are raises the question of the central processes and mechanisms involved in human behavioral development.

Despite the tendency of some to dismiss behaviorism and its emphasis upon learning as irrelevant to an account of behavioral development, there is no question that the ability to form associations (i.e., to learn) is at the heart of any set of developmental mechanisms. It is now also clear that the initial behavioral repertoire gives both possibility and constraint with respect to how learning occurs and what is likely to be learned. Further, the characteristics and development of the organism's interaction with stimulus information undoubtedly are profoundly implicated in shaping the course of learning. And finally, the evolutionary history of the human organism has probably contributed significant determining elements to both the information-processing and the learning domains that contribute to its behavioral development. It is useful to discuss these issues and perspectives in turn and to consider how our knowledge in each of these areas might best be used in constructing a model to account for behavioral development.

When Miller (1959) asserted that the human newborn arrived prepared to learn, there was not then available the kind of firm evidence we now have that the normal human neonate is capable of responding to stimuli in every sensory modality. It was only then just becoming apparent that the newborn infant was able to respond discriminatively to repeated stimulus events and to novel events, again in every sensory modality. The evidence with respect to these areas is now well established. We thus have the basis to say that at least from the very beginning of extrauterine life the human organism attends selectively to stimulus information in the environment and "records" or encodes in at least a short-term memory store information about the environment that can be used for comparative and associational purposes (e.g., Antell, Caron, & Myers, 1985). In the literature documenting learning in the newborn (Lipsitt, 1979) it is clear that a simple S–R paradigm involving reinforcement of responding and classical conditioning paradigms (Rovee-Collier, 1986) result in learned associations in the laboratory. Although there may be qualitatively different aspects affecting neonatal conditioning and although the role of ecologically valid parameters remains to be further understood (Papoušek & Papoušek, 1984), the basic importance of conditioning as a mechanism involved in behavioral development is unassailable.

The question that must be asked with respect to the processes and mechanisms responsible for behavioral development in the natural environment is: Do the information-processing characteristics in the human organism, combined or in concomitance with the ability to learn from the systematic juxtaposition of environmental information and the organism's responses, constitute the necessary and sufficient conditions for the development of the human behavioral repertoire given a physically normal and intact organism? There are several issues inherent in this question.

Are Learning and Development Synonymous?

One issue, and the one that is of great recent popularity, is the relevance of laboratory demonstrations of infant learning and generally of child learning as an analog to how development occurs in the natural environment. To discuss this, a set of subordinate issues with respect to learning must be considered. There is, basically, the question of the learning paradigm as an analog of developmental process. Most laboratory demonstrations related to learning involve either the systematic delivery of reinforcing consequences or observational opportunities for learning to occur as the result of contiguity of events. Is the learning paradigm that requires a reinforcer analogous to what happens in that natural, normal, complex environment? Would it be possible to claim that what is not learned in the natural environment as a result of reinforced responding can otherwise be accounted for by observational learning? Or is it more reasonable to assume that response acquisition is largely determined by intra-organic factors that control the development and organization of response characteristics albeit using the elements of the environment to form the content of behavioral transactions? In this latter characterization "learning" represents the high potential pre-program that only incidentally utilizes information from the environment. In the former instance, environmental events, either by systematic sequencing or observational conjunction, serve to shape and determine both the topography and the content of behavioral development. What evidence exists to help us decide the issue?

There is no single direct test we can make to address the problem of what is essentially a learning-maturation question. There are, however, two indirect sources of evidence that may be cited. One is, as we have noted, the extensive application of learning principles in situations and with populations where significant intervention or remediation has been needed and for purposes of enhancing school achievement. A second source of evidence comes from observations of mother–infant and mother–child interactions where the occurrence of contingent responsiveness on the part of the mother appears to be associated with better developmental outcome for the child. However, neither of these constitutes, by itself, a strong antidote to the skepticism concerning the operation of reinforcement principles in the natural environment. In the first instance, as we have alread commented, direct manipulation to make something happen in controlled and semi-controlled environments does not necessarily mean that the same principles are operating in the natural environment. In the second instance, it is not clear whether maternal contingent responsiveness can be claimed as carrying the major weight for behavioral development, especially as the consistency of maternal responsiveness in the natural environment is probably much less than in the laboratory. Additionally, is it conceivable that each mother shapes up the same basic behavioral repertoire as all other mothers? Or is the role of learning in shaping the behavioral repertoire more restricted to the quality, specific content, and extensivity of the responses being acquired and not responsible for the total selection of specific responses that will constitute the behavioral repertoire? Alternatively, or perhaps concomitantly, is the evolutionary history of the organism such that behavioral development is highly overdetermined in the human organism and that there is a variety of pathways, processes, and mechanisms that function simultaneously to foster development?

An Evolutionary Perspective Within Behaviorism

The evolutionary perspective is an important one in considering these issues. It has been brought to bear upon the question of learning in relation to whether or not it is reasonable to believe that learning is a general process whereby in any organism "any emitted response and any reinforcer can be associated with approximately equal facility" (Seligman, 1970, p. 407). This belief, referred to as "the assumption of equivalence of associability" or the "equipotentiality premise" involves the idea that there are general laws of learning to account for acquisition, extinction, discriminative control, shaping, and generalization gradients for all responses and reinforcers (Seligman & Hagar, 1972). The equipotentiality premise has been called into question and an alternative view proposed. Namely, that each organism brings to the situation of learning an evolutionary history and a genetic makeup that have prepared the individual to learn some things and not others and to learn under some circumstances and not others, thus reflecting species-specific biological and evolutionary constraints on learning. Such "preparedness" would mean not only that some things are learned more readily, but that some associations are not acquired systematically. For example, social stimuli are more easily associated with reinforcing conditions than non-social stimuli. The mother and the spoon are both involved in feeding situations, but the learned associations are stronger to the mother's face than to the spoon.[3] Further, some behaviors may be acquired under a broad range of circumstances, others under a more limited range. Evidence brought to bear upon this position has come largely from the animal literature (Seligman & Hagar, 1972). Some recent analyses with respect to language learning in children are relevant (Gleitman, Newport, & Gleitman, 1984). It appears that learning language may be highly overdetermined for the normal child so that language learning occurs relatively easily under a broad range of stimulating and reinforcing conditions. If, in fact, this kind of "preparedness" notion is a more valid characterization of learning in the human organism, what does this mean for any general proposition with respect to the role of learning in behavioral development?

There are several implications to be drawn out of a position that assumes preparedness in an evolutionary context as relevant to human behavioral development. First, some stimuli in the environment should be preportent for eliciting responsiveness on the part of the organism. For example, the human face as compared with a dog's face. Second, the values of the

---

[3]One might argue that the strength of the association to social stimuli is a function of the larger number of elements and a greater complexity of elements in the social stimulus of the face than in the non-social stimulus (the spoon) so that on a purely quantitative basis the social stimulus will have more associative strength.

elements in the laws of learning should vary with how important or central the responses to be learned are to the survival and maintenance of the organism. In this regard, instinctual responding would be at one end of a continuum (automatic responses are assured) as among the oldest, perhaps once more important responses in the historic evolution of the human organism. More recent responses in the human behavioral repertoire would be at the other end of the continuum where natural acquisition is not highly probable and carefully arranged opportunities for learning are necessary if learning is to occur. Preparedness, in fact, has been discussed in relation to the notion that "learning is continuous with instinct" (Seligman & Hagar, 1972). Feldman (1980) has suggested that there is a continuum of behavioral acquisition from universal to unique. This is entirely compatible with these ideas. It seems plausible, on several accounts, to suggest that the more culturally based a behavior is in the behavioral repertoire the more subject it is to the laws of learning and the more dependent it is for its acquisition on opportunities for learning to occur. Charlesworth (1986) has noted that although evolutionary forces have culminated in particular organismic structures, learning ability and cultural factors are as relevant to an evolutionary perspective on human adaptability as are genes, a position not dissimilar from that taken by Cavalli-Sforza and Feldman (1981).

Is learning then "a" or "the" mechanism that produces development? In the picture we have been sketching in the last several paragraphs the answer is both "yes" and "no." This is not so much an equivocation as a qualification. The qualification requires further consideration. It is stimulated by evidence from comparative studies of learning placed in an evolutionary perspective. Rozin has suggested that there are likely a number of adaptive specializations in learning and memory, some of which may be reflected in "quantitative variations on basic laws of learning, or, in some cases, as qualitative differences" (Rozin & Kalat, 1972, p. 93). Rozin has also proposed that in some species important survival skills and associations form into what he has called a "cognitive unconsciousness" whereby there are "tightly wired" response systems specific to particular stimuli and domains. Additionally, the role of experience with respect to these "prewired" elements of intelligence may be to calibrate the system or to facilitate the connection of the system with other systems or with acquired, non-prewired responses or response systems.

Evolutionary advances, according to Rozin (1976), are reflected in (a) the increasing accessibility of elements of the cognitive unconscious for incorporation into the cognitive conscious; and (b) the growth of plastic mechanisms "sensitive to environmental factors which, in varying combinations with genetically determined programs, lead to successful solutions to problems" (p. 258). Mammals, and humans in particular, may not so much differ from other animals with respect to "the complexity and plasticity of their behavior in any particular situation, as in the range within which they can apply their complex plastic programs" (p. 259), learning paradigms being among the most important general mechanisms available. Development, according to Rozin and as taken up by Brown (1982) in her discussion of learning and development, involves the notion of ontogeny recapitulating phylogeny. This involves the proposition that the components of intelligence first acquired in our evolutionary history have the most constrained domains of functioning in their initial appearance in the behavioral repertoire of each individual. This is followed by a gradual extension and connecting together of these initially isolated skills. Then, as development proceeds, there is a growing awareness of the functioning of the cognitive system per se (metacognition). With this comes an increasing flexibility in accessing knowledge.

Developmental Trajectories and Behavior Potentials

By integrating a number of the perspectives sketched out in the preceding sections, learning can be thought of as a mechanism or a set of mechanisms whereby relationships between pre-wired cognitive domains are established with response repertoires that are themselves acquired by learning. Learning thus operates on a base of "givens," on a base of a partially "pre-wired cognitive system." In this view, stimulus elements involved in learning are handled according to rules of information processing that are in some aspects likely to be species-specific. Further, there may be developmental constraints on the sequencing of what can be learned and on the parameters that enter into the learning paradigms. These constraints or determinants may sometimes be quantitative in nature and sometimes qualitative in nature.

The point of view being developed here retains learning as a central process in development but places it in the context of organismic characteristics. It fits well with the growing body of literature on the development of information processing systems (Siegler, 1983), with recent work on the development of intelligence (Sternberg & Powell, 1982), and with the notion of many intelligences (e.g., Gardner, 1983) and skill theory (Fischer, 1980). Brown (1982) has used this perspective to consider what she believes is the essential developmental question with respect to learning; namely, how does the knowledge base grow, change, and reorganize, and what mechanisms promote the change and growth. The answer, she believes, will be found in research that is based upon a model of learning adapted from proposals by Jenkins (1979) and Bransford (1979). In this model, characteristics of the learning, specific learning behaviors, the task involved, and the nature of the materials and task are all important dimensions determining whether and how learning occurs. Such a program of research could well reveal the manner in which what Sternberg and his associates call "transparadigmatic principles of intellectual development" (Sternberg & Powell, 1982) come to develop. These principles involve the idea that with age the organism develops more sophisticated "control strategies" or executive functions. Information processing becomes more nearly exhaustive, comprehension of relations of successively higher orders develops, and there is increasing flexibility in the use of information-processing strategies and information.

From the point of view being proposed here we would say that the general trajectory of these developments may be set by the evolutionary history of the organism and its resultant general genetic characteristics; each individual course may be heavily influenced by environmental opportunities to learn. Thus, learning is a central interactive element in the developmental process, made possible by evolutionary history and development and making development possible. An example of how this may work can be found in a recent evaluation of the evidence with respect to the role of environmental input on language development wherein the contribution of the environment in the learning of language appears to be modulated by characteristics of the child as learner. These characteristics, most probably species characteristics, determine that the child will be selective in what is used from the environment, selective in when, in the course of language acquisition, the child chooses to use particular input, and selective in what use is made of the information to which the child attends (Gleitman, Newport, & Gleitman, 1984). Thus, the child learns language not according to a tabula rasa operation of basic laws of learning, but as a function of the operation of laws of learning qualified by species-specific dispositions to select or attend to particular aspects of environmental input in a particular sequence. The environmental input must be there, the laws of learning must be operative, but the functionality is circumscribed by the characteristics of the organism doing the learning. The evidence that learning of the species-specific birdsong occurs in the critical period before hatching illustrates this point well (Marler, Zoloth, & Dooling, 1981).

All of this may well describe how development is fostered by learning in the natural environment. It still leaves open the potential for making development happen by the special use of learning principles when the events of the organism–environment interaction do not naturally result in normal developmental progress. It still leaves open the possibility that what we observe as the normal, natural course of development may in actuality represent the "high probability," "overdetermined," developmental course— which requires learning for development to happen. However, it is not the only such course possible.

The idea that the developmental course thought typical of a species may, in fact, be only one of a number of such possibilities has been discussed extensively by Kuo (1967). He proposed that a basic set of factors determines one course of behavioral development. Significant modification of one or more of the factors will produce different behavioral characteristics. According to Kuo, behavior at any point in time reflects the interaction of five factors: organismic morphology, biophysical and biochemical makeup, stimulating objects, developmental history, and environmental context. The course of behavioral development begins prenatally so that by the time an organism is born a behavioral trajectory or a set of "behavioral potentials" has already been established. Significant intervention prior to birth would change the behavior potentials just as significant intervention postnatally could be made to change these potentials. Kuo believed that the range of possible behavioral patterns available to an organism was much broader than was commonly believed. He set out to demonstrate this experimentally with a number of different species. He raised kittens to relate affiliatively with rats and birds; he altered seemingly instinctual behaviors in a number of animals—using conditioning to establish what he called "behavioral neophenotypes" or novel patterns of behavior. The point of view adopted by Kuo is reflected in what has been called the "psychobiological" approach (Gottlieb, 1983). Using an experimental strategy, Gottlieb (1983), Schneirla (1966), and others, like Kuo, have attempted to untangle the role of external influences on development, keeping in mind the species-typical developmental course that occurs in the organism's natural habitat and focusing upon the processes that determine that natural course.

Kuo considered processes of development not in terms of the usual nature–nurture analysis, but with respect to the interaction of the organism and its environment in which there was mutual modification; the result was a modified and reorganized organism, and a modified and reorganized environment. There is here some of what has been propounded as a "transactional" model of development (Sameroff & Chandler, 1975), but with a much stronger emphasis upon process analysis backed up by an experimental strategy designed to take apart and reassemble the components of the interactional or transactional process. Kuo's theory of behavior potentials involves the recognition that there are a large number of possibilities or potential behavior patterns in each newborn organism given the limits of the normal morphological structure of the species. This is not equivalent to asserting that there are inborn behavioral predispositions, but rather sets out the notion of a potential of behavioral gradient patterns that have differential probabilities of development. Learning, in this scheme, is a central but not a sole mechanism determining which potentialities develop and at what level.

A more sophisticated analysis of the relationship between potential and actuality has been taken up by Oyama (1985) in her attempt to once and for all dispense with the nature–nurture analysis and with the parsing out of percentage responsibilities to genes and environment. She notes that the concepts of biological plans and constraints on development can only be taken seriously if they are understood in terms of "contingent phenotypic processes" and not in terms of a preformed code. Ontogeny, in this view, is not genetically directed development; it is inherently a contingent outcome, depending on environmental actualization. Kuo repeatedly emphasized that each organism and each species has many behavior potentials. Those that are actualized are "chosen" by the processes and the set of environmental conditions that obtain. The import of this perspective cannot be underestimated because it places the controlling elements neither in the organism nor in the environment but in the process.

RECAPITULATION

The discussion of processes and mechanisms and the role of learning and development is, in some ways, far from radical Watsonian behaviorism. Yet, it is close to some of the essential tenets in other ways. The emphasis upon process is a strength of behaviorism that, when combined with methodological behaviorism, has resulted in a large and reliable data base concerning behavioral functioning. The weakness of theoretical behaviorism is largely in evidence with respect to developmental analyses. It should be possible to combine the methodological and the process aspects with a theoretical framework for developmental analysis that incorporates ideas from developmental biology and organismic theory. What is not clear is how the stage-structure-system approach can or should be integrated into what might be described here as a neo-neo-behavioristic and psychobiological analysis of development and developmental processes.

REFERENCES

Alexander, J. F., & Malouf, R. A. (1983). Intervention with children experiencing problems in personality and social development. In P. H. Mussen (Ed.), *Handbook of child psychology* (4th ed., Vol. 4, pp. 913–981). E. M. Hetherington (Ed.), *Socialization, personality and social development*. New York: Wiley.

Antell, S. E., Caron, A. J., & Myers R. S. (1985). Perception of relational invariants by newborns. *Developmental Psychology, 21,* 942–948.

Baer, D. M. (1973). The control of developmental process: Why wait? In J. Nesselroade & H. W. Reese, (Eds.), *Life-span developmental psychology: Methodological issues* (pp. 185–193). New York: Academic Press.

Baer, D. M. (1976). The organism as host. *Human Development, 19,* 87–98.

Bandura, A. (1977). *Social learning theory.* Englewood Cliffs, NJ: Prentice-Hall.

Bergmann, G. (1957). *Philosophy of science.* Madison, WI: The University of Wisconsin Press.

Bijou, S., & Baer, D. M. (1961). *Child development* (Vol. 1). New York: Appleton-Century-Crofts.

Bijou, S., & Baer, D. M. (1978). *Behavior analysis of child development.* Englewood Cliffs, NJ: Prentice-Hall.

Bower, G. H., & Hilgard, E. R. (1981). *Theories of learning* (5th ed.). Englewood Cliffs, NJ: Prentice-Hall.

Bransford, J. D. (1979). *Human cognition: Learning, understanding and remembering.* Belmont, CA: Wadsworth.

Bridgman, P. W. (1927). *The logic of modern physics.* New York: Macmillan.

Bronfenbrenner, U. (1979). *The ecology of human development: Experiments by nature and design.* Cambridge, MA: Harvard University Press.

Brown, A. L. (1982). Learning and development: The problems of compatibility, access and induction. *Human Development, 25,* 89–115.

Brown, A. L., Bransford, J. D., Ferrara, R. A., & Campione, J. C. (1983). Learning, remembering and understanding. In P. H. Mussen (Ed.), *Handbook of child psychology* (Vol. III, pp. 77–166). J. H. Flavell & E. M. Markman (Eds.), *Cognitive development.* New York: Wiley.

Cavalli-Sforza, L., & Feldman, M. (1981). *Cultural transmission and evolution: A quantitative approach.* Princeton, NJ: Princeton University Press.

Charlesworth, W. R. (1986). Darwin and developmental psychology: From the proximate to the ultimate. *Human Development, 29,* 22–30.

Dollard, J., Doob, J. L., Miller, N. E., Mowrer, O. H., & Sears, R. R. (1939). *Frustration and aggression.* New Haven: Yale University Press.

Dollard, J., & Miller, N. E. (1950). *Personality and psychotherapy.* New York: McGraw-Hill.

Emde, R. N. (1980). Toward a psychoanalytic theory of affect. In S. I. Greenspan & G. H. Pollock (Eds.), *The course of life: Psychoanalytic contributions toward an understanding of personality development. Vol. I: Infancy and early childhood* (pp. 63–83). Washington, DC: U.S. Government Printing Office.

Etzel, B. C., & Gewirtz, J. L. (1967). Experimental modification of caretaker maintained high-rate operant crying in a 6- and 20-week-old infant (*Infants tyrannotearus*): Extinction of crying with reinforcement of eye-contact and smiling. *Journal of Experimental Child Psychology, 5,* 303–317.

Feldman, D. H. (1980). *Beyond universals in cognitive development.* Norwood, NJ: Ablex.

Fischer, K. W. (1980). A theory of cognitive development: The control and construction of hierarchies of skills. *Psychological Review, 87,* 477–531.

Gagne, R. M. (1968). Contributions of learning to human development. *Psychological Review, 75,* 177–191.

Gardner, H. (1983). *Frames of mind: The theory of multiple intelligences.* New York: Basic Books.

Gewirtz, J. L. (1967). Deprivation and satiation of social stimuli as determinants of their reinforcing efficacy. In J.P. Hill (Ed.), *Minnesota Symposium on Child Psychology* (Vol. 1, pp. 3–56). Minneapolis: University of Minnesota Press.

Gholson, B., & Beilin, H. (1979). A developmental model of human learning. In H. W. Reese & L. P. Lipsitt (Ed.), *Advances in child development & behavior* (Vol. 13, pp. 47–81). New York: Academic Press.

Gholson, B., & McConville, K. (1974). Effects of stimulus differentiation training upon hypotheses, strategies and stereotypes in discrimination learning among kindergarten children. *Journal of Experimental Child Psychology, 18,* 81–97.

Gleitman, L. R., Newport, E. L., & Gletiman, H. (1984). The current status of the motherese hypothesis. *Journal of Child Language, 11,* 42–79.

Gottlieb, G. (1983). The psychobiological approach to developmental issues. In P. Mussen (Ed.), *Handbook of child psychology* (4th ed., Vol. II, pp. 1–26). M. M. Haith & J. J. Campos (Ed.), *Infancy and developmental psychobiology.* New York: Wiley.

Hall, R. V., Lund, D., & Jackson, D. (1968). Effects of teacher attention on study behavior. *Journal of Applied Behavior Analysis, 1,* 1–12.

Hart, B., & Risley, T. R. (1980). In-vivo language intervention: Unanticipated general effects. *Journal of Applied Behavior Analysis, 13,* 407–432.

Hebb, D. O. (1980). *Essay on mind.* Hillsdale, NJ: Lawrence Erlbaum Associates.

Horowitz, F. D. (1968). Infant learning and development: Retrospect and prospect. *Merrill-Palmer Quarterly, 14,* 101–120.

Horowitz, F. D. (1984). The psychobiology of parent-offspring relations in high-risk situations. In L. P. Lipsitt & C. Rovee-Collier (Eds.), *Advances in infancy research* (Vol. 3, pp. 1–22). Norwood, NJ: Ablex.

Hull, C. L. (1943). *Principles of behavior.* New York: Appleton-Century-Crofts.

Jenkins, J. J. (1979). Four points to remember: A tetrahedral model and memory experiments. In L. S. Cermak & F. I. M. Craik (Eds.), *Levels of processing in human memory* (pp. 429–446). Hillsdale, NJ: Lawrence Erlbaum Associates.

Kendler, H. H., & Spence, J. T. (1971). *Essays in neobehaviorism.* New York: Appleton-Century-Crofts.

Kendler, T. S. (1979). The development of discrimination learning: A levels of functioning explanation. In L. P. Lipsitt & H. W. Reese (Eds.), *Advances in child development & behavior* (Vol. 13, pp. 83–117). New York: Academic Press.

Kirigin, K. A., Wolf, M. M., Braukmann, C. J., Fixsen, D. J., & Phillips, E. L. (1979). Achievement Place: A preliminary outcome evaluation. In J. S. Stumphauzer (Ed.), *Processes and behavior therapy with delinquents* (pp. 116–145). Springfield, IL.: Charles C. Thomas.

Kuenne, M. R. (1946). Experimental investigation of the relation of language to transposition behavior in young children. *Journal of Experimental Psychology, 36,* 471–490.

Kuo, Z.-Y. (1967). *The dynamics of behavior development.* New York: Random House.

Langer, J. (1969). *Theories of development.* New York: Holt, Rinehart & Winston.

Lichtenberg, J. (1983). *Psychoanalysis and infant research.* Hillsdale, NJ: The Analytic Press.

Lipsitt, L. P. (1979). The newborn as informant. In R.B. Kearsley & I. Sigel (Eds.), *Infants at risk: Assessment of cognitive functioning* (pp. 1–22). Hillsdale, NJ: Lawrence Erlbaum Associates.

Locke, J. (1936). An essay concerning human understanding. In B. Rand (Ed.), *Modern classical philosophers* (pp. 215–262). New York: Houghton Mifflin. (Originally published, 1690)

Marler, P., Zoloth, S., & Dooling, R. (1981). Innate programs for perceptual development: An ethological view. In E. Gollin (Ed.), *Developmental plasticity* (pp. 135–172). New York: Academic Press.

Masling, J. (Ed.), (1983). *Empirical studies of psychoanalytical theories.* Hillsdale, NJ: The Analytic Press.

McCandless, B. R., & Spiker, C. C. (1956). Experimental research in child psychology. *Child Development, 27,* 75–80.

Meichenbaum, D. (1977). Cognitive-behavior modification: An integrative approach. New York: Plenum Press.

Miller, N. E. (1959). Liberalizations of basic S-R concepts: Extensions to conflict behavior, motivation and social learning. In S. Koch (Ed.), *Psychology, a study of a science* (Vol. 2, pp. 196–292). New York: McGraw-Hill.

Miller, N. E., & Dollard, J. (1941). *Social learning and imitation.* New Haven, CT: Yale University Press.

Miller, S., & Konorski, J. (1928). Sur une forme particuliére des relexes conditionnels *C.R. Soc. Biol. Paris, 99,* 115-157.

Mussen, P. H. (1983). *Handbook of child psychology* (4th ed.). New York: Wiley.

O'Leary, K. D., Becker, W. C., Evans, M. B., & Saudargas, R. A. (1969). A token reinforcement program in a public school: A replication and systematic analysis. *Journal of Applied Behavior Analysis, 2,* 3-13.

Overton, W. F., & Reese, H. W. (1973). Models of development: Methodological implications. In J. R. Nesselroade & H. W. Reese (Eds.), *Life-span developmental psychology: Methodological issues* (pp. 65-86) New York: Academic Press.

Oyama, S. (1985). *The ontogeny of information.* Cambridge: Cambridge University Press.

Papoušek, H. (1967). Experimental studies of appetitional behavior in human newborns and infants. In H. W. Stevenson, F. H. Hess, & H. L. Rheingold (Eds.), *Early behavior: Comparative and developmental approaches* (pp. 249-278). New York: Wiley.

Papoušek, H., & Papoušek, M. (1983). *The evolution of parent-infant attachment: New psychobiological perspectives.* Unpublished paper presented at Second World Congress on Infant Psychiatry, Cannes, France.

Papoušek, H., & Papoušek, M. (1984). Learning and cognition in the everyday life of human infants. In J. S. Rosenblatt, C. Beer, M-C. Busnel, & P. J. B. Slater (Eds.), *Advances in the study of behavior* (Vol. 14, pp. 127-163). New York: Academic Press.

Papoušek, H., & Papoušek, M. (1985). *Precursors of control beliefs, their determinants and significance during human infancy.* Unpublished paper presented at meetings of Society for Research in Child Development, Toronto, Canada.

Patterson, G. R., & Gullion, M. E. (1968). *Living with children: New methods for parents and teachers.* Champaign, IL: Research Press.

Pavlov, I. (1927). *Conditioned reflexes.* London: Clarendon Press.

Reese, H. W. (1980). A learning theory critique of the operant approach to life span development. *Human Development, 23,* 368-376.

Rosenthal, T. L., & Zimmerman, B. J. (1978). *Social learning and cognition.* New York: Academic Press.

Rovee-Collier, C. (1984). The ontogeny of learning and memory in human infancy. In R. Kail & N. E. Spear (Eds.), *Comparative perspectives on the development of memory* (pp. 103-134). Hillsdale, NJ: Lawrence Erlbaum Associates.

Rovee-Collier, C. (1986). The rise and fall of classical conditioning research: Its promise for the study of early development. In L. P Lipsitt & C. Rovee-Collier (Eds.), *Advances in infancy research* (Vol. 4, pp. 139-159). Norwood, NJ: Ablex.

Rozin, P. (1976). The evolution of intelligence and access to the cognitive unconscious. In J. M. Sprague & A. N. Epstein (Eds.), *Progress in psychobiology and physiological psychology* (pp. 245-279). New York: Academic Press.

Rozin, P., & Kalat, J. W. (1972). Learning as a situation-specific adaptation. In M. E. P. Seligman & J. L. Hagar (Eds.), *Biological boundaries of learning* (pp. 66-96). Englewood Cliffs, NJ: Prentice-Hall.

Sameroff, A. J., & Chandler, M. J. (1975). Reproductive risk and the continuum of caretaking casualty. In F. D. Horowitz (Ed.), *Review of child development research* (Vol. 4, pp. 187-244). Chicago: University of Chicago Press.

Schneirla, T. C. (1966). Behavioral development and comparative psychology. *The Quarterly Review of Biology, 41,* 283-302.

Self, P. A., & Horowitz, F. D. (1979). Neonatal assessment: An overview. In J. D. Osofsky (Ed.), *Handbook of infant development* (pp. 126-164). New York: Wiley.

Seligman, M. E. P. (1970). On the generality of the laws of learning. *Psychological Review, 77,* 406–418.

Seligman, M. E. P., & Hagar, J. L. (1972). (Eds.). *Biological boundaries of learning.* Englewood Cliffs, NJ: Prentice-Hall.

Siegler, R. S. (1983). Information processing approaches to development. In P. H. Mussen (Ed.), *Handbook of child psychology* (Vol. I, pp. 129–211). W. Kessen (Ed.), *History, theory, and methods.* New York: Wiley.

Skeels, H. M. (1966). Adult status of children with contrasting early life experiences: A follow-up study. *Monographs of the Society for Research in Child Development, 31* (Serial No. 105).

Skeels, H. M., & Dye, H. B. (1939). A study of the effects of differential stimulation on mentally retarded children. *Proceedings and Addresses of the American Association on Mental Deficiency, 44,* 114–136.

Skinner, B. F. (1938). *The behavior of organisms: An experimental analysis.* New York: Appleton-Century-Crofts.

Spence, K. (1937). The differential response in animals to stimuli varying within a single dimension. *Psychological Review, 44,* 430–444.

Spence, K. W. (1956). *Behavior theory and conditioning.* New Haven: Yale University Press.

Spiker, C. C., & Cantor, J. H. (1977). Introacts as predictors of discrimination performance in kindergarten children. *Journal of Experimental Child Psychology, 23,* 520–538.

Stern, D. (1985). *The interpersonal world of the infant.* New York: Basic Books.

Sternberg, R. J., & Powell, J. S. (1982). Theories of intelligence. In R. J. Sternberg (Ed.), *Handbook of human intelligence* (pp. 975–1005). Cambridge, MA: Cambridge University Press.

Sternberg, R. J., & Powell, J. S. (1983). The development of intelligence. In P. H. Mussen (Ed.), *Handbook of child psychology* (Vol. III, pp. 341–419). J. H. Flavell & E. M. Markman (Eds.), *Cognitive development.* New York: Wiley.

Stevenson, H. W. (1972). *Children's learning.* New York: Appleton-Century-Crofts.

Sulzer, B., & Mayer, G. R. (1972). *Behavior modification procedures for school personnel.* Hinsdale, Il.: Dryden Press.

Watson, J. B. (1970). *Behaviorism.* New York: W. W. Norton & Co. (Originally published 1924)

Watson, J. B., & Rayner, R. (1920). Conditioned emotional reactions. *Journal of Experimental Psychology, 3,* 1–14.

White, S. H. (1965). Evidence for a hierarchical arrangement of learning processes. In L. P. Lipsitt & C. C. Spiker (Eds.), *Advances in child development and behavior* (Vol. 2, pp. 187–220). New York: Academic Press.

White, S. H. (1970). The learning theory tradition and child psychology. In P. H. Mussen (Ed.), *Carmichael's manual of child psychology* (3rd ed., Vol. 1, pp. 657–701). New York: Wiley.

4 Environment and Development

A central question for any developmental theory is the role that is assigned to environmental experience. What effect does it have on the course of development and on the level of developmental outcome? Where a theory comes down on this issue is what determines where it rests on the continuum that describes the parceling out of heredity and environment in resolving the nature–nurture controversy. Those at the nature end of the continuum typically believe that evolutionary and hereditary variables control both the course of behavioral development and the level of developmental outcome. Those at the nurture end of the continuum give a far greater functional role to environmental stimulation. In fact, however, all theoretical accounts of behavioral development give some functional role to the environment. The differences lie in the nature of that functionality and the determining role it plays in accounting for individual differences.

Piagetians and structuralists who constitute the organismic approach typically assume that a normal environmental surround is necessary for development. In this view, the child uses environmental stimulation in a sequenced and selective manner to foster the successive creation of behavioral structures. However, variations in environmental experience are not thought to be terribly relevant either in affecting the natural course of development or in determining individual differences in developmental outcome. Organismic theorists thus lean more heavily toward the "nature" side of the nature–nurture controversy.

For organismic theorists the environment is functional in the sense that it provides the stimulation for behavioral growth much as food stimulates physical growth. Only extreme variations in environment that deprive the organism of some minimal threshold level of stimulation will stunt growth or deflect it from its natural course. Within the organismic approach no great effort has been made to define the nature of the functional environment above threshold or even to specify threshold. It would be viewed as an unnecessary task for two reasons. First, the environmental surround is a gestalt; analyzing it into its components when the child's relationship to it is as a whole would not be very meaningful. Second, if the principle of equifinality is accepted it means that there are many paths to the same outcome. Specifying those paths in terms of the many different ways in which the environment is functional for different children could involve one in identifying as many paths as there are children—a task of enormous proportions without any clear scientific rationale. Environment, then, for the organismic approach is a given and not the object of major analysis.

Behaviorists, on the other hand, view the "stimulus" as one of the critical elements in the laws that govern behavior. Behaviorists view the stimulus as a critical functional element in learning. They give learning a strong role in determining both the course of development and the level of developmental outcome. They are thus clearly more aligned with the "nurture" end of the continuum than with the "nature" end. Stimuli in the natural environment are assumed to function in precise ways in the equation that accounts for behavioral development. This is particularly true for reinforcing stimuli. It follows, then, that one of the givens in the research strategy of the behaviorist is the necessity to define the stimulus as specifically as possible. This is most evident in the descriptions of stimuli that accompany reports of laboratory experiments. It is believed that the laws that describe how environmental stimuli function in a controlled laboratory situation will eventually be generalized to account for behavioral acquisition in the natural environment. This belief is not simply an abstract hope. There has, in fact, been considerable attention given to the study of stimuli in the natural environment.

Social learning theorists, applied operant psychologists and those interested in mother–child and child–environment interactions in natural and semi-natural settings have all made significant attempts to focus on the definition of the critical environmental stimuli affecting behavior. This has involved observations of the natural environment at different levels of analysis. The more microanalytic approach is exemplified by observations such as the number of occurrences or the contingent occurrence of such stimuli as maternal smiling, eye contact, touching, and so on. The more macroanalytic strategy is exemplified by rating scales that might score maternal contingency from 1 (rarely) to 7 (frequently and consistently) or that might rate non-social stimulation with respect to the amount or variety observed. The large number of observational coding schemes for environmental stimuli in the literature is ample testimony to the importance of environmental variables in behaviorism and social learning theory and in the more "mechanistic" developmental theories. As well, the number attests to the lack of consensus about where in the environment and at what level of analysis one should be looking to discover the functional role of environmental stimulation in behavioral development.

The goal of this book is to arrive at a model of behavioral development that incorporates the most promising evidence and ideas from a number of different research strategies and theories. Some kind of an integration of the essential characteristics of the organismic and the mechanistic points of view must be one component of this model. On the question of environment, these two major positions differ greatly. Is it possible to propose a way to reconcile the two views partially for purposes of incorporating them or some extension or elaboration of them into a coherent and consistent model of development? In order to address this question it is necessary to consider a number of different ways of looking at the environment and to review the kind of evidence that might be brought to bear upon each of these strategies. A discussion of some of the general considerations related to defining the environment is the first step. It is followed by seeing how the environment might be defined as a stimulus array, as a set of learning opportunities and as a set of patterns. Special consideration is given to the concept of culture as environment, and to analyzing some of the schemes that give a role to environment in developmental outcome. Finally, there is an attempt to specify, from all of these different analyses, how one might best conceptualize the notion of a functional environment for developmental outcome.

DEFINING THE ENVIRONMENT

Bronfenbrenner and Crouter (1983), in their extensive review of the evolution of environment models in the study of human development, used the following working definition for the term *environment: "Environment"* encompasses any event or condition outside the organism that is presumed to influence, or be influenced by, the person's development" (p. 359). Using that definition and other key terms, their review takes them back to the early 1870s and to the systematic research on the effect of environmental variables on human development that was carried out in Germany and in England. Their very complete historical survey renders any such review here unnecessary. Suffice it to say that there has been an evolution of environmental models over this period that is consistent with the different strands of theory formulation in developmental psychology.

Bronfenbrenner and Crouter confined their discussion of environmental models to those that focus upon "development-in-context" or what one might think of as natural environments. The development-in-context research appears to be characterized by three stages. The first spans the period from the early 1870s to about 1930. It involved research that was focused upon relatively gross environmental variables such as "social addresses" or neighborhoods differing in socioeconomic characteristics and on family characteristic variables that were thought to constitute the "nurture" side of the nature–nurture discussion. The second, from 1930 to the present, uses more sophisticated conceptualizations of environment in the form of developmental paradigms involving person–process relationships. These range from Lewin's notions of environment and life space to social learning theory's use of environment as a socialization context to Hebb's discussion of environment as perceptual stimulation to Vygotsky's concept of changing society as providing the context for cognitive development. The third stage, overlapping with the second from 1950 to the present, represents more emphasis upon environment as structure. This is exemplified by Bronfenbrenner's (1979) scheme for parsing out environmental structure as a function of the extent of developmental settings and the relationships between settings. At the simplest level is the microsystem that involves a particular setting over time that contains a pattern of "activities, roles and interpersonal relations" (Bronfenbrenner, 1979, p. 22). The infant at home with parents and caregivers in a relatively stable physical environment is an example of a microsystem. At the next level of complexity is the mesosystem. This involves two or more microsystem settings simultaneously affecting the development of a child. Home, a microsystem, and school, a microsystem, both affect the child's development. Taken together in their separate contributions and in their relationships they form a mesosystem as the context for development. Finally, there is the exosystem. It is comprised of the micro- and mesosystems experienced directly by the child and the effects of the micro- and mesosystems experienced by those who interact with the child although the child does not experience them directly. Thus, the occupation and work-setting of the father, which the child may not contact directly, affects the child for it forms the contexts that shape the father's behavior which, in turn, affects the father's interaction with his child. In totality, the child is involved in an exosystem.

Bronfenbrenner's description of levels of environment for development-in-context is admirable for the many hypotheses it generates and for the complexity it attempts to encompass. Bronfenbrenner sees developmental contexts as forming the basis for launching and maintaining particular developmental trajectories. In this he begins with his simplest level—the microsystem. However, it is not clear that the microsystem as he describes it is really the simplest level for the purposes of analysis of environmental effects on behavioral acquisition. A simpler definition of environment would begin at the level of the single stimulus impinging upon a sensory receptor. This was, of course, the focus of much of early experimental psychology. It is still of considerable interest in neurobehavioral studies and in the analysis of learning and perception. The single stimulus imping-ing upon a sensory receptor, repeated in a set of stimuli that form the basis for a stable pattern of stimulation, probably constitute the most basic level of environmental stimulation as it affects cognitive and perceptual devel-opment. For purposes of building a developmental model that includes environmental stimulation as an important dimension it is important to begin at this level even while recognizing that the micro-, meso-, and exosystem analysis proposed by Bronfenbrenner offers one potentially useful way of chunking environmental stimulation.

At the other end of the complexity continuum it is possible to extend Bronfenbrenner's exosystem. One can take the exosystem as macroanalysis of environment. This forms the large-scale system for socialization. One can extend Bronfenbrenner's exosystem into the realm of culture and cultural variation so as to encompass ideational domains as well as behavioral domains (Kluckhohn, 1962). Thus, the environment, in a developmental model that recognizes the importance of the interaction of the organism with the environment, can be defined at a number of levels of complexity and characterization. This becomes particularly important for mechanistic models of development where it is assumed that one will understand the nature of environmental impact in terms of the processes that govern behavioral development. If one posits different levels of complexity for environment is it expected that the same processes will characterize all levels or will different processes be found at different levels? For example, does environment at the most complex level of "culture" impact individual development through the base processes of conditioning?

Another question that must be posed about defining the environment is whether the functional environment is determined by the nature of the organism interacting with the environment who, in turn, defines the envi-ronment by his or her own behavior. Recently, it has been proposed that individuals make their own environments as a function of their geneotype by selecting out the components of the environment that will be functional for them (Scarr & McCartney, 1983). If this is the case does it make any sense to parse out levels of environmental complexity? If individual devel-opment results from an organism–environment interaction or transaction is there an objective, organism–independent environment to be described? Is the answer to this question the same for all domains of development and in all periods of development?

The schematic used to define the environment is very important. It will set the strategy for asking questions about the functional role of environ-mental stimulation and about organism–environment interactions. Although Bronfenbrenner's (1979) proposal has many attractive features and does take one from a more micro level to a more macro level, the continuum from microsystem to exosystem is not really synonymous with microanalytic to macroanalytic. The levels of analysis in Bronfenbrenner's system are not functional in the sense of relating the different levels to either different processes or to some systematic scheme of a growing complexity in the basic equations that describe development. As noted earlier, it offers a system for chunking together units of experience and for looking at the relationships between units of experience. These units may, however, embody within them principles of organism–environment interaction that generalize across settings that may provide for a more basic understanding of the processes involved. For example, is the behavior being reinforced in one setting also being reinforced in another setting in a mesosystem? How does the consistency or inconsistency of reinforcement across settings affect the acquisition of responses? Is level of developmental outcome affected by consistencies or inconsistencies if they are generalized phenomena?

The concept of levels of analysis from microanalytic to macroanalytic applied to the environment that is used in this discussion takes us from the simple level of environment as a stimulus array to the environment as culture. The reason for choosing this organization is that it permits us to ask a number of different questions about the role of environment in the acquisition of responses and in the effect that environment as experience has on the level of developmental outcome. This strategy involves the implicit recognition that environmental stimulation may have different effects depending on the domain of behavior involved, individual organismic differences, and the point in the developmental course of the behavioral system that is being impacted. There is also a recognition that environmental stimulation may have an effect on response acquisition but not developmental outcome and vice versa.

For our purposes, it is useful to discuss "environment" in relation to three levels of conceptualization. The effort here is partly driven by the desire to make the analyses of environment compatible with issues related to concepts of stage, structure, and system and with the dimensions of processes and mechanisms that we have already discussed. The three levels may be constituted on a continuum from simple to complex although there is no intent to assume equidistance between levels or to quantify the relationship from one level to another. Rather, each level is proposed in terms of a functionality with respect to development. The first level considered simply involves stimuli and stimulus patterns that impinge upon the receptors and that interact with the organism's own processes of stimulus organization and neurological development. The second level is conceptualized in terms of patterns of repeated stimulation or dimensions of environmental stimulation that are organized in relation to the organism's interactions or transactions with the environment. This level of environmental analysis is probably the most common of all in developmental and behavioral studies as it is reflected in variables such as mother–infant interaction, adult–child relationships, school and neighborhood characterizations, and particularly in discussions of the effects of "early experience." It is possible that Bronfenbrenner's scheme of micro- and mesosystems may be incorporated as a further chunking of environments at this level.

Finally, the third level of the environment is considered in terms of patterns of stimulation or experience that are guided and arranged by principles of organization and emphasis that might be referred to as having the superordinate characteristics of "culture." Obviously, the levels are not discrete and the initial distinctions being proposed here are basically convenient devices to facilitate discussion. It is important to consider some of the issues related to the levels being described and the notion of "development-in-context." There is an attempt to determine if the manner in which environment is conceptualized permits an investigation of functional relationships with the organism that helps account for the acquisition of behavior and for developmental outcome.

Concern for the idea of "development-in-context" lies at the heart of much of the criticism of laboratory studies of child behavior. It is thought that such analyses have little relevance to development that occurs in the noisy, uncontrolled, variable, complex environment. Development-in-context implies that the environmental context changes in relation to the behavior of the developing organism. This defines the essential characteristic of a transactional model of development as compared with an interactional model (Sameroff, 1983). Any analysis of environmental surround as a static composition of stimuli would be sure to fall short of the dynamic elements that are part of the developmental process. From this point of view, a mother and an infant in interaction are mutually modifying each other's behavior; the child in the preschool is having an effect on the behavior of the other children and the adults and on the physical environment, which in turn are affecting the child's behavior. There is an assumption being made here that the principles controling the course of such mutually modifying transactions cannot be identified by studying the more simplified cases of interaction. Further, it is assumed that the simpler instances do not in any cumulative manner come to constitute an adequate description of the complex transactional patterns. A recent entry of counterproposals is to be found in Lerner's use of *contextualism* (Lerner & Kaufman, 1985) in which development is assumed to reflect the progress of the "organism in transaction."

These assumptions, of course, could be cast in the form of empirical questions. As questions, all of the issues just raised relate to the earlier discussions of the relation of sub-systems or closed mechanistic systems to open systems and to structural organizations. For example, are the seemingly more "dynamic" concepts of transactional relationships important to consider with respect to all levels of environmental variables? Are some levels less susceptible to the mutual modification principles than others? Might the transactional model be more relevant to the individual–environment interaction that is involved in the acquisition of situation-specific behavioral patterns, but less relevant to the organism in relation to superordinate factors of cultural dimensions except in a longer evolutionary time-frame? These are the kinds of questions that can be addressed by organizing the discussion of the environment as stimulus array, as variation in stimulation and opportunity for learning and as patterns of stimulation.

Environment as Stimulus Array

The normal newborn organism is assaulted at birth with what must be a dazzling world of sights, sounds, and smells, of tactile sensations and vestibular cues. Locke's tabula rasa notion now has no viable support. The sensory experiences do not impinge upon an undifferentiated slate. It is known that the human infant is born with a response repertoire that imposes some organizational structure on environmental stimuli. William James' (1890) assertion that the organism's initial contact with environmental stimulation is characterized as an experience of confusion also appears untenable. Somewhat the opposite appears to be true. The normal human infant not only responds to stimuli in every sensory modality but discriminates some stimuli from others, categorizes some stimuli into groups, prefers some stimuli over others, and exhibits behavior that appears to be organized according to certain principles in relation to stimulus characteristics. The evidence is particularly strong in the visual domain (Banks & Salapatek, 1983) and auditory domain (Aslin, Pisoni, & Jusczyk, 1983). Whether the organizing principles are of the kind that Haith (1980) has described (i.e., that visual scanning patterns in the newborn are governed by an overriding principle to maximize cortical firing), or are of the more general nature advocated by the Gestaltists remains to be seen. Some stimulus elements or attributes such as movement may be prepotent for eliciting infant attention (Nelson & Horowitz, 1987).

It is entirely reasonable to take as a given the fact that the human newborn reflects an evolutionary history at birth that results in the human organism being inclined to perceive the sensory world discriminatively and preferentially. Several questions, however, follow from this. Given these predispositions or characteristics, how does the stimulus world the infant experiences affect development? Is it meaningful to discuss the functional stimulus environment for the human infant as different from one infant to another? Or, are the dispositions and characteristics uniform across normal human infants? Is the base of environmental stimulation so universal for all infants that any discussion of a functional variation in level of sensory stimulation is rendered moot? How best should we parse and categorize sensory stimulation?

Experimental Analyses of Environmental Stimuli.   Much of the analysis of the environment as a stimulus array for children has taken place in the context of experimental studies of infant responsivity to sensory stimulation in laboratory settings. From this body of work it has been possible to describe the perceptual capabilities of newborn and older infants. It is clear from the animal literature that a minimal level of sensory stimulation is necessary for the maintenance of perceptual abilities. It is not clear whether changes in perceptual abilities over the course of early development are a function of an unfolding and growing capability of the nervous system that invariably occurs as long as the necessary level of ambient stimulation exists. Or, is variability in level and type of sensory stimulation an immediately functional dimension that sets the organism on a particular course of perceptual–cognitive development?

Hebb (1949) originally suggested that enriched early sensory environments would foster greater neural density and organization that, in turn, would contribute subsequently to better information-processing abilities and more efficient learning. Since Hebb's original formulation, several lines of research, entirely with infrahuman organisms, have substantiated some of the general aspects of his ideas, although the direct relationship between neural characteristics such as synaptic density and behavioral capacity is still not clear. However, the evidence has implications for thinking about human early experience and developmental outcome. For example, in cats, rodents, and a number of other species the level of stimulation experienced by the animal in the early postnatal period affects such aspects as dendritic and synaptic organization. Summarizing some of the recent work in this area, Goldman-Rakic, Isseroff, Schwartz, and Bugbee (1983) noted that limiting the level of environmental stimulation results in reductions in synaptic density and in length of branching of dendrites while enhancing the level of stimulation has the opposite result. Such effects appear to be restricted to the sensory modality stimulated or deprived and are most pronounced during the seemingly sensitive periods in early postnatal life although there will be variance from one cortical area to another. Sensory stimulation also appears to facilitate neuronal metabolic activity in relation to the production and action of important neurotransmitter substances (Parmelee & Sigman, 1983). It is not unreasonable to suppose that the density of sensory stimulation in the early postnatal period for the human organism has similar effects. One question that comes to mind, however, is whether almost all normal environments are sufficiently above threshold in this regard as to make any variations from environment to environment trivial in their impact upon any individual infant.

The question of the importance of variation from environment to environment needs to be evaluated in terms of how stimulation is related to learning. There is no doubt that sensory experience activates specific and non-specific brain systems. As the result of such experience, neurobiological processes are affected, not only morphologically and chemically, but also in relation to general arousal of the organism. This has its own consequences with respect to hormonal activity and such things as the efficiency of memory processes (McGaugh, 1983). We also have evidence that the organism's associational or learning experiences produce alterations in neural structure and affect electrical and chemical activity in the brain (Rosenzweig & Bennett, 1976). The earliest developmental period can thus be characterized as offering extensive opportunities to be in contact with the stimulus array of the environment and, through repeated conjoint occurrences of stimuli and attentional patterns, to acquire many simple associations. Early sensory stimulation and early associational opportunities are thereby linked. The infant attends to and learns on the one hand while the level, adequacy or "richness" of the sensory and associational map is being formed on the other hand.

The functional effect of stimulus array may be embedded in opportunities for associational learning. Although every normal environment may contain above threshold levels of sensory stimulation, qua stimulation, the critical dimension of variation from environment to environment that affects developmental outcome may be in the variety and level of stimulation available that is hooked into opportunities to learn. Further, the amount and variety of stimulation to which the infant attends may be increased or decreased by how extensively attention is reinforced. This, in turn may determine whether the functional level of stimulation above threshold extends or enriches the potential of the perceptual and cognitive systems to enter into more elaborated behavioral repertoires. There may be important constraints on the basic parameters of the perceptual–cognitive systems. There is growing evidence from experimental studies of non-human species that a species-specific, genetically determined program specifies which stimuli will receive attention and which are the more highly probable associations that will be formed. Marler and his colleagues (Marler, Zoloth, & Dooling, 1981) have summarized their view on the relation of these programs to early perceptual development:

> As we conceive of such programs, they focus the developing infant's attention on particular aspects of environmental stimulation that will form the fundamental building blocks of perceptual organization (Marler, 1977). Among the genetic specifications for such attention-focusing programs, some are broad,

such as those that establish levels of receptor sensitivity. Others are highly specific, allowing selective responsiveness to only certain key features of the environment. Whereas some operate generally, others are state dependent. Some specifications are absolute, others are relative, and manifest only in choice situations. Such preferences may be durable, or they may be transient. They may be resistant to environmental influence, or highly subject to modification by experience. (p. 136)

Marler and his colleagues say, further:

According to this view, young birds and mammals have the potential to acquire responsiveness to most if not all perceptible features of a stimulus object. In many circumstances, they will nevertheless be prone to attend to certain features of natural situations in preference to others, as though these were endowed with an innate salience, thus serving to canalize perceptual development. In species-typical environments, the consequences for adult perceptual organization may be highly predictable in certain respects. Even though there is a potentiality for a range of types of perceptual organization, as manifest in individuals growing up in typical environments or with unusual social histories, most species members will come to share a similar perceptual organization, as a result of the nature and timing of these innate perceptual constraints, operating in environments typical of the species. (p. 165)

The identification of innate programs of attention and of the specific kinds of learning that may occur does not obviate the idea that there are mechanisms that function to actuate the programs. Experimental investigations by Marler (e.g., Marler, 1976, 1977) and others have been directed at specifying the particular environmental cues that activate the mechanisms. The idea that there are innately determined probabilities that given cues will have pre-potent roles in perceptual organization and in early learning is entirely compatible with Kuo's (1967) theory concerning behavior potentials. These are laid down during the prenatal period and form the nature of the postnatal course of development in a species-typical normal environment. Oyama (1985) would take the argument further by eliminating the concept of a genetic "program" in favor of the "construction" of form in developmental processes.

The species-typical normal environment is, however, essential for the behavior of the organism to be maintained or developed, no matter how high the probabilities are. Some aspects of early perceptual development and associational learning may have particularly high probabilities. These have been referred to as "hard-wired" and may be part of what Rozin (1976) has called the cognitive unconscious. Others may be less probable but still quite likely. Others may be probable, requiring a more active role of environmental stimulation to develop. Gottlieb (1983) has attempted to specify some of the characteristics of the mechanisms related to the different probability levels. They are based in early experience with the environment but the role of the environment is different for different levels of probability. The most highly probable behaviors, those that are in the behavioral repertoire at birth as fully developed achievements, require the stimulation of a species-typical environment to maintain the behaviors. Behaviors in the behavioral repertoire that are only partially developed or underdeveloped will occur in the species-typical normal environment no matter what the level of stimulation as long as it is above a minimal threshold. However, early experience with more or more effectively presented environmental stimulation can facilitate the development of the behavior so that it occurs earlier or at a faster rate. However, in the absence of these facilitating conditions the behavior will come to its full development anyway. Other probable behaviors will not come into the behavioral repertoire or develop unless they are induced by environmental experience.

An example for each of these may be helpful. (a) The human newborn already can discriminate among some different stimuli in all the sensory modalities. This ability is maintained by the environment to the extent that the environment continues to provide instances of sensory stimulation in each modality. (b) There is evidence that the early appearance of walking behavior can be facilitated by special stimulation of the walking reflex and early stepping movements (Zelazo, Zelazo, & Kolb, 1972). Such facilitation is not necessary as the normal environment provides the experience that is required for walking to develop (e.g., nutritional for physical growth, vestibular for balance, practice opportunities, etc.). (c) Examples of induction are more difficult to come by. Gottlieb notes the induction of species-typical behavioral development may generally occur within a context of organismic characteristics that themselves have required maintenance. Imprinting may be an example of induced behavior because specific stimulus context is necessary for the behavior to appear, although Gottlieb has reservations about this example. There are, of course, no clearly identified human behaviors that fit an imprinting model. A possible general example of induction for the human organism might be the development of language. Assuming a normal hearing apparatus, experience with the language community of which the child is a member is necessary to induce language development on the part of the child.

The Functional Role of the Environment as Stimulus Array.   The environment as stimulus array, from the point of view developed here, appears to have functionality largely with respect to providing the ambient stimulus surround that maintains sensory functioning in the organism and that activates sensory information-processing mechanisms. These information-processing mechanisms/dispositions are likely of the "hard-wired" type in being species-typical in their operation, selectivity, and organization. One of these mechanisms is habituation. Repeated instances of stimulation tend to result in a diminution of attending behavior. For example, if an infant is shown a black-and-white checkerboard square the infant will attend to this stimulus on its first presentation and on subsequent presentations. However, over the course of repeated exposure to the stimulus the amount of visual attention will decline. The effect is not due to sensory organ fatigue because the presentation of a different stimulus, such as a red bullseye, will serve to re-recruit the infant's looking behavior. This is a primitive mechanism that is present at birth in the human organism and appears to be fully functioning in every sensory modality. It is a significant mechanism because it permits the human infant to recognize when stimulation is the same or different and thereby provides the infant with a behavioral repertoire for regulating his or her attentional behavior. It may also be the mechanism that starts the chain of events that produces neural coding of information. This is where one might try to determine if enrichment of the stimulus array above some minimal threshold in early infancy might lead to different densities of coded information available to the infant and subsequently to the child. This is the basis of Hebb's proposal about early experience establishing a bank of "cell assemblies" upon which the child can draw for later learning. These proposals are consonant with what we know about the effects of stimulation on neural growth and organization.

In analyzing the environment as "stimulus array," the organism should not be considered as "passive" and simply the object of stimulus bombardment. Arousal mechanisms activate attentional and search behavior on the part of the child. These are necessary partners in any functional role attributed to the environment. It is the organism's own behavior that determines whether the environment will have the functionality described here. Individual differences may also determine how efficiently the infant makes the environment functional. For example, some infants may habitually exhibit a greater range of alert state behavior that may, in turn, affect how efficiently the infant habituates to repeated stimulation.

From a developmental point of view, the environment as stimulus array is not static. Repeated attention to its elements and components results in the formation of neural representations and the mapping of environmental information. Habituation results in the infant moving on developmentally with respect to the aspects of the array that elicit and/or maintain attention. In this sense the effective or functional stimulus environment for a 1-month-old infant is different from that which is the effective environment for a 10-month-old infant. Not only are some aspects of the environment well mapped and coded, but the learned associational network to environmental arrays at 10 months is vastly larger and different than at 1 month. Thus, environment as pure stimulus array without an associational context likely does not exist past the most initial sets of environmental experiences, if then.

It is in this realm of associational context where it is reasonable to raise questions concerning the dimension of functional variability in relation to developmental outcome. Is there a level of sensory stimulation and early associative learning beyond which variations in environmental opportunities have differential effects on the quality of behavioral development and/or the level of developmental outcome? Or, put another way, if one partials out the "givens" under normal circumstances, is there a degree of environmental influence that can be determined above and beyond the base? And, of what sort? Obviously, some behaviors that are universal occur in different context for different children in different environments. Many of those differences are likely trivial, almost decorative differences. But others may not be. Some rudimentary behaviors are universal but in different environments and for different children they are differentially elaborated and developed. How can we identify the role of the environment in producing such differences with respect to the levels, components, and/or characteristics that contribute to individual variation in combinations or separately from the genetic contribution to individual differences? It is to a discussion of these issues that we now turn.

Environment as Variation in Learning Opportunities

There has been increasing emphasis upon the idea that development occurs in context (i.e., in the natural environment). As we have seen, the natural environment as stimulus array appears to the infant as a discriminable set of stimuli with some stimuli more likely to command the infant's attention than others. Environments as stimulus array vary in the amount and variety of stimulation, although it is probable that all normal environments contain sufficient threshold of amount and variety of stimulation to maintain that aspect of the infant's behavioral repertoire that is relatively well developed at birth and to support the course of behavioral development that is a high probability phenomenon in all normal children and in all normal environments. From this point of view, one can develop the following position. The general course of behavioral development that one sees in all normal children and in all normal environments is activated by a minimal threshold of stimulation. But, this is not the whole story.

There are several dimensions upon which behavioral development can be described and evaluated. First, there is a universal set of behaviors that all normal children possess or acquire. Second, there are variations in this common set of behaviors. The variations are to be found in individual differences with respect to the rate at which the behaviors are acquired, the quality of the behaviors once acquired, and the degree to which the universal behaviors are elaborated, generalized, and related to behaviors that are not universal. Third, there are behaviors that are not universal and there are differences in the level of competence achieved in this set of non-universal behaviors.

Some examples may be useful here. Walking is a universal human behavior acquired by all normal infants sometime within the first 18 months of life. Productive language is a universal behavior acquired by all normal children by about the end of the first 2 to 2½ years of life. The rate of acquisition of these behaviors varies from child to child. Some children walk gracefully, some not so. Some elaborate the motor skill of upright locomotion into dancing, racing, and so on. Some children speak clearly and a lot; others do not. Some children develop a high proficiency in productive language, others minimal proficiency. Some children elaborate their productive language abilities into oratory and into a sophisticated writing style, and so on. There are many behaviors that are not universal that are acquired by some children—playing the violin, doing mathematics, reading, and so on. It is possible that one could make the case that underlying all the non-universal behaviors is a basic behavioral skill that is universal.

The rate of behavioral acquisition of the behaviors acquired and the extent and level of achievement reflected in the non-universal behavioral repertoire varies greatly. What accounts for the variations that one sees? As Bronfenbrenner and Crouter (1983) have noted, one of the oldest research traditions is based upon the hypothesis that variations in the environments in which children grow are partially responsible for the differences in the level of competence and in the range of non-universal behaviors acquired. What dimensions of environmental variation might be cited as being responsible for the observed differences?

Observed differences in school achievement and in long-term developmental outcome and assigning of responsibility for these to environmental experience have formed the basis for the mounting of intervention programs. The theoretical bases for these have not always been well articulated. Some of the rationales employed have also been theoretically inconsistent. For example, most intervention programs have been aimed at young children in infancy or during the preschool period. Two theoretical sources are often cited. One is from Hebb and his notion that stimulus enrichment in the early years results in better learning in later years. The second is from Piaget although it is, typically, vaguely stated. The Piagetian rationale usually refers to the fact that infants have been shown to have much greater cognitive competence than was once thought. However, the Piagetian model of development, as we have repeatedly noted, involves the assumption that all normal environments provide the basic level of threshold stimulation necessary to normal sensorimotor development. Variations in this development, according to Piaget, are attributed to individual differences in the organism and not to the environmental experience of the child. Recent advances in cognitive theory, such as Fischer's skill theory, however, place much more emphasis on the functional role of the environment not only in terms of mechanisms but with respect to individual differences.

The Hebbian model has been somewhat more logically employed as a rationale for environmental intervention. Enriched stimulation should result in a larger bank of coded information that can become the basis of later learning. However, as we have seen, there is some question whether sheer levels and variety of stimulation, unrelated to learning, is a reasonable basis for predicting faster rates of development or the acquisition of a more elaborated behavioral repertoire. In fact, most intervention programs do not provide only increased stimulation. Rather, they tend to provide enriched stimulation in the context of social relationships. The programs more oriented toward improving cognitive development usually provide for systematic and structured opportunities to interact with materials and cognitively challenging problems. It is interesting to note, however, that in programs everyone considers were of very high quality, there were no differences in the effectiveness of the programs as a function of whether the intervention was or was not cognitively oriented (Consortium for Longitudinal Studies, 1983; Lazar, Darlington, Murray, Royce, & Snipper, 1982), although there was generally better outcome for children who participated in programs than those who did not. The failure to find outcome differences as a function of program orientation could be due to a number of reasons. One of them involves the possibility that all these early intervention programs, despite their avowed orientations and special activities dictated by those orientations, provided stimulation embedded in effective social learning contexts.

Development-in-Context.   The emphasis upon "development-in-context," which we have mentioned previously, involves two notions. One is that there is a complex environmental surround with multiple sources of influence on development; the other is that the environmental context changes in relation to the behavior of the developing organism. This, as we have noted, represents the assumptions that underlie a *transactional* model in which the environment modifies the child's behavior and the child's behavior modifies the environment, and, more recently, notions about contextualism (Lerner & Kaufman, 1985). We focus for the moment on the first of the two notions by posing a series of questions. Is it possible to analyze the complex environmental surround in terms of its components with respect to stimulation and learning opportunities? Is there one combinatorial model of stimulation and learning opportunities that accounts for the development of all behaviors or are there multiple models? Can environmental input be parcelled out in terms of learning and thereby account for some of the variations in the behavioral repertoire that is acquired and the differences in level of competence or development outcome? An analysis of environment as learning opportunity is attempted to see if these questions can be answered in such a way as to begin to build toward a model of development that factors in environment along the dimensions of our analysis.

The human infant is born into a social system that has arranged itself to provide food, cleaning, and other forms of nurturance. Although the organization of a social system may be considered, for this purpose, as universal, it is clear that in some portions of most societies a breakdown in the operation of the social system can result in serious neglect, abuse, and even death. Hence, the fact is that the social system into which the infant is born is itself maintained or not maintained by a system of social mechanisms. These are modified by the presence of the infant even as they function to affect and modify the behavior of the infant. Here we have the essence of a transactional model. However, if a transactional model is to be anything more than a metaphor for complex interrelationships of mutual modification it is necessary to consider the mechanisms that are involved in the model. It is also necessary to attempt to specify those system concepts involved in a transactional model that contribute to the support, shaping, and facilitation of the course of development. The mechanisms are discussed first and then the system concepts.

The mechanisms may be described as follows. First, as has been noted, some stimuli in the environment are pre-potent for attracting and maintaining the infant's attention. The human face appears to function in this manner. The human face provides information to the infant that is important for socialization as well as for intellectual/cognitive development. It is reasonable to attribute the potency of the human face to survival advantage in the evolutionary history of the organism. Infant attention to a caregiver's face is also important to the caregiver, hence mutual benefit is derived in face-to-face infant-caregiver interaction. However, as Hinde (1983) cautions, care must be taken about such explanations. As a stimulus, the human face is superbly constructed of the elements that elicit and maintain infant attention: The face has coloration, variety in shape, movement, sound, and changing perspective. Additionally, it is immediately associated with food, physical comfort, and the reduction of disturbing stimulation. This combination of a powerful stimulus and the learning opportunities it occasions probably sets the conditions that result in what has been referred to as *attachment* or *bonding* of parent and child.

One hypothesis concerning mother–infant bonding is that there is, immediately after birth, a sensitive period during which mother–infant interaction (involving mutual gazing and also bodily contact) results in the formation of an emotionally charged social bond that has long-term consequences for the mother–infant relationship and for developmental progress of the child (Klaus & Kennell, 1976). A number of studies have been reported with seemingly confirming evidence. However, the hypothesis has been called into question and some of the evidence is not as strong as at first thought (Campos, Barrett, Lamb, Goldsmith, & Stenberg, 1983; Leiderman, 1978). It is not yet clear how this issue will finally be resolved, especially with respect to whether there is a sensitive period immediately after birth. However, there is no doubt that in the mother–infant interactive system the human face along with bodily contact plays a very central role in the mutual learning of mother and infant, beginning in the initial days of life or whenever mother and infant first come together.

Patterns of interaction that involve eye contact, mutual gazing, and mutual aversion in a somewhat rhythmic pattern have been discussed in terms of mother–infant synchrony and identified as an indicator of a mutually rewarding, facilitating mother–infant relationship (Brazelton, Koslowski, & Main, 1974). In the context of this complex stimulus package that characterizes such an interaction it is possible to specify the stimulus parameters that are significant components and to quantify the nature of the interactive sequence (Gottman, Rose, & Mettelal, 1982). Attachment, bonding, and synchrony can be seen as summary labels for complex interactions that occur in, and partially constitute, the natural, normal environment in which development occurs. There are emotional components involved that contribute to heightened arousal that makes these interactions ripe for analysis as learning opportunities.

Development-in-context has been of major interest to ethologists who attempt to describe the nature of the behavioral patterns that occur in the natural species-typical habitat of the developing organism. They also put great emphasis on trying to understand the critical salient stimuli that control the behavioral patterns. Thus, the attempt to identify the mechanisms of learning as part of the process by which environmental factors exert control over the development course is not at odds with an ethological approach. In fact, recent representations of the ethological point of view include a clear recognition that development-in-context is the result of processes of learning. These processes interact or are "interdigitated" with the existence of biologically constrained behavioral patterns. Together they determine the developmental trajectory of the organism in the natural environment (Chizar, 1981; Hinde, 1983).

If one accepts this point of view as reasonable (and the weight of the data suggests it to be so), then the question becomes one of how the environment functions as learning opportunity and what role(s) does it play in the acquisition of the human response repertoire, in its maintenance, in its elaboration and qualification, in its developmental course. From the animal observational and experimental literature there are many suggestive paradigms and insights. The human species, however, possesses capacities beyond other animals; the capacity to develop language, the ability to build language and communication in an extensive verbal and nonverbal symbolic system. Are principles related to development-in-context for non-humans applicable to human development? Vygotsky (1978) and others have been quite skeptical about the ultimate relevance of animal data to human behavioral development. On the other hand, the animal literature is revealing extremely complex accounts of behavioral development that, if not complete analogs to human processes, may well offer important parts of the story that must be told. For example, in the study of bird-song behavior it appears that the elemental components of the song are "given" in the bird's repertoire. How the components are structured to form the song and the contexts in which existence of the songs will develop and occur will depend on the timing of acquisition, the presence of a model that can be imitated, and the existence of situationally reinforcing conditions (Green & Marler, 1979). Bird-song development-in-context builds upon elements that are given. Its realization as mature song, however, requires the processes of imitation and reinforced learning. This is an important example for our consideration because bird song was once thought to be a behavior totally determined by innate factors, including its expression in mature form. The manner in which this behavior is acquired may serve as one prototype for human behavioral development.

Learning and Development.   If, even in the case of the relatively stereotyped adult behavior of a bird, innate components require opportunities for learning in the natural environment for the development of that behavior, what weight should be given to environment and learning opportunities in accounting for the acquisition of the human behavioral repertoire? What processes are implicated and how and when do they function as critical determinants of behavioral development? Answering these questions in light of the evidence and the perspective we have been developing involves a number of rather complex issues. Additionally, it is important to shape answers in such a manner as to contribute toward the specification of a model of human development in which the role specified for environmental variables can be used as the basis for formulating a research agenda. For these reasons, a set of issues must be considered that may not seem, initially, obviously connected.

Three considerations are relevant to the discussion. First, given the complexity of the behavioral repertoire acquired by the human organism it is reasonable to assume that there is a multiple set of processes that are involved in behavioral acquisition. Imitation, observational learning, association by contiguity, reinforced learning, each partially constrained by innate factors characteristic of the human species, are all involved. Second, keeping in mind von Bertalanffy's (1968) notion of an open system model, any given behavior or behavioral system probably can develop via several possible pathways. In some behavioral domains multiple pathways may be more characteristic than in other domains; some pathways may be more prevalent in some populations than in others. Additionally, some aspects of one process may account for behavioral development if they occur at one point in developmental time, but other aspects may dominate at another point in time. Third, behaviors or behavioral domains that are very important to species survival have a tendency to be overdetermined. This means that more than one process and more than one pathway can provide the basis for behavioral acquisition. The more important the behavior for species survival the more likely this is to be the case.

As we have already noted, the environment exerts its effects on the acquisition of the behavioral repertoire through the operation of a number of different processes. Gottlieb (1983) proposed three general environmental strategies that are operative in the early phases of development: maintenance, induction, and facilitation. There must be mechanisms that will describe how these strategies function. Maintenance is probably best explained by the role of the relevant ambient stimulation to keep behavior at a level of responsivity necessary for function. This ambient stimulation may be thought of as having a reinforcing function at a sufficient schedule of occurrence to keep the behavior at threshold.

Induction involves environmental stimulation that results in the behavior appearing in the behavioral repertoire. The social smile of the infant may be one example of this kind of environment–behavior relationship. The normal course of smiling behavior and the systems controlling smiling have been well described by a number of investigators (e.g., Emde & Harmon, 1972). The infant social smile will appear in the normal behavioral repertoire anywhere from about 4 or 5 weeks of age to about 9 weeks of age. After initial onset of the behavior (referred to as spontaneous social smiling because it is easily elicited by almost all social stimuli) the normal developmental course is described by an increase in frequency and spontaneity for a period of time and then a decline from peak frequency. The point at which decline appears is when a stranger awareness/wariness begins to develop. There is evidence that the age at which smiling first appears and the course of its increase in frequency and then decline is a function of different constellations of caretaking environments (Gewirtz, 1965).

It is not known how environmental stimulation functions to induce smiling. Clearly, there is an innate component to its form because it is a universal human behavior. Prior to the onset of social smiling there is a form of smile behavior that has a reflex-like quality when elicited by certain stimuli. There is also evidence of a neonatal smile that may be endogenously controlled (Emde & Harmon, 1972). It is possible that the neonatal reflex smile is shaped into an operant social smile although there is presently no evidence to support this scenario. Whether or not such turns out to be the case, the course of smiling appears to be induced and facilitated by environmental events. The facilitative aspect is reflected in the fact that the rate of the course of the spontaneous social smile through a period of increased frequency and then a period of decreased frequency is a function of the environment in which the child is being reared.[1] One may invoke operant conditioning to account for the increased rate of smiling after initial appearance with the different environments providing different schedules of reinforcement. It is not as easy to account for the decline in spontaneous smiling simply in operant conditioning terms although a form of operant conditioning of other incompatible behaviors might be claimed as a contributor to the decline. From a developmental point of view, however, it is possible to maintain that the conditioning is one process involved. A parallel and interacting process in perceptual development may be taking place. This would involve the increasing ability of the infant to discriminate familiar and unfamiliar people along with learning that involves better prediction (more reinforced expectancy) on the part of the infant of the behavior of familiar people than unfamiliar people. Familiar people, associated with predictable events, may continue to elicit social smiling; unfamiliar people, now associated with more unpredictable behavior, elicit a longer period of initial visual regard (often labeled *wariness*), which is sometimes followed by crying behavior. The more cautious responding to unfamiliar people, resulting in a decline in spontaneous social smiling, appears in the behavioral repertoire of normal infants anywhere from 7 to 9 months of age. When it is accompanied by vigorous crying it is sometimes called *stranger anxiety* and in its more strident forms peaks in intensity at about 13 months of age. After the initial onset of stranger wariness and the accompanying decrease in spontaneous social smiling the course is highly individual. From a process point of view this is a developmental phenomenon in perception, a developmental phenomenon in terms of the course of increase and decrease in spontaneous smiling and stranger wariness and highly individualistic parameters with regard to the rate of behavioral change and the intensity of the behavior displayed. Fischer's (1980) skill theory is applicable to the analysis of smiling as a skill (operant) that

---

[1]There is evidence that in severely depriving social environments the behavior will be extremely delayed and once in the repertoire will occur rarely (Spitz, 1946). In this instance the environment eventually induces the behavior but is not sufficiently above threshold to maintain or facilitate the behavior through a normal developmental course.

undergoes a developmental sequence in relation to environmental experience although its initial appearance and the shift from endogenous to exogenous control require further explanation.

This somewhat extended example serves to illustrate the interrelationship of learning and development, the environmentally controlled mechanisms that are involved in Gottlieb's induction and facilitation functions, and the environmentally controlled functioning of those mechanisms to produce different rates and intensities of the behavior. Additionally, another parameter must be introduced: individual differences in responsivity. Some infants go through the developmental course we have described with little or no intense crying behavior; others have extremely emotional responses. Some of this difference is attributable to individual differences in temperament or reactivity to environmental stimulation. Some of the difference is attributable to the infant's operant use of crying to control the environment. Stranger anxiety for one infant may largely be an expression of temperament; for another infant it may be a strongly operant behavior. In the first instance, environmental control of stranger anxiety behavior will be more difficult to exert than in the second instance.

The learning analysis invoked in the previous example is fitted with a description of developmental course in a perhaps more explicit manner than the evidence to date warrants. It is not unusual for those who have puzzled over the relationship between learning and development to acknowledge, quite inexplicitly, that learning is a key factor. For example: "it is the job of human developmentalists to understand what processes, across ontogeny, link the individual to its context. Reinforcement processes, cognitive developmental processes, and social relational processes, such as attachment and dependency, may *all* be involved" (Lerner & Busch-Rossnagel, 1981). Learning is one of the processes. But we must go beyond this kind of assertion and reach for a functional analysis of how learning opportunities operate in the natural environment to affect development and developmental outcome. Skinnerians have maintained that the program for such an understanding rests upon the demonstration of how a behavior is acquired in the laboratory and the determination that it occurs in the same manner in the complex natural environment (Baer, 1973). There are numerous examples of evidence that the same principles account for behavioral changes in natural environment settings such as a preschool classroom as have been shown to obtain in the more controlled conditions of the laboratory. However, typically, these demonstrations involve behaviors that are already in the repertoire but are being increased or decreased or generalized or extinguished by the application of operant techniques. Is such evidence sufficient for asserting that the normal developmental course is similarly controlled? Answering this question, however, requires a definition of what is meant by the "normal developmental course." First, this usually refers to the appearance of behaviors in the behavioral repertoire that are thought to be universal. Smiling would be such a behavior; reading would not be, although the individual skills necessary to learn to read might be. Conservation would be such a behavior but formal algebra would not be.

Both smiling and conservation are, in Gottlieb's terms, induced by environmental factors. Piaget would put the control the other way around by giving the child the controlling function in the biologically programmed strategies used to act on the environment. Even so, the environment must function in a systematic fashion in relation to the child's behavior. Once a behavior such as smiling is in the repertoire, environmental consequences can determine its frequency, the situations in which it will be exhibited, and what other behaviors will be associated with smiling. Parallel developmental phenomena and environment control of them, as we have already described, affect the course of smiling. Smiling cannot be extinguished once in the repertoire, although its occurrence can obviously be environmentally controlled to occur at a very low rate. Development, in this sense, has been said to be *irreversible.* Kuo (1967), however, demonstrated that by imposition of extreme environmental conditions it was possible to produce patterns and courses of behavior not normal to the species. This is reason to always exercise basic theoretical caution about what is and is not possible even though testing such propositions with humans is ethically out of the question.

When we are dealing with developmental phenomena such as Piaget described, the regularity of appearance of the behaviors involved leads to conclusion that the behavior is acquired without "training." The cognitive skill of conservation or the appearance of productive language have been used as examples. However, the supposed "natural" occurrence of a behavior or skill in the absence of specific training experiences does not provide sufficient reason to dismiss a learning analysis of the acquisition. The natural environment may well have all the elements necessary for the learning paradigm to operate. To come back to the simple example of smiling, it is probably rare that anyone sets out to deliberately increase the rate of spontaneous smiling in a young infant. Yet, casual observation of what happens when a baby smiles at an adult reveals that this behavior is usually consequated with a great deal of social stimulation. These naturally occurring contingencies easily meet the criteria of a learning paradigm to account for an increased rate of smiling. Similarly, the acquisition of conservation can be accounted for in terms of a shaping of a behavioral repertoire that occurs in the normal course of the child's interaction with the environment. A definitive answer to such a question requires observational evidence that such a shaping program occurs in the child's natural environment. Piaget clearly recognized the normal feedback that occurs in the process of environmental concourse. In the case of many of the Piagetian cognitive skills such feedback is a natural consequence of the child's interaction with the physical environment. This, however, does not account for the timing of the development of conservation during middle childhood as opposed to during infancy unless one wishes to invoke the notion that conservation itself cannot be shaped into the repertoire unless prior cognitive skills have been shaped (e.g., Fischer, 1980).

Two considerations mitigate against learning as the only model to account for development. One is the sudden appearance of some behaviors in the repertoire. The other is the growing evidence of the role of biological constraints on learning. This involves the fact that the parameters of conditioning are partially determined by biological characteristics of the species. Also, some stimulus cues have much more salience than others for different species. The sudden appearance of behaviors could be the result of an internal organismic reorganization of response potential or an instance of induction by environmental cues. In either case, the learning analysis applies only after the appearance of the response to explain how it is elaborated and becomes embedded in a context. The seemingly sudden appearance of a behavior could exemplify our ignorance about the natural program for shaping the response. Response chains may be involved but we may not know about them. There is no evidence to support or refute such a hypothesis. There is no reason to necessarily push it in this context except to suggest that a set of different analyses to explain the seemingly sudden appearance of behaviors is not out of the question. Fischer's (1980) transformation rules provide some interesting possibilities for explaining the seeming appearance of new, more mature behaviors in the repertoire.

The evidence for biological constraints on learning and the existence of specially and sequentially valenced environmental cues related to the acquisition of some behaviors is persuasive. Knowledge of early language acquisition is quite suggestive of the presence of biological constraints that contribute to the sequencing of acquisition. A review of recent evidence leads to the conclusion that some cues related to learning language are salient and used by the child for learning at one point in time; other cues are salient and used by the child at another point in time even though all the cues are available to the child and are discriminable from the beginning (Gleitman, Newport, & Gleitman, 1984). This is a reasonable picture if one assumes that behavioral acquisition in the human organism will eventually be explained by several different processes. Under these circumstances the challenge will be to parcel out the environment's role in terms of a number of different paradigms having various functions. To sum up this discussion of the relationships between learning and development it can be said that in light of the data available from experimental analyses of response acquisition, from natural observations, and from normative descriptions,

the most reasonable position is the following: First, the biological constraints and genetic potential for behavioral development set a general
development trajectory of the outlines of behavioral development. Second,
the environmental contribution to actuating this trajectory may well rest in
the general maintenance, facilitation, and induction roles described by
Gottlieb. Third, the elaboration of the response repertoire over and above
a kind of species-typical developmental base may be best accounted for by
learning paradigms. There may well be an interactive component between the
base level and the elaborated repertoire that is modulated by organismically
based individual difference characteristics. In looking at the course of
human development and the relative amounts of the behavioral repertoire
that can be apportioned out to one of the three aspects just described, the
largest apportionment must be given to the elaboration of the response
repertoire—to opportunities for learning in natural and in specially arranged
environments. Here is where most of the determinants of developmental
outcome or developmental plasticity will be found. We do not presently
understand how and when such determinants operate for maximal or
minimal results. However, much of what is seen with respect to individual
differences in outcome (although certainly not all) is probably the result of
the availability and use of the learning opportunities that permit the
elaboration of the base developmental behavioral repertoire of the organism.
Much of the elaboration probably occurs as "development-in-context";
significant aspects of "development-in-context" are embedded in socially
mediated situations.

Environment as Social System

It was Sears who many years ago urged that a developmental perspective
required focus upon dyadic interactions. His discussion of the importance
of the dyad for understanding personality development and social interaction
further stimulated the formulation of current conceptions within social learning theory (Cairns, 1983; Sears, 1951). Erikson (1950) and Bronfenbrenner
(1979) have tried to describe the influence of the social system as broadening
out from the dyad to a variety of interpersonal relationships in larger and
larger social contexts such as family, neighborhood, school, and community.
The elements in these social systems are variously defined at different
levels of analysis (micro- to macroanalytic levels), depending on theoretical
inclinations. Sears (1951) placed the dyadic interaction within a social
learning framework; Bandura (1977) has continued that tradition, focusing
largely on learning and social settings that afford opportunities for observational learning. Recently, in recognition that children not only are influenced by opportunities to learn in a social context but also learning about
the social context, some attention has been given to social cognition and its

development (Flavell & Ross, 1981). As the cognitive system develops and matures children can apply cognitive skills with increasing sophistication to an analysis of the social environment that is influencing their behavior. These reflective processes permit the child to selectively approach social influences, so that some social elements in the natural environment exert an effect while others do not, partly as a function of the level of the child's cognitive abilities.

The social environment is organized on a number of dimensions. Some relate to the physical well being of its members by providing for food, shelter, and clothing. Some reflect the developmental expectations in terms of education, work roles, and play. All human social systems contain these dimensions but some are more emphasized than others and some are expressed in particular ways depending on the group that is involved in the development and maintenance of the social system. Which elements in the social system come to have particular salience and which do not is heavily determined by values. The values held by the parents and other adults in the child's world influence strongly which dimensions of the social world will be emphasized in the social learning context. Although we discuss the cultural issues in our next section, it is relevant here to note some recent work by Goodnow and her colleagues (1986). Goodnow has challenged using the traditional Piagetian analysis of development for both the physical and social world. In Piaget's analysis, developmental progress comes about as the result of the child's "intrinsic curiosity" in interacting with the environment where information is "freely available" and there is "minimal interference or help from others" in obtaining that information. Goodnow has suggested that such a model is quite appropriate to the content areas where: "Other people have few vested interests in making sure that particular ideas are acquired. . . . Other people have an interest but consider that information does not need to be managed because the ideas are expected to be acquired easily or without effort on their part. . . . A number of alternative views do not conflict with one another. . . . It is feasible to acquire information by direct manipulation of the material . . . " and experimentation is feasible and permissible (Goodnow, Knight, & Cashmore, in press).

Goodnow accepts the proposition that the traditional Piagetian cognitive achievements can be explained by the presence of these factors. However, many of the phenomena related to ideas about the social world, friendships, honesty, social reciprocity, and so on, are exactly where other people have vested interests. Therefore, they are motivated to manage the child's acquisition of a belief and value system that is consonant with the family and/or culture in which the child is developing. It is exactly in these social domains where principles of social learning such as Bandura has described would be most critical. Parents and adults in the child's world often model approved behavior and establish elaborate direct and indirect reinforcement systems in an attempt to shape the child's social behavior and social belief repertoire over the course of development. Obviously, some parents and some cultures succeed better than others. There are the more and the less effective patterns that determine the efficiency with which one generation transmits values and behavioral practices to the next generation. It has been suggested that the relative efficiency of these processes determine the rate of cultural evolution (Cavalli-Sforza & Feldman, 1981). The particular elements involved in cultural transmission will vary as a function of the age of the child and the organization of the particular social system. Many of the processes, however, are analyzable in terms of the complex of mechanisms associated with learning.

The phrase "a complex of mechanisms" is used here deliberately so as to emphasize that these learning mechanisms are deeply embedded in a social system. The system exerts constraints over the saliency of the mechanisms likely to be used at a particular point in the history of the system, at a particular point in the development of the child, and with respect to the content that is to be learned. The use of the term *system* is partially modeled on von Bertalanffy's (1968) discussion of open systems as a way of describing the growing and reorganizing biological system. Here we are mapping onto the social system, as von Bertalanffy did (1975), some of the ideas developed with respect to dynamic biological systems.

When the developing child is considered as a biological system we discussed the fact that with growth there is increasing internal organismic differentiation into subsystems. One of the characteristics to be expected in some of the subsystems was the functioning of learning systems. In an analogous way, the child is a subsystem within a social system. Part of the child's developing characteristics is reflected in the increasing organization and differentiation of learning mechanisms. These learning mechanisms, in turn, as they are exemplified by the child, function within the social system and are affected by the social system. Just as the nature of the biological organism exerts constraints on parameters of the learning process that characterize parts of the biological organism, so the social system imposes constraints on parameters of the learning processes that exert their influence on the child and on the child in relation to the social system. Those constraints are visible in the patterning of stimulation that the system makes available to the child and in relation to how and when information is socially mediated. The constraints are also likely to be influenced by the degree to which the child's behavior is permitted to or does affect the elements and/or organization of the social system.

A comparative example helps make these points concrete. One child grows up in a nuclear family arrangement, another in an extended family arrangement. Each family type represents historically stable patterns of social organization (as compared to more recently developed alternative lifestyle communities). The extended family system will typically provide quite different patterns of social stimulation for the child than the nuclear family. This will be reflected in terms of numbers of individuals in the child's daily life, in the definition of roles with respect to the child's care, in the kinds of observational learning opportunities available to the child, and in the quite different complex of social relationships that the child experiences and observes in each family. In turn, the kind and extent of influences each child can exert on the system will be quite different. Von Bertalanffy (1968) noted that systems evolve in accordance with a "principle of progressive mechanization." This involves a transition from "undifferentiated wholeness" to higher function, made possible by specialization and "division of labor." With mechanization there is a tendency for "leading parts" to be established. These are components of the system that tend to dominate the behavior system. A small change in the characteristics of the leading part will cause disproportionately large changes in the total system via what von Bertalanffy calls "amplification" mechanisms. Thus, in one social organization the dominant component might be different than in another social organization. The mother in the nuclear family is a much more dominant component of that social system than is the mother in an extended family. A change of comparable magnitude related to the mother will have a much larger effect in the nuclear family than in the extended family. The child's behavior in the nuclear family will be calibrated to affect the social organization of the family and the functioning of the family to a larger extent than is true in the extended family. Many obvious examples come to mind to elaborate this concept. A retarded or handicapped child in a nuclear family will occupy a much more "leading part position" than in an extended family. A system analysis thus involves processes that are modified or constrained by the nature of the system.

Significant changes in leading parts of systems can have the effect of producing a major reorganization of the system and of establishing new subunits and mechanized subparts. Once established, these then function according to known sets of processes. For example, when the children are grown and leave home in our society, the patterns of social organization of the parents typically undergo significant change. Older children later returning to the family home often disturb those patterns causing a still further system change. Once the system comes into homeostasis the basic processes that regulate behavior and that preclude behavioral change reassert themselves. The concept of the large, complex social system is Bronfenbrenner's exosystem in its full elaboration. Our discussion of the environment as social system was designed to specify some of the variables that characterize the operation of social systems qua systems, taking into account the dimensions of systems as discussed by von Bertalanffy. At the same time, there has been an emphasis in this discussion on the fact that the processes within systems are not necessarily different processes than those found in the analysis of the functioning of individual behavior. In recent years it has become fashionable to refer to development-in-context in terms of the mutual modification of behavior by child and caregiver, by system and individual. As we have indicated previously, it is an attractive metaphor. However, unless we can view the transactional model in terms of its constituents and processes we cannot hope to establish a meaningful research agenda related to behavioral development.

A developmental perspective here does not come easily in relation to systems. An analysis of development-in-context, given the fact of system organization, requires looking at development from the point of view of its relationship and role in the system, from the point of view of the species-typical developmental trajectory, and from the point of view of the cultural parameters that characterize the system. A consideration of culture and cultural parameters as aspects of environment needs to be undertaken.

Culture as Environment

After examining many definitions of culture, Kroeber and Kluckhohn (1952) asserted that the following encompassed what most behavioral scientists considered culture to involve:

> Culture consists of patterns, explicit and implicit, of and for behavior acquired and transmitted by symbols, constituting the distinctive achievement of human groups, including their embodiments in artifacts; the essential core of culture consists of traditional (i.e., historically derived and selected) ideas and especially their attached values; culture systems may, on the one hand, be considered as products of action, on the other as conditioning influences upon further action. (as cited in Kluckhohn, 1962, p. 73)

Cavalli-Sforza and Feldman (1981) used the Webster Dictionary definition of *culture:* "The total pattern of human behavior and its products embodied in thought, speech, action, and artifacts, and dependent upon man's capacity for *learning* and *transmitting* knowledge to succeeding generations." (p. 3). Cavalli-Sforza and Feldman, however, noted that limiting the concept of culture to the human species may be unjustified even though culture, by any definition, is developed to a higher and more extensive degree and probably transmitted more complexly by humans than is true for any other species.

The definition of culture in terms of "patterns" and the notion of cultural transmission from generation to generation raises questions of how the patterns are identified and formed and how transmission occurs. Cole and his colleagues discuss some of this in the context of what they define as the "sociohistorical approach" to how "culturally organized social inter- actional patterns can influence the psychological development of the child" (Laboratory of Comparative Human Cognition, 1983, p. 334). Some of the most profound considerations of the relation of culture and development were carried out in Russia by Lev Vygotsky and his student and colleague, Alexander Luria, during the 1920s and 1930s. Recent translations of their work have stimulated growing attention to the kinds of syntheses they attempted in trying to understand development-in-context with "context" defined as *culture* (Luria, 1976, 1981; Vygotsky, 1962, 1978).

Four sources of cultural influence are proposed by Cole and his colleagues: Culture 1) arranges for the "occurrence or non-occurrence of specific basic problem-solving environments embodied in cultural practices," . . . 2) orga- nizes the "frequency of the basic practices; . . . 3) shapes the patterning of co-occurrence of events . . . (and) 4) regulate(s) the level of difficulty of the task within contexts" (Laboratory of Comparative Human Cognition, 1983, p. 335).

Thus, culture involves specially arranged environmental opportunities for learning, mediated always in the context of social interactions that facilitate the development of speech and the internalization of sign and symbol systems. In turn, language will structure cognitive activity, which then operates on the environment that has been culturally organized in ways compatible with the language structures of the culture. This intimate relationship between developing structures in the child and social inter- actional processes is regulated in the developmental context of what Vygotsky called the zone of proximal development. The zone of proximal develop- ment is essentially a teaching/learning environment arranged for the child by a member (usually older) of the child's culture in which language in a social context is typically used to regulate the child's attention to compo- nents of problems, to their use and sequencing. By a combination of physical, symbolic, and speech activities the level of task difficulty just ahead of the child's developmental level is thus defined. In turn, such successive encounters not only produce learning in the conventional sense but help to shape and restructure the child's cognitive activity so that it matches the culturally defined patterns of task analysis and problem solv- ing behavior in a social and emotional context of interpersonal relationships. Culture, then, is a profound and pervasive organizer of patterns of environ- mental stimulation, patterns of interpersonal relationships, and the defini- tion of behavioral goals.

The evidence is generally supportive of the implications that such organizing influences begin early and affect every developmental domain (Field, Sostek, Vietze, & Leiderman, 1981; Leiderman, Tulkin, & Rosenfeld, 1977; Werner, 1979). Vygotsky placed particular emphasis on language as shaping the basic structure of the child's thinking. Symbolic activity, as the child develops, has an organizing function and is one of the fundamental sources for shaping new forms of behavior. Thus, culture is depicted in terms of patterns of environment that become part of internal representations through the development of symbolic systems. Vygotsky developed a particular view with respect to behavioral transformation and development in relation to learning. He considered learning to be an extremely important variable, but not synonymous with development. Learning stimulates mental development, which stimulates developmental processes that would not otherwise occur. The environmental (i.e., cultural) context essentially defines the learning that will occur, its timing and the forms by which development will be expressed in behavioral patterns.

This view of culture makes culture the most pervasive factor in the organizational structure of the environment. It includes things that range from the arrangement of the physical environment into which the child is born to the socio-historical context that defines, regulates, and elaborates the learning opportunities available to the child. It is not clear what level or levels of analysis will be most useful for revealing the patterning of the environment as culture nor whether various dimensions of cultural experience differentially influence different domains of development and/or periods of development. The human species has a prolonged period of infancy in which the infant is extremely dependent on the social system and on interpersonal relationships. The early cultural context of development may thus be particularly effective and important in shaping the basic cognitive and emotional structures that subsequently organize the child's relationship with the environment and that influence the manner in which the environment can affect the child. Culture may therefore represent a kind of overriding dimension of environmental experience as a component in the transactional model. It can only be modified gradually and over long periods of time. In the modern era, however, rates of cultural change have increased vastly over previous periods of history. This raises the intriguing possibility that the instability of the cultural dimension during such times changes the relationship of culture and development. Additionally, if children grow up in functionally conflicting cultural contexts their developmental progress may be adversely affected. Alternatively, such pluralism of cultural experience, if the conflicting elements are not developmentally destructive, may define new cultural composites that result in new or different forms of behavior. The effect of these kinds of variables on a child's development probably is partially dependent on the timing of their occurrence with respect to the developmental stage of the child in different domains.

Consequences of rapid social change with conflicting components have been identified as affecting parent–child interactions (Werner, 1979), but there is no systematic evidence about the kinds of developmental effects that result from placing children in radically different cultures at different points in their development. If all the data pointing to the profound influence of culture on development is to be taken seriously, then it is reasonable to believe that extreme alterations of cultural context will affect the individual although one need not presuppose whether the effects will be negative or positive. Some of the sources of the "cohort" effects discussed by Baltes, Cornelius, and Nesselroade (1979) may be found in the changing cultural parameters that affect development.

At the level of culture, environment is to be seen as a system with all the concepts of system organization thereby relevant to an analysis of culture. Culture is constantly evolving, even if it is not undergoing rapid change. Some of the evolution is the result of ecological changes wrought by changes in physical nature; some of the evolution is the result of variations that occur in the process of transmission of cultural patterns; some of the evolution may well result from unique and creative events associated with an individual which then get adopted and generalized across a population (Feldman, 1980). It is easier to see cultural differentiation when comparing obviously unrelated and noninteracting cultures—although in the modern era opportunities for such comparisons are rapidly disappearing. It is not as easy to identify and analyze cultural differentiation between groups that are in contact but have maintained autonomy in the important aspects of their cultural systems that are implicated in behavioral development. Some of the issues that face a pluralistic society like the United States are rooted in these difficult to specify dimensions of difference.

Most of the investigation of cultural influence on development has been done on cognitive development. There is reason to believe that culturally based organizing patterns of emotional development are as important or perhaps more important than the influence of culture on cognitive development. In fact, the interaction of emotional and cognitive factors, stressed particularly in Freudian theory, has been largely neglected in the context of formal developmental theory. It has been argued that Freud's use of emotion was based entirely upon Western culture concepts and thus questionable as to its universality. Nevertheless, cultural determination of emotional patterns may underlie the organization of a number of other behavioral domains, giving culture a profoundly pervasive role in behavioral functioning and amplifying behavioral patterns in culturally specific ways (e.g., Berland, 1982).

Does an emphasis on the role of environment as culture in shaping cognitive and emotional structures conflict with the basic question of universality, especially as it is related to cognitive development? Not if one takes a developmental point of view that involves several sources of organizing influences on the organism. One of those sources is clearly biological/

genetic in nature, reflecting the phylogenetic history of the organism as well as an ontogenetic history. The high probability dispositions, the "hard wiring" of elements of a cognitive unconscious represent the phylogenetic legacy; the proximate factors of the individual's genetic background and the individual's environmental surround (which begins prenatally) combine with the phylogenetic history to produce the ontogenetic expression of development. The phylogenetic history can be seen as providing the potential for the universal aspects of cognitive, emotional, and language development. These are expressed (constructed, according to Oyama, 1985) in a particular physical, social, and cultural environment that, in turn, shapes the non-universal dimensions of each individual's behavior. Some of the universal characteristics may be immutable, others plastic. The immutable elements contain the most visible universal elements; some universal components are more subject to environmental influence. Universality may be retained as an overall characteristic but its degree of elaboration may vary from individual to individual. Some aspects of the individual's genetic inheritance may constrain how the environment can operate on or elaborate universal characteristics thus determining the magnitude of developmental benefit from environmental input. Any structural model of development must take into account the multiplex of these interacting dimensions and must involve the recognition that multiple principles may be operating with respect to different domains and different developmental periods.

THE FUNCTIONAL ENVIRONMENT
AND DEVELOPMENTAL OUTCOME

No topic has had a longer history in the discussion of behavioral development than the environment. Laymen and professionals alike recognize that environmental experience is critical to development. There is, however, no consensus on the questions of how critical, critical for what and when it is critical. Nor is there agreement on the level of analysis of environmental events for identifying the functional units of experience that should form the basis of our measurements of environmental variables. Propositions on the role of environmental experience range, as we have noted, from viewing the environment largely as a necessary ambient surround that permits behavioral development to occur in an essentially predetermined fashion, to giving environmental experience the significant role for both the particular behaviors that develop and for the level of competence achieved. For the purposes of our discussion here it is useful to review some of the questions and considerations of environment that we have already noted and to extend our explanation of them briefly.

Does environment/experience play the same role in different domains of development? For example, are environmental variables more critical for cognitive and intellectual development than for personality and emotional development or vice versa? Within a domain, does it have different functions with respect to motivational influence on performance as opposed to determining basic levels of capability? Zigler and his colleagues (Zigler, 1968; Zigler, Butterfield, & Capobianco, 1970) have shown that using environmental events to increase motivation results in improved performance in retarded individuals although they remain basically retarded with respect to intellectual capability. Is there a need to specify different kinds of environmental influence on behavior similar to what Gottlieb (1983) has attempted, but extend it beyond the early developmental period?

The question of timing of experience has received the most theoretical attention. Kuo (1967) as we have seen, placed experience in the prenatal period as critical to the development of the basic species-typical behavioral repertoire as well as to the form of the developmental trajectory that would occur postnatally. Massive environmental intervention at any point in time, however, could change behavior although the normal concourse with the normal environment insured a mutually interacting functional relationship between genetic predispositions and environmental experience. The experimental ethologists have focused upon prenatal and early postnatal periods as particularly sensitive periods for the acquisition of species typical behavior, giving as we have seen an important role to environmental experience as providing critical learning opportunities (Marler et al., 1981). Hebb (1949) proposed a neurologically based theory in which he claimed that early perceptual experience would enhance latter learning and thereby affect the level of intellectual achievement that could be attained. Bloom (1964) claimed that the majority of one's intellectual competence was determined by the time a child reached 4 years of age, although this has been challenged. Evidence from the animal experimental literature and from the imprinting literature along with the influence of Bloom's analysis and Hebb's theory, stimulated many of the early intervention efforts designed to improve intellectual development for children from poor homes. White (1965) has claimed that it is in the first three years of life that environmental experience is most critical in determining the level of developmental outcome.

A somewhat opposite point of view on timing has been taken by Kagan (1978) and Scarr (1981) who believe that the behavioral repertoire of the human infant is so highly canalized that environmental experience, although clearly important for behavioral development to occur, is not a critical element in individual differences observed during the first two years of life: "For the development of sensorimotor skills, nearly any natural human environment will suffice to produce criterion-level performance" (Scarr, 1981, p. 96). Variations in environmental experience after the first two years of life play a much more determining role with respect to level of competence although both Kagan and Scarr have increasingly, in the last several years, given more weight to genetic and constitutional variables as affecting developmental outcomes.

Except in experimental ethology, there is very little empirical work that addresses the issues of timing of experience on development. The human behavioral repertoire is extraordinarily complex; one can expect that environmental influences and the myriad variations in which they occur exert their impact in many different ways. It is not clear that there is any single environmental event or any specifically timed experience that functions in a rigid manner to produce a particular behavioral outcome. For example, the study of social bonding in the first few days of life initially led to claims by Klaus and Kennell (1976) that extended contact between mother and infant immediately after birth had lifelong impact upon the nature of the emotional relationship between mother and child and on the child's intellectual development. However, some of the research on which these claims were based has been criticized for over-generalization. Klaus and Kennell, themselves, have recently been a bit more equivocal on the long-term developmental significance of early extended contact (Klaus & Kennell, 1982). Evidence from research such as Werner and Smith's (1982) study of early individual differences in response to environmentally adverse conditions should help qualify how we conceptualize the nature of environmental influences on development in the early years of life.

The most theoretically elaborated model on the impact of the timing of environmental experience is to be found in Freudian theory that posits stages of development defined by the nature of the critical experiences that must occur during each period. In Erikson's (1950) stages, based upon Freudian theory, but extended to the life span, critical experiences during different periods of time are also identified as resulting in lifelong personality characteristics for each individual. Empirical verification of the stages and the critical nature of particular environmental experiences does not exist although the scheme suggested by Erikson is intuitively appealing. Most of the concern for developmental outcome has focused on intellectual and cognitive achievements although the most theoretically elaborated attempt, represented by Freudian theory, deals largely with personality and emotional functioning. There has been little discussion of the possiblity that environment impacts development differently in different domains of behavior.

Canalization has been an attractive concept recently because it provides a way of dealing with the observed regularity of behavior under a wide range of environments. However, canalization provides a way of thinking about the regularity of the form or topography of the behaviors that come into the repertoire; it does not provide a way to try to understand individual differences in level of achievement or rate of achievement. Even if one accepts the proposition that all normal infants in normal environments eventually acquire sensorimotor skills to some criterion, the criterion does not capture the individual differences in the quality of the behavior. Nor is it known how to conceptualize the developmental implications of these individual differences over the course of the life span.

One of the most popular recent developmental metaphors has been "transactional theory." As originally discussed by Sameroff and Chandler (1975), it was based largely on the Piagetian notion of the child as an active participant in his or her own development through the use of the environment, in contrast to the more "passive" model of the child as reactant to environmental input. More recently, the model has been elaborated to stress the continuous mutual modification that goes on between environment and organism (Sameroff, 1983) and the term *contextualism* has been added (Lerner & Kaufman, 1985). It is not clear what gains these conceptualizations provide in terms of specifying the processes involved or the functional role of either organism or environment in the transaction except to induce a greater appreciation for the complexity of the phenomena that we are trying to understand.

Deciding on how to best unitize environmental events has proved to be extremely difficult. As has already been discussed, there is no agreement on the level of analysis of environmental stimulation that will be most fruitful. A variety of conventions has grown up around different research strategies. Laboratory investigators typically use relatively simple nonsocial stimuli or relatively controlled social stimuli. Those who investigate in natural and seminatural environments deal with more complex stimulus events although they may choose to make measurements at relatively different levels of analysis in the manner we have already described. It is possible that the proper conceptualization of the functional units of environmental stimulation should be thought of in terms of the level of complexity of the behavior under study. For example, a single stimulus such as a checkerboard square may be proper for studying the single behavioral response of eye fixation. A complex stimulus such as maternal warmth, defined by a rating scale made up of relatively gross behavioral descriptors, may be appropriate for studying social skills in children or the general level of intellectual competence. There is little theory to guide such a discussion although the child development literature tends to break out into these kinds of matches.

After the physical principles that govern the functioning of the physical world on this planet, the most pervasive source of organization of environmental stimulation that distinguishes one general environmental context from another is culture. The empirical work on the influence of culture on behavioral development has been confined to the study of cognitive development (Laboratory of Comparative Human Cognition, 1983). The theoretical treatment of the relationships between culture and behavioral development is to be found mainly in the work of Vygotsky (1962, 1978). Again, it is not clear at what level of analysis culture as an organizing principle of environmental stimulation would be best understood.

There is no one who denies that the environment is an important partner in behavioral development. However, for those who adopt the organismic point of view, individual differences in developmental status has not been of interest and the nature of the processes by which environment affects general behavioral development have not been investigated. Social learning theorists and many who are interested in the transactional model do focus upon the nature of environmental input and they have been more concerned about how we come to understand individual differences in developmental status. The recent interest in developmental outcome for high-risk infants is an example of this. Because of all the problems that have been identified with respect to consensus on defining environmental variables the equations proposed for accounting for developmental outcome which factor in the environment have been quite imprecise and generally based on relatively weak theory.

In many of the models of development, the environment has generally been conceived of too simply and too unidimensionally. There are several reasons for making this assertion. First, it is likely that the role of environmental input is different in different domains of behavior both in terms of what dimensions are affected and at which points during development environmental input is functional. Second, it is likely that there are points in development, again different ones in different domains, at which major behavioral reorganization occurs, changing the qualitative relationship of the individual to the environment for development. Third, and finally, the functional input of the environment may be governed by different organizational principles depending on the level of "organism-environment interaction." These range from the environment as stimulus array and its relation to hard-wired routines, to the environment as culture and its relation to the individual as an organizing principle of patterns of stimulation. In light of this and all that has preceded, it is time to undertake consideration of the kind of structural model of development that is recommended by a full consideration of the factors and variables we have identified as important for building a model to account for developmental outcome.

RECAPITULATION

In this chapter the manner in which environment has been conceptualized as a functional element in the development of the human behavioral repertoire has been reviewed. Four levels of environmental organization were proposed: the environment as stimulus array, the environment as variation in learning opportunities, the environment as a social system, and the environment as culture. Each level functions differently with respect to behavioral development. The stimulus array level provides for discrete and patterned stimulus input to the organism. The organism is "hard-wired" to organize these inputs in particular ways. At the next level the environment is patterned sequentially and associatively so that it forms the context for learning. The social system is a more complex level of environmental organization in which the environment is embedded as learning opportunity. Finally, a superordinate set of organization principles represented by cultural systems provides for a pervasive and profound patterning of stimulus and response patterns. Taken together these four levels become the functional environment contributing to behavioral development. The behavioral variables associated with individuals selectively influence how the organism samples the environment creating an interactive system that defines the functional environment.

REFERENCES

Aslin, R. N., Pisoni, D. B., & Jusczyk, P. W. (1983). Auditory development and speech perception in infancy. In P. H. Mussen (Ed.), *Manual of child psychology* (4th ed., Vol. 2, pp. 573-687). M. M. Haith & J. J. Campos (Eds.), *Infancy and developmental psychobiology.* New York: Wiley.

Baer, D. M. (1973). The control of developmental process: Why wait? In J. Nesselroade & H. W. Reese (Eds.), *Life-span developmental psychology: Methodological issues* (pp. 185-193). New York: Academic Press.

Baltes, P. B., Cornelius, S. W., & Nesselroade, J. R. (1979). Cohort effects in developmental psychology. In J. R. Nesselroade & P. B. Baltes (Eds.), *Longitudinal research in the study of behavioral development* (pp. 61-87). New York: Academic Press.

Bandura, A. (1977). *Social learning theory.* Englewood Cliffs, NJ: Prentice-Hall.

Banks, M., & Salapatek, P. (1983). Infant visual perception. In P. H. Mussen (Ed.), *Manual of child psychology* (4th Ed., Vol. 2, pp. 435-571). M. M. Haith & J. J. Campos (Eds.), *Infancy and developmental psychobiology.* New York: Wiley.

Berland, J. (1982). *No five fingers are alike.* Cambridge, MA: Harvard University Press.

Bloom, B. (1964). *Stability and change in human characteristics.* New York: Wiley.

Brazelton, T. B., Koslowski, B., & Main, M. (1974). The origins of reciprocity. In M. Lewis & L. Rosenblum (Eds.), *The effect of the infant on its caregiver* (pp. 49-76). New York: Wiley.

Bronfenbrenner, U. (1979). *The ecology of human development: Experiments by nature and design.* Cambridge, MA: Harvard University Press.

Bronfenbrenner, U., & Crouter, A. C. (1983). The evolution of environmental models in development research. In P. H. Mussen (Ed.), *Handbook of child psychology* (4th ed., Vol. 1, pp. 357-414). W. Kessen (Ed.), *History, theory, and methods.* New York: Wiley.

Cairns, R. B. (1983). The emergence of developmental psychology. In P. H. Mussen (Ed.), *Handbook of child psychology* (4th ed., Vol. 1, pp. 41-102). W. Kessen (Ed.), *History, theory, and methods.* New York: Wiley.

Campos, J. J., Barrett, K., Lamb, M. E., Goldsmith, H. H., & Stenberg, C. (1983). Socioemotional development. In P. H. Mussen (Ed.), *Handbook of child psychology* (4th ed., Vol. 2, pp. 783–915). M. M. Haith & J. J. Campos (Eds.), *Infancy and developmental psychobiology.* New York: Wiley.

Cavalli-Sforza, L. L., & Feldman, M. W. (1981). *Cultural transmission and evolution: A quantitative approach.* Princeton, NJ: Princeton University Press.

Chizar, D. (1981). Learning theory, ethological theory and developmental plasticity. In E. S. Gollin (Ed.), *Developmental plasticity* (pp. 69–99). New York: Academic Press.

Consortium for Longitudinal Studies, (1983). *As the twig is bent... Lasting effects of preschool programs.* Hillsdale, NJ: Lawrence Erlbaum Associates.

Emde, R. N., & Harmon, R. J. (1972). Endogenous and exogenous smiling systems in infancy. *The Journal of the American Academy of Child Psychiatry, 11,* 177–200.

Erikson, E. H. (1950). *Childhood and society.* New York: Norton.

Feldman, D. H. (1980). *Beyond universals in cognitive development.* Norwood, NJ: Ablex.

Field, T. M., Sostek, A. M., Vietze, P., & Leiderman, P. H. (1981). *Culture and early interventions.* Hillsdale, NJ: Lawrence Erlbaum Associates.

Fischer, K. W. (1980). A theory of cognitive development: The control and construction of hierarchies of skills. *Psychological Review, 87,* 477–531.

Flavell, J. H., & Ross, L. (1981). *Social cognitive development.* Cambridge, MA: Cambridge University Press.

Gewirtz, J. L. (1965). The course of smiling in four childrearing environments in Israel. In B. M. Foss (Ed.), *Determinants of infant behavior* (Vol. 3, pp. 205–248). London: Methuen.

Gleitman, L. R., Newport, E. L., & Gleitman, H. (1984). The current status of the motherese hypothesis. *Journal of Child Language, 11,* 43–79.

Goldman-Rakic, P. S., Isseroff, A., Schwartz, M. L., & Bugbee, N. M. (1983). The neurobiology of cognitive development. In P. H. Mussen (Ed.), *Handbook of child psychology* (Vol. 1, pp. 281–344). M. M. Haith & J. J. Campos (Eds.), *Infancy and developmental psychobiology.* New York: Wiley.

Goodnow, J., Knight, R., & Cashmore, J. (1986). Adult social cognition: Implications of parents' ideas for approaches to development. In M. Perlmutter (Ed.), *Minnesota Symposium on Child Development* (Vol. 18, pp. 287–320).

Gottlieb, G. (1983). The psychobiological approach to developmental issues. In P.H. Mussen (Ed.), *Handbook of child psychology* (4th Ed., Vol. 2, pp. 1–26). M. M. Haith & J. J. Campos (Eds.), *Infancy and developmental psychobiology.* New York: Wiley.

Gottman, J., Rose, F. T., & Mettelal, G. (1982). Time-series analysis of social interaction data. In T. Field & A. Fogel (Eds.), *Emotion and early interaction* (pp. 267–289). Hillsdale, NJ: Lawrence Erlbaum Associates.

Green, S., & Marler, P. (1979). The analysis of animal communication. In P. Marler & J. Vandenbergh (Eds.), *Handbook of behavioral neurobiology. Vol. 3. Social behavior and communication* (pp. 73–158). New York: Plenum Press.

Haith, M. M. (1980). *Rules that babies look by.* Hillsdale, NJ: Lawrence Erlbaum Associates.

Hebb, D. O. (1949). *The organization of behavior.* New York: Wiley.

Hinde, R. A. (1983). Ethology and child development. In P.H. Mussen (Ed.), *Handbook of child psychology* (Vol. 2, pp. 27–93). M. M. Haith & J. J. Campos (Eds.), *Infancy and developmental psychobiology.* New York: Wiley.

James, W. (1890) *Principles of psychology.* New York: Holt.

Kagan, J. (1978). *Infancy.* Cambridge, MA: Harvard University Press.

Klaus, M., & Kennell, J. (1976). *Maternal-infant bonding.* St. Louis, MO: Mosley.

Klaus, M., & Kennell, J. (1982). *Parent-infant bonding.* St. Louis, MO: Mosley.

Kluckhohn, C. (1962). *Culture and behavior.* Glencoe, IL: The Free Press.

Kroeber, A. L., & Kluckhohn, C. (1952). *Culture: A critical review of concepts and definitions.*

Papers of the Peabody Museum of Archaeology and Ethnology (Vol. 47, No. 1). Cambridge, MA: Harvard University Press.

Kuo, Z.-Y. (1967). *The dynamics of behavioral development.* New York: Random House.

Laboratory of Comparative Human Cognition (1983). Culture and cognitive development. In P. H. Mussen (Ed.), *Handbook of child psychology* (4th Ed., Vol. 1, pp. 295–356). W. Kessen (Ed.), *History, theory, and methods.* New York: Wiley.

Lazar, I., Darlington, R., Murray, H., Royce, J., & Snipper, A. (1982). Lasting effects of early education. *Monographs of the Society for Research in Child Development, 47* (1–2 Serial No. 194).

Leiderman, P. H., Tulkin, S. R., & Rosenfeld, A. (Eds.). (1977). *Culture and infancy: Variations in the human experience.* New York: Academic Press.

Leiderman, H. (1978). The critical period hypothesis revisited: Mother to infant social bonding in the neonatal period. In F. D. Horowitz (Ed.), *Early development hazards: Predictors and precautions* (pp. 43–77). Boulder, CO: Westview Press.

Lerner, R. M., & Busch-Rossnagel, N. A. (1981). Individuals as producers of their development: Conceptual and empirical bases. In R. M. Lerner & N. A. Busch-Rossnagel (Eds.), *Individuals as producers of their development* (pp. 1–36). New York: Academic Press.

Lerner, R. M., & Kaufman, M. B. (1985). The concept of development in contextualism. *Developmental Review, 5,* 309–333.

Luria, A. R. (1976). *Cognitive development. Its cultural and social foundations.* Cambridge, MA: Harvard University Press.

Luria, A. R. (1981). *Language and cognition.* New York: Wiley.

Marler, P. (1976). Development and learning of recognition systems. In T. H. Bullock (Ed.), *Recognition of complex acoustic signals.* Berlin: Dahlem Konferenzen.

Marler, P. (1977). Sensory templates, vocal perception, and development: A comparative view. In M. Lewis & L. A. Rosenblum (Eds.), *Interaction, conversation, and the development of language* (pp. 95–114). New York: Wiley.

Marler, P., Zoloth, S., & Dooling, R. (1981). Innate programs for perceptual development: An ethological view. In E. Gollin (Ed.), *Developmental plasticity* (pp. 135–172). New York: Academic Press.

McGaugh, J. L. (1983). Hormonal influences on memory. *Annual Review of Psychology, 34,* 297–323.

Nelson, C. A., & Horowitz, F. D. (1987). Visual motion perception in infancy: A review and synthesis. In P. Salapatek & L. B. Cohen (Eds.), *Handbook of infant perception. Vol. 2.* (pp. 123–153). *Cognitive aspects.* New York: Academic Press.

Oyama, S. (1985). *The ontogeny of information.* Cambridge, MA: Cambridge University Press.

Parmelee, A. H., & Sigman, M. D. (1983). Perinatal brain development and behavior. In P.H. Mussen (Ed.), *Handbook of child psychology* (Vol. 1, pp. 95–155). M. M. Haith & J. J. Campos (Eds.), *Infancy and developmental psychobiology.* New York: Wiley.

Rosenzweig, M. R., & Bennett, E. L. (Eds.). (1976). *Neural mechanisms of learning and memory.* Cambridge, MA: MIT Press.

Rozin, P. (1976). The evolution of intelligence and access to the cognitive unconscious. In J. M. Sprague & A. N. Epstein (Eds.), *Progress in psychobiology and physiological psychology* (pp. 245–279). New York: Academic Press.

Sameroff, A. J. (1983). Developmental systems: Contexts and evolution. In P.H. Mussen (Ed.), *Handbook of child psychology* (Vol. 1, pp. 237–294). W. Kessen (Ed.), *History, theory and methods.* New York: Wiley.

Sameroff, A. J., & Chandler, M. J. (1975). Reproductive risk and the continuum of care-taking casualty. In F. D. Horowitz (Ed.), *Review of child development research* (Vol. 4, pp. 187–244). Chicago: University of Chicago Press.

Scarr, S. (1981). *Race, social class and individual differences in I.Q.* Hillsdale, NJ: Lawrence Erlbaum Associates.

Scarr, S., & McCartney, K. (1983). How people make their own environments: A theory of genotype-environment effects. *Child Development, 54,* 424–435.

Sears, R. R. (1951). A theoretical framework for personality and social behavior. *American Psychologist, 6,* 476–483.

von Bertalanffy, L. (1968). *General system theory.* New York: Braziller. (Rev. Ed.).

von Bertalanffy, L. (1975). *Perspectives on general system theory.* New York: Braziller.

Vygotsky, L. S. (1962). *Thought and language.* Cambridge, MA: MIT Press.

Vygotsky, L. S. (1978). *Mind in society.* Cambridge, MA: Harvard University Press.

Werner, E. E. (1979). *Cross-cultural child development.* Monterey, CA: Brooks/Cole.

Werner, E. E., & Smith, R. S. (1982). *Vulnerable but invincible: A longitudinal study of resilient children and youth.* New York: McGraw-Hill.

White, B. L. (1975). *The first three years of life.* Englewood Cliffs, NJ: Prentice-Hall.

Zelazo, P. R., Zelazo, N. A., & Kolb, S. (1972). "Walking" in the newborn. *Science, 176,* 314–315.

Zigler, E. (1968). Mental retardation. In P. London & D. Rosenhan (Eds.), *Foundations of abnormal psychology* (pp. 519–566). New York: Holt, Rinehart & Winston.

Zigler, E., Butterfield, E. C., & Capobianco, F. (1970). Institutionalization and the effectiveness of social reinforcement: A five and eight year follow-up study. *Developmental Psychology, 3,* 255–263.

5

Synthesis:
A Structural/Behavioral
Model of Development

Early in our discussion it was noted that the major theories of development were largely formulated prior to 1930, while the bulk of our data on behavioral development has become available since that time. A small recapitulation of some previous observations may be useful here. There has been no major revision of grand developmental theory in light of data, although data have served to bolster allegiance to one theoretical disposition over another. The exception is seen in recent attempts to alter or adjust Piagetian theory given evidence challenging the stage-structure analysis proposed by Piaget. From one point of view, it could be said that the theories have served the field well in generating research. Disconfirming evidence has not provided sufficiently serious challenge to any given theory to necessitate theory revision or theory generation. Alternatively, developmental theories may be viewed as currently irrelevant in the formal sense to the generation of research. The theories can be seen as serving, instead, as a kind of background ambience for the choice of problems, for the selection of terminology, and as an umbrella rationale for a strategy of investigation. Although neither position, in its extreme form, properly characterizes the field with respect to theory/research relationships, the intellectual tradition from which most developmentalists operate is closer to the latter orientation than to the former.

Developmentalists tend to become aligned with clusters of other investigators interested in a particular problem, behavioral domain, or period of development, using mini-theories as the basic source for identifying their research questions. An overall integrative theoretical perspective is either largely missing or takes the form of a choice of world view described by

Reese and Overton (1970) as organismic or mechanistic. Practically, this has come down to either opting for behaviorism and looking at development in terms of response acquisition or championing cognitivism and characterizing development in terms of the organization, system, and structure of behavioral functioning. A recent variation of the organismic approach using terms of contextualism and transaction has been proposed (Sameroff, 1983). In these two world views it is claimed that the child is seen quite differently. The mechanistic world view has the child as an essentially passive, reactive recipient of environmental forces that shape a developing behavioral repertoire; in the organismic world view the child is an active participant who uses the environment to shape his or her own developmental course, albeit every child shapes the same basic course. In a mechanistic orientation behavioral development is regarded as linear and cumulative; in the organismic view stages, systems, structures, and organization are arrayed in a developing spiral or succession of overlapping sets.

Has the umbrella use of theory and/or the general adoption of a world view been productive? Has the strategy of formulating mini-theories aimed at understanding particular phenomena either over time or during a given developmental epoch provided a sufficiently rich source for the generation of important research questions and the advancement of our knowledge concerning behavioral development? If the answers are positive then the status quo is affirmed. If the answers are negative then either one begins to resurrect an existing theory or one attempts to formulate a new theory. One might, however, be equivocal and opt for a mixed approach. The mini-theory, world view strategy has not been unproductive—witness the expansion of the Mussen *Handbook* from two volumes to four between 1970 and 1983, a period when the mini-theory, world view orientation has been particularly dominant. On the other hand, as has been indicated, this era has not been one in which there has been a tendency to ask strong developmental questions. There has not been an integrative framework to guide analyses of developmental status, of continuity–discontinuity, or of interactions between behavioral domains. We have not had a theory-based rationale for relating mirco- and macrolevel phenomena, or for considering how process and organization might best be unified into a developmental analysis. Combining the so-called mechanistic and organismic world view without diluting the strengths of either could, at this point in the history of developmental science, be useful. In other words, by equivocating in the answer to the question of the sufficiency of the status quo, it is possible to consider a synthesis that might result in proposing a structural/behavioral model of human behavioral development that would foster stronger and more programmatic developmental research.

The purpose in this chapter is to propose such a structural/behavioral model of behavioral development and to explore some of its implications for a developmental research agenda. Cairns (1983) recognized the need for this when he called for the development of more precise models than we now have and for trying to determine the limits of models with respect to integrating and predicting across different behavioral domains. More precise models will be useful if they permit us to deal with issues and to undertake analyses that are not now fostered by the theories and models we are using. This does not mean that we must obviate the use of mini-theories for investigating particular phenomena or abandon essentially empirical efforts on specific topics. Rather, assuming the data generated by mini-theory strategies or in the context of empirical investigations are reliable and replicable, any proposed model needs to be tested by its ability to accommodate the data thus provided.

Kuhn (1970) noted that for purposes of pushing a science ahead, it is sometimes convenient and important to ignore discordant data until the full parameters of a particular theory have been explored. At that point, discordant data may become the basis for considering theory revision or scientific revolution. However, it is one thing to strategically ignore data for the time being and another to dismiss data as "wrong." In the behavioral sciences and in psychology in particular, there has been a tendency to dismiss data when they are not in agreement with a prevailing theory or model. Dismissing or quarrelling with an interpretation of data is one thing. But, the facts, themselves, assuming they are reliable and replicable, cannot be declared wrong. Some will argue, of course, that there is no such thing as fact without interpretation, but that is not the view being taken here. Discordant data should always be taken as a source of information about the parameters of a particular theory or model that at some later point in time will need to be accommodated through either theory revision or scientific revolution. Such a programmatic strategy has tended to be more typical in the biological and physical sciences than in the behavioral sciences—perhaps a measure of the difference in the relative maturity of the enterprises.

It is important to make some distinctions concerning models and theories and the use of these terms. The structural/behavioral model of behavioral development discussed here does not fit neatly any of the four categories of model/theory proposed by Marx (1976), although it may be useful here to consider his analysis. A model, according to Marx, is largely an informal metaphor for how elements relate. It is used heuristically by investigators as a general guide for formulating research questions. Data are not formally used to modify or expand the model although in some unspecified manner models do change as data accumulate and are interpreted to suggest alternative or revised models. Theories, in Marx's analysis, take one of three forms: deductive, functional, and inductive. Inductive theory involves the statement of general law or principle based upon a set of data without further interpretation. Skinnerians typically use theory in this manner although Skinner foresaw that more formal theory building might one day be possible when enough descriptive laws had been accumulated. Hull, however, envisioned psychology as operating in a deductive theory mode whereby a formal set of propositions is devised, experiments are designed to test aspects of the theory and the theory is revised in light of the results (Hull, 1943, 1951). Functional theory, which Marx believes characterizes most theory building in psychology today and is perhaps analogous to the mini-theory approach mentioned, involves a general statement or hypothesis that is tested and then revised on the basis of evidence. The new hypothesis now undergoes testing and is further revised, and so on. Functional theory may well be embedded in a particular model and more often than not can be assigned to one or another of the "world views" we have described.

In choosing the modifier of "structural/behavioral" for the model being discussed here, it is meant to imply a wedding of the organismic and mechanistic approaches. Although some believe that this juxtaposition is now outdated and that a more ecumenical climate exists, a perusal of most of the developmental journals and many of the books will not support this belief. The behavioral S-R approach is typically dismissed as "mere" stimulus-response in the organismically oriented literature, if mentioned at all, and the organismic perspective is typically totally ignored in the behaviorally oriented literature. Few investigators working in the context of organismic theory or with transactional system theory really take learning and the mechanisms of learning seriously; almost no investigators working in the behavioral S-R tradition consider the organization of behavior and how organization and sequences affect learning. (Fischer, 1980, makes a similar point.)

There is a further consideration in the posing of the structural/behavioral model. The growing appreciation of gene action and gene structure has emboldened the parsing of behavior into percentages accounted for by genetic factors. This behavioral genetics tradition has helped to increase a tendency to consider "organismic" variables as synonymous with "genetic" variables. Although lip service is played to the interaction of environment and genes, predominance has been subtly and not so subtly assigned the genetic influences (for example, see Scarr and McCartney's, 1983, proposal that genes drive behavior). In fact, however, as Oyama's (1985) penetrating analysis makes clear, the gene–environment interactional paradigm has been too simply represented. She stresses that organismic form is not transmitted in the gene; rather, as has already been noted, it is constructed in the course of development. "A program for simulating ontogeny ... would have to include not only the genomic structure but descriptions of all the conditions, parameters and interactions internal and external to the organism, that constitute the developmental system in transition" (Oyama, 1985, pp. 61–62).

Like Kuo (1967), Oyama refers to the perspective that the action of cells is constituted and controlled by the tissues constructed; similarly, the behavioral system is constituted and constructed by the interactions with the environment. For this reason, Oyama takes the position that it is not possible to distinguish between the inherited and the acquired. Universal characteristics are dependent for their actualization on sufficient "developmental interactants." This point of view is extremely compatible with the model of structural/behavioral development described here.

In coming to a description of the structural/behavioral model of development, first consideration is given, based upon all that has been discussed in the previous chapters, to the kinds of phenomena that the model needs to encompass. Then it is possible to describe the model and show how it accommodates what it must accommodate. Finally, an attempt is made to determine how the structural/behavioral model affects the kinds of questions that are asked and how it changes or amplifies some of the metaphors that have been used.

THE NECESSARY INGREDIENTS OF A STRUCTURAL/BEHAVIORAL MODEL

Behavioral development and developmental outcome are obviously complexly determined. Moreover, it is likely that there is a certain amount of redundancy in the determining systems such that failure of one system is compensated for by a higher amplitude of functioning in another system that has the capacity for effecting the same or a modified outcome. Depicting this in any graphic manner is not easy. Figure 5.1 is an attempt to identify the elements that must be encompassed by a structural/behavioral model of development, if that model is to help generate hypotheses about relationships and help specify the conditions that will produce particular developmental outcomes. The shape of the diagram in Fig. 5.1 is purposely abstract; the specific form of the contour is of no particular significance except that it is non-representational of any particular object. The elements included in the model are of mixed kinds—some are events, like "B" for birth and "C" for conception; some like the inner-most contour representing the prenatal period, some are schedules such as "stages and developmental program"; some are conditions such as "functional environmental surround"; and some are processes such as "learning." Each is included as an ingredient that must go into a structural/behavioral model of behavioral development. At the risk of a seeming mixed metaphor, these ingredients are specified as the base contributions to behavioral development.

The non-universals and universals outside the contour of the figure represent two general classes of behaviors in the behavioral repertoire of the human organism that result from one or more of the ingredients of the model. Each of the ingredients needs to be described before the interrelationships that are being proposed can be discussed.

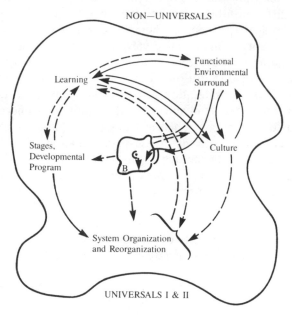

FIG. 5.1. The elements that must be taken into account in a developmental theory or model.

At the center of the figure is "C" for conception and the uniting of the sperm and the egg. Included here is the entire gamut of genetic material, genetically determined parameters and developmental programs that exist as potential in the human germ plasma. This is the "given" for the organism—a given reflecting not only the proximate hereditary factors from the donor parents but also a long evolutionary history that has shaped the nature of what constitutes genetic structure. The space between "C" and the inner contour, is the prenatal period reflecting a uterine environment that surrounds, protects, feeds, and affects how the given at conception is developed and expressed. During the 9-month prenatal period the organism is involved in a highly significant developmental journey influenced by the genetic material of the organism in interaction with the environmental surround not only in terms of the mechanical features of the uterus and its transport systems, but also the environment. Environment is determined by the behavior of the mother with respect to her nutrient and alcohol intake, smoking, and possibly other behaviors. In turn, some of the constitutional characteristics of the fetus will determine what and how much of the environment affects organismic growth and development. It is almost common sense to observe that what will be detrimental for one child may not be detrimental for another. Some infants whose mothers consume relatively large quantities of alcohol during pregnancy will be born with fetal alcohol syndrome; others will not. This may be a result of differential metabolism of alcohol by the mother and differential passage to the fetus. It may also be influenced by the degree to which the fetus has the capability of buffering against the effects of the alcohol. This kind of organism–environment interaction is a prototype of organism–environment interaction throughout development. The term *transaction* might well be substituted here as the nature of the fetus may affect the functional nature of the fetal environment. Not all interactive relationships, however, are transactive.

The line intersected by "B" represents birth. The double portion of that line is meant to highlight the fact that the perinatal period is a potentially hazardous one that can profoundly alter the subsequent developmental potential of the organism. Severe oxygen deprivation during birth and other perinatal complications can influence particular systems of behavior and/or result in general effects that are less dramatic but important nevertheless. However, as indicated in Sameroff and Chandler's (1975) classic review of this literature, the nature of the child's postnatal environment significantly modifies the nature of the effects of perinatal trauma unless major and currently irreparable physiological insult has occurred. Because the factor of relative organismic vulnerability was not well recognized when Sameroff and Chandler did their review, they did not stress differential individual susceptibility to the effects of perinatal complications and to the subsequent environment. Any attempt at a comprehensive analysis of development in any structural model of development must include such individual differences in vulnerability in the developmental outcome equation.

Some of the ingredients of behavioral development depicted in Fig. 5.1 are heavily weighted by the evolutionary history of the human species. Some include influences from individual hereditary factors. Some are more environmentally determined. For example, the program of behavioral development with rough stage division and the elements of system organization and periodic reorganization reflect the strong species characteristics that involve a course of high probability behavioral development or behavior potentials. The rate of development through this course, and some of the parameters that determine how robustly behaviors are acquired, are influenced (not determined) by the individual's personal hereditary background. The functional environmental surround, namely the ambient environmental background that contains the functional or effective environmental stimulation is environmentally weighted, although both species characteristics and individual hereditary factors will contribute to the determination of what is and is not functional stimulation. For example, the human species may be particularly sensitive to certain sounds and not others, language sounds especially; for any given individual auditory stimuli may be a stronger stimulus dimension in the environment than visual stimuli or vice versa. Both species and individual hereditary factors influence functional environmental stimulation. However, over time, opportunities for learning will shape responsiveness to some stimuli and not others. So, what constitutes functional environmental stimulation for an individual is a reflection of species characteristics, individual constitutional characteristics, and the individual's learning history.

Culture represents the overriding organization of stimulation in an environment through emphasis on certain patterns and not others. It is reflected in the more global behaviors that positively valence and negatively valence behaviors and different aspects of the organization of environmental patterns. Culture contributes to the aspects of the environment that serve as functional, that set the agenda for some of what is learned, that influence the organization and reorganization of behavior patterns in conjunction with the control exerted by species characteristics and by individual hereditary factors.

The processes of learning are ubiquitous in the acquisition of the behavioral repertoire. They are constrained by species characteristics, they are influenced by individual constitutional characteristics, they are affected by culture and by the discriminative characteristics of the functional environmental surround. Learning, in turn, influences progression through stages, the evolution of culture and the progressive definition of the functional environmental surround.

Both the prenatal and postnatal course of development are controlled by the relationships among the ingredients shown in Fig. 5.1. The "given" of conception influences the prenatal developmental course. The prenatal environment and the conditions surrounding the perinatal period combine with the initial genetic structures to define the infant's developmental status at birth. Culture influences some aspects of prenatal environment through nutritional patterns, activity patterns, and medical practices. The effects of the relationships are bi-directional even during the prenatal and perinatal periods. The infant's developmental status at birth begins to affect the functional postnatal environment just as the environmental factors affect the infant. This complex of relationships, not necessarily exerting equal influence from different directions, constitute strong determining influences on how the genetically programmed developmental course will be played out. The effects will be seen in the timing and nature of system organization and behavioral reorganization. They will be seen in how the nature and adequacy of learning opportunities are sorted out for individual children and they will help give a general definition to what is the functional environmental surround. In turn, cultural parameters and parental behavioral will highlight some aspects of environment, underplay other aspects. However, the child's own characteristics will partly determine the degree to which environmental influence plays a determining role in behavioral development. This will hold for those domains and for those behaviors where environmental variability is a factor in behavioral acquisition.

What will be affected by the organism's characteristics and what will, in turn, affect the growth and development of the child and the interactions among these elements are all shown within the boundaries of the picture presented in Fig. 5.1. Some effects are represented by dashed lines, others by solid lines. The solid lines are meant to indicate the more direct influences, the dashed lines the more indirect relationships. Indirect influences are presumed to involve one or more intervening variables although these are not shown in the figure. The choice of solid or dashed lines was somewhat arbitrary, influenced by a general estimate about the weight of the evidence and also by hypotheses related to whether the mechanisms for the influences were likely to be more direct (solid) than less direct (dashed). In both cases the data base is not sufficient to defend these decisions staunchly at the present time. Bi-directionality and, ultimately, multidirectionality is the rule rather than the exception, again pointing to a complexity that is developmentally cumulative. Additionally, the relative strength of organismic and environmental contributions may not be the same in different developmental periods or for different behavioral domains.

Universals I and II

At the borders of the figure are the terms *universals* and *non-universals.* They represent categories of behavior and have particular relationships to the elements shown in the figure. Two types of universals in development are being proposed. Universal I involves behavioral characteristics that have a course of development that is laid down in the phylogenetic inheritance of the organism—shaped, as we have said, by the eons of evolutionary history. The behavioral expression of these universals cannot occur in the absence of a normal species-typical environment. However, given that environment, what will be expressed is largely the same in every normal human organism. The quality of the behavior may be influenced by individual inheritance and/or environmental factors but the base topography of the behavioral capability will not vary from child to child. Those behavioral characteristics that are said to be "hard wired" are assigned to this category of universal as in Rozin's (1976) notion of the cognitive unconscious. Only massive organismic insult or abnormality can dislodge the expression and development of these universal behaviors. Hebb has commented that experience does not write on a blank slate. Rather, "the slate has grooves and indentations that make the appearance of letters inevitable, other letters impossible" (Hebb, 1980, p. 105). In other words, given an intact organism developing in a species-typical environment the probability of the behavior and its course of development is as close to "one" as it is possible to get. This is the type of universal represented in the inherent spatial calculus of the organism and in the capacity to process certain types of environmental information in particular ways. It is lodged in the genetics of the organism with a very high probability of expression in neural characteristics and in neural information processing mechanisms.

Many of the Universal I behaviors involve those responses that are considered to be perceptual capacities. For example, the human organism processes certain portions of the visual and auditory spectra but not others. The development of eye–hand coordination is another example. These are hard-wired behavioral potentials requiring only the normal species-typical environmental surround for their development. Many of the autonomic responses and the reflex responses are Universal I behaviors, although behaviors that fall into these categories are not often thought of as behavioral responses. Nevertheless, they are in the behavioral repertoire, they may play a strong underlying role in the development of other behaviors and they are typically found in all normal human organisms. Fodor's (1983) notion of modularized perceptual processes fits a Universal I categorization.

A Universal II type behavior is one in which the probability of expression and development is also high but somewhat less than "one." It is more subject to variability in environmental conditions and plastic elaboration than is the case for Universal I type behaviors. The high probability is "wired" but less hard wired than with universals of the first type. Universal II behaviors are of the kind described by Kuo (1967) as behavior potentials. They fit Waddington's (1966) concept of "canalization." According to Waddington, certain pathways of development are canalized "in the sense that the developing system has an inbuilt tendency to stick to the path, and is quite difficult to divert from it by any influence. . . . The canalization is . . . not complete. Developing systems do not always reach the fully normal adult state. The point is that they have a tendency to do so, and are not entirely at the mercy of any temporary abnormalities" (p. 48). Thus, some aspects of behavioral development, to the extent that they are canalized, are universal. The path of behavioral developmental course is difficult (but not impossible) to divert. Some aspects of the characteristics of developmental outcome have high probability of being attained. Many of the behaviors we identify as universally human are of this type. For example, erect motor locomotion, the capacity to learn language, and sensori-motor skills in the first two years of life.

Universal II type behaviors may be supported by Universal I type behaviors but they are distinguished from them by two aspects. One, Universal II type behaviors will generally have a longer developmental course to reach maturity; two, environmental factors will exert a greater influence on the variability of the quality of the behavior and its final developmental level than will be true for Universal I type behaviors. For example, many of the features of human cognitive development in the sensori-motor period during the first two years of life may be highly canalized. The developmental course of these behaviors is universal for all normal organisms being reared in a species-typical environment. However, environmental variations may determine the quality of the cognitive achievements during the sensori-motor period, their sequence, and synchrony across behavioral domains. Environmental variations may also determine how the quality of the sensori-motor achievement will contribute to the subsequent quality of cognitive development. Further, some subtle cultural influences may help shape, sharpen, or elaborate aspects of these cognitive behaviors. An organism–environment interaction is also at work here. The same environment will functionally produce differential quality for different individuals. In turn, individual characteristics will affect the nature of what becomes the functional environment.

Another characteristic typifies Universal II type behaviors. This involves Kuo's (1967) concept of "behavior potentials." These are the behaviors that every member of the species will develop if reared in species-typical environments. The factors determining their acquisition can be altered (albeit sometimes only with massive intervention) resulting in the acquisition of less probable behavior potentials. For example, Kuo found that the seemingly natural enmity of birds and cats could be altered by sufficient manipulation of rearing conditions. Demonstrations such as this give one reason to be cautious about attributing universal species-typical behaviors entirely to genetic control and evolutionary history.

The concept of behavior potentials as Universal II type behaviors has application to some kinds of abnormal behavioral patterns. For example, it appears that autistic children typically respond selectively to environmental stimuli in very different ways than normal children. For these children it is possible that behavior potentials that typically have a low probability in normal children have, for unknown reasons, much higher probability in some children. These children's behavior is more easily shaped to non-social stimuli, more easily shaped to highly stereotyped and repetitive behaviors, and less responsive to social reinforcers than that of normal children. A set of atypical behavior potentials interacts with the normal species-typical environment that is geared to shape typical behavior potentials. The result is abnormal development. If these initially much lower probability behavior potentials could be detected very early then it might be possible, à la Kuo, to manipulate the environment in such a manner as to strengthen the normal behavior potentials that are uncharacteristically weak in a particular child and thus prevent or avoid much of the development of the autistic behavior.

The mechanisms of acquisition of Universal II type behaviors can be represented as a conspiracy between the nature of the organism and the nature of the environment. The normal organism is "grooved" to a particular course and not easily diverted given normatively most probable characteristics of the environment. Additionally, using Waddington's notion of canalization, this course is multiply determined and has heavy insurance of "self-righting" in a redundancy of mechanisms that give high probability to the basic developmental course. However, the acquisition is the result of processes that involve "learning." Because of variety in environmental conditions and organism–environment relationships there will be variability in learning from child to child. The variability associated with learning will be expressed in the quality of the behavior acquired and the manner and degree to which it is elaborated rather than with respect to which behavior is acquired.

Behaviors that fit the category of Universal I and Universal II have strong species-typical characteristics. However, the acquisition of these behaviors into the behavioral repertoire, particularly the Universal II behaviors, requires opportunity to learn. Further, the learning opportunities reflect variability in environment and thus environment impacts the quality of the behavior that is acquired. Individual constitutional differences, however, exert a modulating influence on the effect of the environment. A good example of the complexity involved here is to be found in the acquisition of language. Productive language acquisition is a Universal II type behavior. All normal, intact children reared in a normal environment with the necessary minimum conditions for learning will acquire language.

Some aspects of language acquisition are determined by species programs of stimulus selectivity and response organization and reorganization. In addition, however, acquisition will be influenced by non-universal environmental factors that will determine which language will be acquired and the level of language competence that will be achieved. Individual difference characteristics associated with the organism will modulate the environmental effects. The same non-universal environmental conditions will affect different children differently depending on their constitutional characteristics. In other words, how and at what level universals will be expressed is partly under environmental control, especially with respect to the quality and sophistication of the end points of the developmental path and partly under control of individual difference factors.

Oyama (1985), although not using a "universals" dimension, characterizes developmental systems as being more or less reliable and well integrated:

"The more reliable and well integrated a developmental system is . . . the more spontaneous and inevitable, the more 'biological' ontogeny will appear and the more uniform the effects of any given genetic or environmental factor will be. The more unpredictable the system the less programmed it will seem" (pp. 44–45). This is a good continuum to use to understand the Universal I to Universal II to Non-Universal relationships being suggested here.

Non-Universal Behaviors

Non-universal behaviors indicated in Fig. 5.1 encompass all those behaviors that are the result of learning opportunities determined by cultural values and variations in functional environments. The mechanisms of learning lie at the heart of the acquisition process of the non-universal behaviors although the species-typical aspects of stages and system organization influence some of when and how those mechanisms operate and partially determine some of the content of the non-universal behaviors acquired. System organization in some domains and at some points in development may be heavily influenced by cultural factors, especially as cultural factors determine that some environmental elements will be salient over others. For example, the degree to which and the manner in which emotion serves as a constraining or amplifying force in the learning process will be heavily influenced by cultural differences in the organization and use of emotional responses.

The role of emotional factors in behavioral development has not received much systematic study except with the psychoanalytic tradition of Freud's concepts of psychic energy and of developmental progression through psycho-sexual stages. These involved an emphasis on emotional organization as a key factor for all other aspects of behavioral performance and behavioral organization (Freud, 1905/1954). Kurt Lewin (1954) also believed that "needs" or emotional states served to organize behavior. Lewin postulated that "the cognitive structure of the life space is influenced by the state of the needs" (p. 946), but it is not clear to what extent emotional factors influenced structural change or development across time. Lewin made frequent reference to psychoanalytic sources in discussing his theory and obviously saw his approach as compatible with Freudian theory. Lewin stressed an analysis of the behavioral system in terms of sectors of life space organized by field forces of positive and negative valences. The differential boundary permeabilities of the life-space sectors determined the ease with which environmental events could exert an influence on the individual to change, reorganize, and develop.

It is difficult to use Lewinian ideas in a direct manner in formulating a structural/behavioral model of development. There is an obvious intuitive validity to some of his organizational concepts. However, there has been little direct empirical testing of the theory in its developmental context with the exception of Zigler's initial and successful challenge of the theory as applied to the behavior of retarded children. (Zigler, 1961, 1963; Zigler & Williams, 1963).

Recent renewed interest in emotional development, in part stimulated by psychoanalytic theory (e.g., Emde, Gaensbauer, & Harmon, 1976; Emde, Kligman, Reich, & Wade, 1978), is a promising development. It has provided empirical definition for some of the central concepts of emotion and affect. This will enable investigators to incorporate Freud's ideas about the role of emotional organization and the use of affect more systematically into models and theories of development. Lewin's discussion of life-space organizational principles tends still to have metaphorical value. It is related to our discussion of system organization and flexibility of system boundaries, but what is needed is an attempt to identify the empirical strategies that might illuminate how these concepts can best be used. To the extent that emotional variables are played out in the context of learning opportunities, in the context of cultural definitions, and in the context of constitutional differences among individuals, they are significant sources of influence in the acquisition of non-universal behaviors. A basic set of emotional reactions, however, appears to be universal although their developmental course may not be.

A structural/behavioral model should encompass all that we have just discussed here. It must also incorporate and accommodate all the known mechanisms by which behavioral development and change can come about. These mechanisms are partially reflected in Fig. 5.1 to the extent that genetic structure is represented in what is laid down at conception and to the extent that learning mechanisms are obviously present. Learning and genetic mechanisms are involved in information-processing mechanisms. Information-processing mechanisms, in turn, affect learning. Interactions between environmental and biological factors determine when mechanisms function and how elements in mechanisms take on and leave off their functional roles. A model should also accommodate the possibility that the saliency of organizing principles of behavior and of behavioral development may differ for different domains of behavior and in different developmental periods. The model must permit us to test hypotheses about continuities and discontinuities within behavioral systems and across developmental epochs.

THE NATURE OF A STRUCTURAL/BEHAVIORAL
MODEL OF DEVELOPMENT

The choice of the term *structural/behavioral model of development* is intended to convey the notion that behavioral development is the result of a complex structural relationship involving many elements. A model must accommodate the variables that appear to be significant contributors to development. It must permit empirical tests of specific relationships as well as strong developmental questions. As was noted in chapter 1, the model being proposed here has been evolving over several years (e.g., Horowitz, 1978) but it is, however, more extensively developed and elaborated here than in any previous discussions. The model, shown again in Fig. 5.2, is presented here for the convenience of the reader. Some repetition from chapter 1 is also provided for a complete presentation here. The elements of the model are arrayed along two major dimensions, each of which is conceived of as a continuum: characteristics of the organism and characteristics of the environment. The dimension of organism variables has two aspects. One has to do with the physiological integrity of the child, ranging from completely unimpaired to significant impairment. The other involves the degree of organismic vulnerability or, if one wishes, resiliency, in the face of adversity or non-facilitative environmental input. At the invulnerable end of the continuum there is strong resilience and hence relative invulnerability to adversity; at the other end is low resilience and high vulnerability to adversity. The two dimensions that characterize the organism are independent although severe impairment in a behavioral domain will significantly reduce the influence of the vulnerable–invulnerable dimension in that domain.

The environmental dimension ranges from facilitative to non-facilitative of development. The height of the surface represents the adequacy of developmental status ranging from minimal to optimal, whereas the surface of the model itself represents developmental status as a function of organismic and environmental variables. Developmental status is "best" or most adequate if it is lodged in the highest, upper far, quadrant of the top surface of the model and poorest or least adequate if it is found in the lowest, near quadrant of the surface. The shaded inset on the top surface is meant to convey the variables of system organization in one or more developmental domains.

The top surface of the model represents developmental status at any point in time. Organismic variables and environmental variables combine in complex ways to determine developmental status. Developmental status is a composite of the Universal I, Universal II type behaviors, and the non-universal behaviors that have been acquired. Universal I behaviors are expressed in the behavioral repertoire. However,

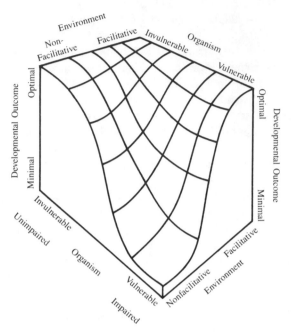

FIG. 5.2. The Structural/Behavioral Model to account for developmental outcome. (Adapted from Gowen, 1952.)

their appearance and maintenance in the repertoire requires only an ambient and supportive normal environment. Variability in environments have little effect on the occurrence and quality of these behaviors. Universal II type behaviors are expressed and developed as a function of more sources of environmental influence. For these behaviors variable environments will affect the timing of their expression, the quality of their expression, and the elaboration of their expression.

Universal II type behaviors will include "behavioral sets" that are triggered by intra-organic factors. These intra-organic factors involve organizational unities and the reorganization of previously existing behaviors into emergent "wholes" which, in their appearance, introduce a new level of organization into the behavioral system. The intra-organic trigger mechanisms may be genetically controlled, biochemically controlled, and/or environmentally stimulated. Nonuniversal behaviors may be mapped onto universal behaviors or may not involve universal behaviors. Non-universal behaviors have a much larger component of environmental input determinants, although variables associated with organismic vulnerability and impairment will interact with the environmental factors to determine not only which behaviors are acquired but the quality and extensivity of the behaviors that become part of the behavioral repertoire. The larger, superordinate factors of the environment represented in the term *culture* may well play a pervasive organizing role in the non-universal behavioral domain.

Some concrete, relatively simple examples may aid the reader in thinking in terms of the model and testing some of the complexities it has been designed to accommodate. In the area of motor development the basic topography is probably significantly laced with Universals I and II type behaviors. Thus, the course of motor development would be highly canalized. We would expect that a normal, species-typical environment is required for the developmental pathway to be expressed. Normal variabilities within the range of normal environments will have little impact upon basic early motor development, except for slight effects on rate as a function of environmental facilitation during the period of infancy and early childhood. The major source of control of individual differences in early motor development will be genetic and perhaps height–weight ratios, although one could argue that nutritional factors affecting height–weight variables are a source of environmental influence. For the motorically impaired infant, however, influence of environmental facilitation will be considerably larger on rate of development and perhaps on whether or not some forms of motor behavior came into the repertoire depending on the degree and nature of motor impairment. For a profoundly motorically impaired child there may be no functionally facilitative environment, given our present state of knowledge. Under these circumstances there is a high probability that the motor development of such a child would end up in the lower near corner of Fig. 5.2. A measure of environmental facilitation would be the degree to which a motorically impaired child who receives special environmental intervention is moved from the lower right near up on the surface of developmental status for motor development. For some impairments normal motoric developmental outcome is currently beyond the technology of environmental facilitation. Alternatively, for some impairments a form of environmental facilitation that operates directly on the neurological or muscular structure of the child is and may become increasingly feasible. Such a model of environmental intervention can be found in prevention of mental retardation due to PKU or the inability of the organism to metabolize phenylalanine. By eliminating or sharply reducing phenylalanine in the diet in the early years of life, the PKU syndrome of severe mental retardation can be significantly ameliorated. This form of environmental facilitation significantly alters the child's intellectual potential. An organism that otherwise would end up profoundly retarded (lower near corner of the model surface) can be expected to reach more nearly normal intellectual status (mid-center area of the model surface).

So far, our analysis is largely pictorially based in the sense that the example is a simple one that is not particularly enhanced by the presence of the model. However, past the period of infancy and early childhood, after the basic motor forms have been expressed and come into the behavioral repertoire of the normal child, the variations in motoric development may come increasingly under control of environmental factors. Opportunities for motor skill training are variable across children and cultures. These opportunities are embedded in a complex fabric of values with respect to what kinds of accomplishments are important in a sub-culture, with respect to individual differences in parental attitudes, likes and dislikes, and ideals for child achievements, and with respect to social structures in schools and communities that do and do not foster motor skill activities in sports and other programs. Individual differences in children feed into this interaction with environmental facilitation. Some children have more natural motoric skill and grace than others and are more easily reinforced for these types of activities. In societies and communities where motor skill and sports are highly valued, programs may be established for early identification and special training (environmental facilitation) leading to an extremely high level of skill development. This often leaves children not selected without similar facilitation and typically they achieve a lower level of skill development even though increased and reinforced opportunities for training might result in considerably higher levels of motor skill development.

The example of motor skill development offers a prototype for a developmental analysis using the model shown in Fig. 5.2. Organismic factors are of two kinds—those heavily influenced by genetic factors and susceptibility to environmental stimulation and those that become characteristic of the organism as a function of a history of environmental experience. Thus, the child chosen for special skill training may well have had a high probability of selection because of early demonstrations of behaviors influenced by genetic factors; e.g., rapid motor development, agility, perhaps an almost intuitive ability that is expressed in the ease with which a child learns from simple observational opportunities. Once selected and given special training, however, the cumulative skill acquisition gives the child a different, more highly practiced behavioral repertoire in the motor area. If, for some reason, the nature of the environment were to change drastically and special opportunities for learning sharply reduced, the strength of the child's level of motor development might propel him or her to still further motoric achievement without further special facilitating opportunities. The child is now placed at the invulnerable or resilient end of the organismic continuum by his or her history. Environmental facilitation thereby becomes significantly less important to subsequent development in this behavioral domain. Alternatively, for some children with strong behavioral dispositions in a certain area, the level of environmental facilitation might be almost minimal, but the child's use of minimal environmental input might be so efficient and facilitating of development as to result in superior development in that area. One can spin out the various combinations and permutations easily using the dimensions of the model with respect to organismic–environmental relationships.

There are a number of relationships, however, that are not so straight-forwardly derived from the model. One has to do with sequence and structure in behavior in relation to environmental input. In some behavioral domains, notably in language and in cognition (as well as in motor development), general sequences are found although not as tightly orga-nized into stages as Piaget and others have thought. Nevertheless, a rough sequence is in evidence. Further, there appear to be points along the developmental path when the behaviors in the repertoire reorganize or get coalesced so that the structural or system organization of the behavioral domain changes. In the area of emotional expression in infants there has been reference to a "bio-behavioral" shift (Emde et al., 1976). Such organizational shifts have been observed in language and in cognitive development. From a developmental point of view, it is possible that two factors are operating. One is the accumulation of a minimal critical mass of behaviors in a "behavioral set" within a particular domain; the other is a neural integration of response organization, perhaps in a Hebbian cell assembly sense, that permanently alters the structure of the behavior. The form of the neural integration/reorganization may be highly canalized for the species, resulting in similar structural emergence across children. Envi-ronmental input is necessary for the behaviors to be acquired, but organismic factors of canalization determine the nature of the structural shift or emergence. However, the environmental input in the form of learning opportunities can serve, as Vygotsky (1978) suggested, to stimulate the mechanisms (genetic "turn-ons" or neural reorganization?) that result in structural shift or organizational emergence. Fischer's (1980) skill theory, applied to cognitive development as well as other domains, is very com-patible with this analysis. He goes further, however, in suggesting some of the transformation rules that may be operating.

There may also be individual organismic factors involved in organizational emergence. These may be reflected in differential sensitivity to environ-mental stimulation that determines the acquisition of the behaviors and defines the minimal critical mass of behaviors in a behavioral set before which the structural reorganization will not occur. For some children, acquisition will be easy under any set of normal environmental input conditions and a few behaviors (exemplars, perhaps) in the behavioral set will be all that is needed for the next emergent structural development to occur. For other children, the specific nature of environmental input in both amount and kind may be more critical to the rate of acquisition. A larger set of behaviors will be necessary for these children before a new structural organization emerges. Alteration of the nature of environmental input for some children may be possible with a resultant effect on the child's acquisition rate and on the nature and degree of the exemplars required for the shift to occur.

In trying to understand the role of environmental facilitation with respect to individual differences a critical issue involves the way in which environmental input is defined and analyzed. Are we talking about gross levels of stimulation, quality of stimulation, variety of stimulation? Yarrow, Rubenstein, and Pedersen (1975) found that variety of stimulation was a factor in infants' performance on the Bayley Scale. Unfortunately, there was no measure of individual differences of infant responsivity to different levels of variety. In a more narrow area of discrimination learning Etzel and her colleagues (Stella & Etzel, 1980, 1986; Stella, Hathaway, Villalba, Navarete, & Etzel, 1981) have found that there are some children, many with learning problems, who are particularly sensitive to failure in the early stages of a learning program. If they make errors on the early trials in a discrimination problem the probability of learning that discrimination declines sharply. On the other hand, if such children can be gotten through the early trials in an errorless fashion their subsequent learning is no different than children for whom early errors are not detrimental. Thus, the nature of environmental input, in this case assuring error-free early trials, is a critical factor in whether the discrimination is learned or not. We have very few demonstrations of this kind of fine-grained attack on the nature of the role of environmental input on learning for different kinds of children, but it is likely that the nature of the organism–environment interaction will be best understood in some domains with such analyses. One of the problems in discussing this kind of issue is that we do not have good guidelines to tell us when we should be working at an analysis of environment that is relatively micro-analytic and when a macro-analytic analysis would serve us just as well or better.

It is also not clear how the nature of organismic variables with respect to relative vulnerability should be categorized and analyzed. The individual difference literature has been much more heavily influenced by the psychometric and correlational traditions than by the kind of functional analysis approach being used here. In two of our studies we found that newborn infants who exhibited variable behavior from one neonatal behavioral assessment to another were more likely to be involved in an interaction with a mother who has been responsive to the infant's behavior than if the infants were highly stable on the two behavioral assessments (Horowitz, Linn, & Buddin, 1984; Linn & Horowitz, 1983). Thus, behavioral variability on the part of the infant in the newborn period appears to be associated with greater maternal responsivity. Behavioral variability within some limits may be an organismic characteristic that enhances facilitative environmental input during the neonatal period. Some more recent evidence from our laboratory strengthens this hypothesis. Newborn infants who had higher scores on the "Range of State" cluster on the Neonatal Behavioral Assessment Scale subsequently showed a greater probability of increasing their visual fixations to new stimuli following habituation of responding to a familiar visual stimulus (Moss, 1985). One question that needs to be asked is the degree to which this kind of individual difference variable is important at different developmental periods and for which kinds of behavioral interactions.

Continuity and Discontinuity

One issue that the model may help clarify relates to the question of *continuity* and *discontinuity.* The terms have been variously defined and used. Claims for continuity in development have usually rested upon correlational evidence of prediction from early to later measures. When such predictions are not found, it is asserted that this is an indication of an essentially discontinuous function in a particular behavioral system. However, as was noted in the first chapter, using the example of normal and abnormal cell development, the presence of normality and then abnormality in a cell is not a question of continuity and discontinuity in cell development, but rather one of a change in processes that control cell functioning. The distinction being made here is not simply semantic. Rather, it is meant to indicate that the continuity–discontinuity discussion has been carried out in the wrong arena because it has given almost sole emphasis to intraindividual consistency across time.

The implications of our model requires a basic reformulation of the continuity–discontinuity discussion. An example in the area of cognitive development serves here. The standard approach to the question of continuity is to use some measure of cognitive development at two different times and to look for significant correlations within a group of children. If relatively high correlations are found, this is usually taken as evidence for continuity in cognitive development. However, this tells us nothing about cognitive development or the factors that produce the consistency in relative ranking within a group. Instead, let us ask a different question. What characteristics of the child in combination with what characteristics of environmental input result in a particular level of cognitive functioning at age 2, 4, 7, and so on? A number of developmental possibilities become obvious. One is that the child's characteristics that are significant in the process remain relatively constant over time, but the nature of environmental input necessary to maintaining, let us say, a high level of cognitive functioning change over time. Under the circumstances where such environmental change occurs and the child's characteristics are stable we would expect to find an intra-individual consistency. But, if the child's characteristics are stable and the environment does not change over time to maintain its facilitative role then we would not expect to find intra-individual consistency. Similarly, some children may show a shift in organismic characteristics over time that requires a different kind of environmental input if consistency in cognitive developmental level is to be maintained. One can easily describe additional combinatorial scenarios that would produce continuity and discontinuity. The recent analysis of the development of depressive behavior by Cicchetti (Cicchetti & Aber, 1986) exemplify exactly this approach.

Vulnerability to continuity and discontinuity may be different in different behavioral domains. For example, where environmental input is a relatively weak part of the developmental outcome equation and individual difference characteristics stronger, variations in environmental input over time that do not approximate the most facilitative level may be less of a factor in whether or not consistent levels of functioning in that behavioral domain are found. The structural model of development that is proposed here does not involve any necessary assumptions about fixed combinatorial functions across behavioral domains or across developmental periods. The question of continuity and discontinuity becomes one of a trajectory of combinatorial functions across time in relation to the functions that are facilitative of different levels of developmental outcome in different behavioral systems.

One would expect a consistently high level of developmental outcome across time and in all behavioral domains for the child who has a strong disposition to a high level of behavioral functioning in all areas and who is either continuously in an environment that is facilitative of optimal behavioral development, changing the nature of its input to maximize facilitation, or who is highly resilient even under conditions where the nature of the environmental input is not facilitative of behavioral development. We would expect a consistently low level of developmental outcome across time for the child whose organismic characteristics have cumulated so as to produce weak behavioral development dispositions and who is continually in environments that do not maximize facilitative input for that child, or where the nature of the child's organismic characteristics are such that there is no functional facilitative environment possible (e.g., for the child with PKU before the metabolic problem was understood and solved). On the other hand, lack of consistency would be found under a variety of circumstances that involve shifts in organismic characteristics over time (perhaps as a function of changes in genetic programs as they switch on and off over the developmental course) and/or shifts or failure to shift levels or kinds of environmental input that maximize facilitation of development given the nature of the child's characteristics. Again, the combinations and permutations are not difficult to imagine.

Using the structural/behavioral model of development suggested here, the question of continuity and discontinuity is framed in a quite different manner than if we were organizing our questions under the traditional theoretical umbrellas. The power of the model and of the kinds of questions it fosters lies in the focus upon process and how processes change across time. This permits stronger developmental questions. The answers to these questions could provide a more truly developmental perspective on behavior.

It is important to comment upon the question of whether or not development and behavior are being used as distinctive or synonymous and to consider how the term *developmental* is being invoked in this discussion. Kessen (1960) defined a characteristic as developmental "if it can be related to age in an orderly or lawful way" (p. 36). This definition tends to give emphasis to a normative, descriptive approach that involves tracking a behavior over time to determine its relationship to age or to sequence over time. Much of the tradition that has informed the research on cognitive development and that previously informed the work on motor development is consistent with this kind of definition. Wohlwill (1973) and McCall (1977), however, in more than a semantic shift of emphasis, have focused their concern for developmental phenomena on change in behavior over time. This gives possibility to the investigation of phenomena not only of the normative and descriptive kind, but also in terms of processes that produce, facilitate, or retard change (i.e., development). It is this broader use of the term *developmental* that the model we are proposing assumes. If the model has any implication for fostering more developmentally oriented research, as McCall has urged, it will be because it establishes a structural basis for looking at processes that produce change in behavior over time.

Behavior and development are thus not synonymous, although obviously behavioral change is a component of development. Developmental change, however, is more over-arching than behavioral change in that it can be based upon intra-organic structural change and by emergent organization that is triggered by genetically guided programming and/or behavioral acquisition. In fact, the "turn on" for some of the intra-organic reorganization may be based upon behavioral acquisition and change, making behavioral change an inherent partner in developmental change. Some developmental change may be more heavily weighted by intra-organic restructuring as the dominant variable; some developmental change may be more defined by behavioral changes. Not all behavioral change is developmental, although developmental as it is used here will always involve behavioral change.

At the present time there is neither a data base nor a set of theoretical guidelines that can help make a firm distinction between behavioral change that is developmental and behavioral change that is not developmental. An initial attempt to do so might involve the following. Behavioral change is developmental when its occurrence signals the onset of potentially different combinatorial relationships between organismic and environmental variables. A behavioral change is not developmental if the potentially functional set of combinatorial relationships is not altered. The word "potentially" is important here for it qualifies the definition by indicating that the combinatorial relationship in effect need not, itself, change but only that the potentiality or set of possibilities from which the combinatorial relationship can be drawn at this point in time has been changed.

An example of this would be as follows. Suppose a child is learning to classify objects in two dimensions and is using a sequential strategy of first one and then the other dimension in a two-step approach to the task. To the extent that the child generalizes this behavior to different objects and even different dimensions there is behavioral change that is not developmental. In this example the generalization of learning involves environmental input of modeling and reinforcement on an intermittent schedule that is quite facilitative in producing the generalization. Then, the child acquires a classification rule that permits the child to do the classification using two dimensions in a one-step approach to the task. Now, generalization to other objects and other dimensions would involve invoking the rule. Environmental input occurs in the form of modeling and reinforcement and there are several equally facilitative schedules for producing generalization. However, for some reason, although the child knows the rule and can use it, the child continues to approach the task as of old and/or the environmental input does not change. In this case a developmental change has occurred, but the combinatorial relationship between the child's characteristics and the environmental input may or may not have changed. What has changed, and what gives the change its developmental character is the different set of combinatorial possibilities that now exist. Further, developmental change is not reversible; the total set of functional combinatorial possibilities from which the operative combination is being drawn cannot revert to the previous combinatorial set.

Another, perhaps more mundane but maybe more intelligible, example is one that contrasts the set of instructional options available to a teacher: When a developmental change has occurred the set of instructional options now contains new members. Another focus on the distinction between behavioral change that does and does not involve developmental change is to indicate that behavioral change without developmental change will be explainable almost entirely in terms of learning; behavioral change with developmental change may be explained by learning and/or intra-organic structural and emergent changes. Behavioral change and developmental change are not equivalents although developmental change will always include capability for behavioral change.

Asking Developmental Questions

Being a Piagetian or being a behaviorist or being interested largely in cognitive development has tended to be linked to particular research strategies. The result, from an eclectic point of view, has been productive. However, selecting individual research strategies and adopting one or the other of the so-called dominant world views have tended to restrict the nature of the developmental questions to a particular domain or model. These practices have not stimulated integrative analyses across behavioral domains. They have not encouraged the asking of strong developmental questions with respect to developmental outcome. This is not to say that the normative data bases that have been amassed and that the knowledge about variables involved in learning is not relevant to a different approach to developmental issues. Any proposal of a model of development must be tested by its ability to accommodate those data bases. But the model should add to the nature of the questions that are formulated if it is to be claimed that the model emboldens or enhances our efforts to enlarge our account of behavioral development. The model proposed here does stimulate questions in addition to those generated by the theoretical umbrellas already available to us. The new questions are focused upon strengthening the depth of an understanding of behavioral development. They involve trying to specify the parameters associated with the main dimensions of a structural model of development. They focus upon identifying the ranges of values those parameters can take and upon specifying sets of combinatorial possibilities for different behavioral domains and for different developmental periods.

It would be an interesting exercise to try to evaluate what is now known in order to determine to what extent we already have answers to some portion of these kinds of questions. This would enable us to determine what portion of the total puzzle we may have already "solved" or approximated in an initial pass at the model with data that were not necessarily generated by the model. In the final chapter of this book there is an attempt to address some of the kinds of research that might most profitably be undertaken using the model as a useful guide but for the moment it is necessary to turn to some of the issues raised in the previous chapters that must be related to the model.

STAGES AND STRUCTURE

As has already been noted, aspects of the sequence of behavioral development are governed by strong genetic factors shaped in the context of the evolutionary history of the species; some sequences may be more the result of canalization acting in concert with environmental input; some sequences may be largely determined by environmental expectations and the arrangement of learning environments, including environments defined by cultural parameters. Behaviors that are of the Universal I type, hard wired and typically with little developmental plasticity potential, are heavily influenced by the human gene structure for their expression, although as has been indicated, a species-typical environment is necessary for their expression and functioning. Behaviors of this type are often expressed soon after birth and do not exhibit an extensive developmental course, although they may underlie Universal II type behaviors and be heavily implicated in the acquisition of learned behaviors. Many of the early perceptual behaviors are of this type, including selective responsivity to certain stimulus features of the environment. Examples are the spatial calculus, the classificatory abilities with respect to visual and auditory stimuli, and the attention to motion and temporal aspects of stimulation. As such, the expression of these behaviors is a function of the nature of the organism; their expression is largely genetically controlled. The genetic influences may be enhanced or compromised by the nature of the prenatal environment via the influence of drug substances, infections, maternal nutrition, or biochemical variables associated with the mother's physiological functioning. As they enter into further developmental combinatorial possibilities these behaviors will be found to weigh into the developmental outcome equation as organismic variables with respect to the model dimensions. Thus, to the extent that stages and sequencing are associated with these behaviors, stages and sequences are organismic variables.

Universal II type behaviors may also be heavily determined by the evolutionary history of the species as it is provided for in the gene structure of the organism. However, they are distinguished from Universal I type behaviors by being less tightly wired, with a more elongated developmental course having some general inherent stage-sequence characteristics. (The distinction between stage and sequence is one of emergent organizational shift. Stages require some emergent organization or reorganization whereas sequences do not.) To the extent that Universal II type behaviors are highly canalized, the normal species-typical environment, with wide variations in its definition, determines the appearance of the behavior in a normal developmental course. Deviations or rate alterations will, in Universal II type behaviors, be temporary because of a high probability of self-righting tendencies, either as a function of system redundancy that insures alternate compensatory routes, or because of the highly assertive nature and subsequently prevailing dominance of the major developmental pathway. For this reason, their expression in sequences or stages, and perhaps more often in stages than sequences, is based on the organismic dimension of the model, but less fully than is true of Universal I type behaviors. This is being claimed for two reasons. One, the role of the environment is more extensive for Universal II type behaviors than simply providing environmental surround at normal, threshold stimulation levels. Environmental variables are more heavily implicated in the rate of the expression and particularly in the quality of the behaviors involved. Two, the role of the environment is more fully implicated in the degree to which Universal II type behaviors are elaborated and involved in the acquisition of non-universal behaviors.

Language acquisition provides a useful example. Learning language may be based upon Universal I type phenomena, Universal II type phenomena and non-universal phenomena. The Universal I elements would be represented in the categorical perception of speech stimuli that appears to be among the capabilities of all normal infants. The Universal II elements would be represented in the developmental sequencing of attention to different cues and parameters of language and communicative interchanges that appear to prevail during the early years of life. Their expression is dependent on the presence of the cues and parameters in the child's environment. In the species-typical normal environment these cues and parameters will be found to exist in sufficient depth as to constitute the threshold conditions for the basic forms of language to be acquired. Nevertheless, there will be considerable variability in the degree to which the elements occur above threshold. This is where the "quality" and "extensivity" of the language acquisition begin to be influenced. Further, above threshold there will be a number of dimensions of the environment that determine the content of what is learned and the organization of that content according to system aspects of the environment that we might summarize as involving cultural variables. Language acquisition is thus multiply determined in the sense that genetic, universal and non-universal elements are all involved. Further, language may be multiply determined in another sense. Any given component of the acquisition process may be backed up by redundant alternatives. There may be alternative sequences of attention to cues that may affect rate of acquisition, but each leads to the same end point. There may be stage-like organization represented in points at which neural integrations occur and emergent structural characteristics develop, but there may be more than one sequence possible, and/or several alternative emergent structural arrangements all of which result in a similar end point. There is probably depth in the possible replicability of systematic organization of language input, because we know that children raised bilingually eventually come to master the components and store the necessary information discretely enough to speak two languages.

Stages and structures, to the extent that they are universals, involve some genetic elements, but how much environmental input is necessary to "kick off" the system, to maintain, facilitate, and induce the behavioral acquisition will vary with whether the universal is of type I or II as described here. In this scheme it is possible to have a behavioral system organized in terms of stage-structural components, which will be found to exist as universal characteristics of a behavioral domain, without there being a universal stage or structure sequence. Further, in most behavioral domains for which a stage-structure arrangement is or will be found, the elaboration of the behavior in the domain beyond its basic topography will be found not to be universal in nature and highly dependent on the characteristics of environmental input. The more specially human the behavior the more likely it is that, in terms of the notion of greater developmental plasticity and elaborated expression, opportunities for learning and cultural patterning parameters will dominate the final level of developmental outcome for each individual. In this sense, developmental outcome will be heavily determined by the nature and range of the organismic–environmental combinations and permutations possible.

Systems

Systems are variously defined depending on the level of analysis under consideration. At one level there are behavioral systems that involve highly associated behaviors that are governed by rules, are made up of response classes, and appear to be affected in similar ways by a given set of variables. This is designated as System Level 1. A System Level 2 is one in which there is a system organization within an organism involving a unit of function that is defined in terms of the whole. Its elements do not define its nature, but the whole can be described in terms of some principles of functioning. The concept of stage in development is similar to System Level 2 but not entirely analogous to Piaget's concept of stages. At System Level 2 system changes are unit changes. There is also a System Level 3. This is the use of system that involves transactional relationships whereby the behavior of one component of the system alters other components of the system and vice versa. Sometimes the cumulative or individual effects of these transactions are to redefine the unit of the whole. Finally, System Level 4 encompasses the cultural dimension of rules, values, and saliencies that organize, constrain, and amplify the functional role of behaviors in a society.

These various definitions of the term *system* can be thought of as representing levels of system organization that affect behavior and development in different ways and to differing degrees. The features that von

Bertalanffy (1968) identified as characteristics of closed systems apply to level 1. System levels 2, 3, and 4 would have the features von Bertalanffy attributed to open systems. Their developmental course qua system would be toward increasing hierarchic differentiation with the development of sub-units that operate as closed systems (System Level 1). They contain "leading parts" defined as *elements* with the power to affect the functioning of the system disproportionately. They are characterized by equifinality in the sense that the same end points in the system can be achieved through different paths from different initial starting conditions. The system levels can also be thought of as being differentially bounded with respect to relative stability/lability in a manner somewhat analogous to Piaget's notion of relative equilibrium of structures. This concept, not as clearly involved in von Bertalanffy's discussion of open systems, is useful for some of our concerns.

It is not possible to portray all four levels of systems and their relationship to development and developmental processes in the pictorial representation of our model. However, Fig. 5.3 can be used to discuss the system relationships of System Level 2 that can be mapped onto the surface of developmental outcome. In Fig. 5.3, four arrangements are depicted for a System Level 2 discussion.

To give content to this discussion we use the behavioral domain of language. The language functioning of four different children of the same age is shown in Fig. 5.3. Child A's language is well developed for that age, the environmental facilitating conditions are either very good or, because the child is relatively invulnerable, the highly facilitative nature of the environment is not critical for this child (although it will be helpful). The developmental level of child A's language is optimal in all its aspects (i.e., the range competence in the language system is small and the level is high). Thus, the system inset on the surface of the model is over a relatively small area of developmental outcome—all at a highly competent level. Child D also has a relatively high level of outcome but this is a child who is much more dependent on environmental facilitation for language development. The range of the child's language competence is somewhat broader than for child A, stronger in some aspects than in others. Children B and C are intermediate in their levels. Different combinations of child–environment variables produce these outcomes. The arrows on the surface represent possibilities of changes in developmental status at the next period of development (stage?). Child A's environment may now become relatively non-facilitative, but child A's organismic characteristics are such as to result in good language development even under conditions considered quite minimal for good language development to occur. In that instance the level of developmental outcome might move in the direction of the arrow with one asterisk—development will stay at a high level. The width of the

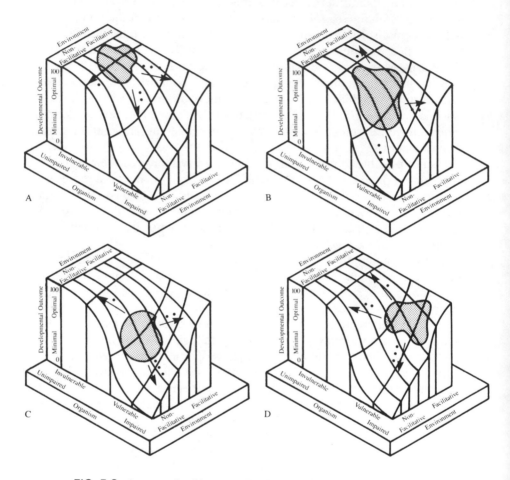

FIG. 5.3. An example of language developmental status or outcome for four children described at System Level 2.

developmental outcome range as represented by the size of the system diversity may change or stay the same. However, suppose child A were to become more dependent on environmental input conditions in this next period and those conditions were facilitative. The direction of the developmental outcome for this developmental period would then be that which is represented by the arrow with three asterisks—development will be relatively optimal. If the environment is not facilitative then the direction of developmental outcome is represented by the arrow with two asterisks.

The schematics shown in Fig. 5.3 represent the idea that the quality and extensivity of language development and some of the content that fills out the forms of language behavior are determined at any given period of development by the interaction of organismic and environmental variables. The value and nature of these variables may change from period to period in development. Some of the changes in the value and nature of the variables associated with the child may be constitutionally determined; some may be the result of a behavioral history. Changes in the environmental dimension may have their source in the nature of the variables that are significant at different periods of development for a particular domain as well as in the values that significant variables take which carry over from period to period. Behavioral change at a particular system level can occur minimally or extensively. Behavioral change in any given domain over proximate points in time is made up of the same combination of organism–environment relationships. However, behavioral development, as compared to behavioral change, involves movement such that the variables and/or values that can be functionally significant have changed from one point in time to the next. This movement can be triggered either by intra-organic factors of genetic programming, or by quantum changes in neurological functioning. It can be made to occur as a result of the cumulative effect of external factors in building up a response system that then undergoes some change. This change now makes it subject to a potentially different set of combinatorial relationships.

System Levels 3 and 4 are not easily schematized in relation to the model in part because they are not so directly mapped on the developmental outcome surface of the model. System Level 3 is characterized by what Sameroff (1983) called "transactional" relationships. Different levels of transactional opportunities can be described by Bronfenbrenner's (1979) description of levels of environments from microsystems to exosystems, from simple dyadic relationships to more complex relationship sets. The environmental components of System Level 3 may very well help define the functional values of the environmental dimension of System Level 2. It is not clear at the present time how directly System Level 3, the transactional system, can affect the developmental progress of different behavioral domains. The transactional effect may be relatively indirect. The system aspect of

Level 3 may be largely internal to the system and not always directly developmentally significant to the system and not always directly developmentally significant for the individual. The direct developmental effect may be found in "leading-part" changes in System Level 3 such that the variables and/or values at System Level 2 are altered.

System Level 4, the cultural system, is not primarily described by transactional characteristics except over a relatively long period of time as a function of transacting forces that produce cultural evolution. Stable cultures would show slow changes over time. These changes alter some of the system rules that constrain, amplify, or moderate System Level 2 and 3 functioning. Some of the source of change in System Level 4, as in other systems, comes from change in leading parts. Different cultural systems will have different elements functioning as leading parts. Leading parts may be individuals, natural events, institutions, or symbolic components.

Leading parts in each of the system levels represent very important sources of system change. At System Level 2 changes in the intra-organic leading parts of different behavioral systems may be the amplification trigger for emergent structural change or structural reorganization. These may be lodged in neurological elements that trigger structural changes in information processing functions and organizations. They may be lodged in biochemical messenger systems that determine onset and offset of genetically programmed events. At System Level 3 the leading parts may actually be aspects of System Level 2, functioning within System Level 3; or they may occur in the context of an element in System Level 3. Different cultural systems (i.e., Level 4 systems), will have different elements functioning as leading parts. To the extent that cognitive and language and socioemotional systems are shaped by and reflect the cultural system the elements that play leading parts in different cultures may be partially culturally determined and/or partially determined by inherent characteristics of the behavioral system being affected. Thus, maternal language input may be a leading part in the language/communication behavioral system in a culture characterized by nuclear families, but the language input may be quite diversified in an extended family culture and thus less subject to a leading-part effect.

Cultures will also differ with respect to the functional valence of critical variables. A developmental change in the cognitive domain for a child might be easily achieved with minimal facilitative input in one cultural system; it may be more difficult to achieve in another cultural system, depending on the importance of the particular cognitive change within each culture. For example, take the emergence of different aspects of formal operations. In a cultural system where all aspects of formal operational thought are highly valued and salient in the adult population a child who needs minimal facilitative environmental input will show strong acquisition of all varieties of formal operational thought. In a cultural system where only some aspects are valued and salient this same or a similar child would acquire easily those that are valued but might require stronger environmental input to acquire the less valued or salient aspects.

Systems may contribute motivational and emotional components as defined by the system organizations. Not all emotional and motivational elements are system dependent. Intra-organic variables associated with emotionality, motivational lability/stability perhaps in part hormonally modulated cannot be discounted. On the other hand, system characteristics may well condition the intra-organic elements to a certain extent.

The system dimensions that affect development cannot be fully represented in a schematic manner in relation to the model. For this, one would need a multidimensional structure. When the knowledge is advanced considerably beyond where it is now, when there is an understanding of the combinatorial possibilities and the system parameters that modify those possibilities, then it will be possible to begin to approach a more nearly complete account of behavioral development. Although such an account may never be fully attainable, in its ideal state it would be analogous to having a set of structural equations. These would specify the nature of the combinatorial interactions. They would also identify the topographical features, and the modifying values of the parameters that define systems that serve to organize the context of development and determine some aspects of the course of development.

System Levels contribute significantly to the content and organization of the non-universal behaviors. These behaviors ultimately constitute large portions of the behavioral repertoire. If there are stage-structure characteristics in some non-universal behaviors these may be a function of the universal behavioral base that underlies some of the non-universal behaviors. Alternatively, or in addition, there may be stage-structure characteristics in the non-universal behaviors. These may be based upon norms and expectations from System Levels 3 and 4. They may be increasingly dominant aspects of development in the later years of the life span. Erikson (1980) described developmental stages that he considered descriptive of the middle and later years of adulthood. The psychosocial crises they cover are "generativity versus self-absorption" and "integrity versus despair." Although Erikson considered these to be of a universal nature, they may well be highly culturally dependent. The universality may lie in the emergence of stages or structures but the specific content, focus and organization may be determined by the cultural system of which the individual is a part. Further, the more embedded an individual is in a given cultural system, the more likely it is that the individual will progress through the stage organizations as defined by the culture or System Level 4. Individuals whose cultural connections are weak or severed may, in fact, not experience the same stage-structure process as those who are culturally well connected.

At System Level 2, some aspects of stage and structure are organismic, some not; some stage-structure components represent human universals, others not. At System Levels 3 and 4 the stage-structure components are more likely to involve non-universals. Changes in System Level 4 would normally be expected to occur gradually. However, the advent of electronic media, the spread of formal schooling, and other aspects of a world pervaded by the forces of modernity are all affecting the rates of change in cultural systems. Undoubtedly there are effects on developmental change, but we do not have a clear enough view of them to propose what the set of transition rules might be. Normative evidence and cross-cultural investigations will aid us in understanding how to parcel the phenomena into categories. To fully understand how they operate in a developmental framework, it will be necessary to see them in relation to the processes and mechanisms that influence behavioral change and development. It is not necessarily the case that a System Level analysis will be applicable to all behaviors or to all aspects of behavioral development. What has been proposed here is an exemplar of how a system analysis might be utilized. It will remain for empirical verification to determine the validity of these ideas.

Many of the ideas discussed here are not novel. They exist in one form or another in the context of Piaget's theory, in the context of developmental biology, and in relation to general system theory. Developmental biologists have found that stage-structure-system relationships describe some phenomena at some levels of organization, but not others. There is reason to believe that there will be a neat nesting of systems within systems in behavioral development. Given the complexity of human behavior, a multiplicity of arrangements is more than likely. Closed systems are probably the most frequent and reliable of the system organizations in the behavioral realm, accounting for behavioral functioning increasingly as development proceeds. To what extent closed systems are implicated and/or characterize behavioral development remains to be seen.

PROCESSES AND MECHANISMS

There is no question that there are intra-organic processes that influence the course of development and the acquisition of behavior. They include gene action systems and biochemical systems, especially as they function with respect to the neural systems in information processing and modification of neural organizational structures. General ambient environmental stimulation and sleep–wake cycles play an important part in modulating these mechanisms. A full account of behavioral development will have to be compatible with the data base of these intra-organic processes. Behavioral acquisition itself is probably an element in the operation of these processes and mechanisms.

The demonstrations involving biofeedback phenomena provide ample evidence for the interplay of behavioral and intra-organic processes. Some aspects of biofeedback are undoubtedly implicated in behavioral development as behavioral dimensions stimulate and shape some of the biochemical, neural, and physiological functioning of the individual. The evidential base for these assertions is sparse. It rests largely on speculation, especially in terms of the relevance to behavioral development. However, with respect to processes and mechanisms involved in learning, the evidential base is of considerable magnitude. As has already been indicated, a great deal is known about many of the variables and parameters that affect the acquisition of responses from laboratory studies of children's learning. There is evidence that the use of these principles in natural and semi-natural environments produces similar outcomes, albeit affecting particular behaviors rather than behavioral systems. With respect to the structural/behavioral model proposed here, significant portions of the parameters involved in mechanisms of learning (such as reinforcement and punishment) are to be found on the environmental input dimension. Their effects, however, are constrained or amplified by species and individual organismic characteristics. The theoretical guidelines for parsing the environment or for identifying at what level of environmental analysis the processes are best described are extremely weak. The model proposed here does not really speak to this problem. The productive investigation of this issue needs to be carried out in empirical contexts until there are sufficient data on which to base the formulation of theoretical guidelines.

As noted, it is not clear at the present time how micro-analytical versus how macro-analytical one should be in postulating the significant components of environmental input. There are relatively high correlations between variables such as maternal education or parental socioeconomic status and developmental outcome. These variables are amplified in importance for children considered at risk for developmental outcome. How these variables operate in a process manner in the combinatorial relationships with organismic variables is unclear. There is some discordance between the level of knowledge concerning environmental contributions to behavioral acquisition and the complexity of the behavioral systems to which that knowledge might be applied. The strongest evidence with respect to learning comes from the behavioristic tradition. The extensive investigation of operant learning has provided a great deal of information about the effect that different schedules of reinforcement have on response acquisition, about the influence of certain stimulus and response parameters, about the formation of response classes and generalization, about classes of reinforcers. This information has not yet been put in a developmental context. Until recently, little of this information has been related to knowledge about specific behavioral domains, such as cognition and language. There are important exceptions. Some integration has occurred in the context of developmentally oriented research on information processing strategies and learning strategies used by children (e.g., Bransford, 1979; Brown, 1982; Brown, Bransford, Ferrara, & Campione, 1983; Gholson & Beilin, 1979; Kendler, 1979). The work of the Papoušeks' is another important exception (Papoušek & Papoušek, 1983, 1984, 1985). They have applied an analysis of learning to mother–infant interaction in the natural environment that is quite forceful.

One of the complicating aspects of looking at learning from the point of view of the structural/behavioral model is that learning is initially on the environmental dimension. Once learning has occurred it becomes a characteristic of the organism. For example, in the learning of a particular behavior the environmental dimension involves the arrangement of stimuli, the occurrence and schedule of reinforcement, and perhaps the opportunity for observational learning. Following Bandura (1977) and others, however, the process of learning also involves cognitive factors that are organismic characteristics. Once a behavior has been learned it joins with the existing behavioral repertoire as the organismic variable of learning history. The next episode involving learning now contains a combinatorial arrangement of a changed organism. That change may or may not have moved the individual along the organismic continuum depending on the significance of the behavior that was acquired. In this sense, behavior itself can serve as a leading part in the organization of the behavioral system with changes in some behaviors having much more of an effect than changes in other behaviors.

The idea of a leading part may be analogous to cognitive structural changes and/or to significant changes in information processing strategies. In fact, information-processing strategies may be a better representation of cognitive structure than the standard Piagetian formulations. They probably are more easily utilized in the model than cognitive structures. Whether one refers to cognitive processes or information-processing strategies they are probably processes that act as system organizers at various of the system levels in the sense that they help to define stimulus saliency, reinforcer effectiveness, and probabilities of generalization and discrimination. In turn, learning stimulates reorganization of information-processing strategies and/or cognitive structures so the interplay between the environmental input dimension and the organismic dimension produces a kind of dynamic, rolling progression. Such a progression is punctuated by developmentally organizing epochs at System Level 2. These may be determined by genetic programs and/or environmentally defined stage/structures inherent in the definition of behavioral accomplishments according to the context in which the learning occurs. One of the challenges from a developmental point of view is to try to specify the developmentally organizing epochs and to identify the processes that result in their occurrence, how they relate to stage-structure organization and to what extent they are constrained or amplified by system considerations. The structural/behavioral model enables the generation of these kinds of questions, although it would be less than candid not to note that specifying the programmatic effort to be designed to address these problems is not easy. Nevertheless, an attempt to organize the available data base from such a perspective might be informative. There may be commonalities across different data bases that were not heretofore appreciated. Such an attempt is beyond the scope of this book but hopefully this discussion stimulates efforts in that direction.

There has been frequent reference to the juxtaposition of open and closed systems, or organic and mechanistic traditions throughout. The presence of open and closed systems is a fundamental tenet of system theory. Nevertheless, as has been observed, developmental theorists appear to emphasize one over the other (open is currently in more vogue). There is no doubt that the open system, organic point of view introduces perspectives and dimensions that were not considered in the so-called mechanistic tradition of behaviorism. The structural/behavioral model, however, rests on the assumption that human behavioral functioning is based upon both open and closed systems and that both the organismic and the mechanistic points of view are valid—although they may be valid for different points in behavioral development and for different domains at different times. The mechanistic analysis involves finite possibilities, feedback loops, and highly routinized organization. Much of human behavior is of this kind and von Bertalanffy (1968), himself, claimed that the more highly differentiated and developed a system the more it would be characterized by closed sub-systems.

If one were to inventory the behavioral repertoire of a normal child or adult on a daily basis, one would probably find that major portions of the behavioral day of the organism could be described in terms of closed sub-systems. From a developmental point of view, however, the developmental principles that may be in control of behavioral acquisition are not fully described by a closed system, even though some portion of the processes are probably well described by closed system principles. Certainly one of the major characteristics of open systems, the increased differentiation within a hierarchic organization, is amenable to a closed system analysis. The elements of the open system model that provide us with important developmental functions include the operation of leading parts, features of emergent organization, and the principle of equifinality. The principle of equifinality, wherein similar outcomes are achieved via different paths, is probably at the basis of some of the major inconsistencies in the developmental outcome literature. Failure to recognize equifinality as an important characteristic of human behavioral development results in feelings of frustration over results that do not appear to permit us to make differential predictions of outcome.

There are many elaborations and examples that can be developed using the structural/behavioral model described here. It is not important at the present time that this model be "right," only that it help formulate questions that might not otherwise be formulated in a systematic manner. The reader will recognize that the model does not contain anything completely novel and that many of the ideas generated by the model are to be found in existing theories and discussions of development. This is particularly true with respect to the structural/behavioral model and transactional approaches to development. However, discussions of transactional models have tended to ally with open systems as "opposed" to closed systems and to leave unspecified the issues of processes and mechanisms in the manner dealt with in this volume.

Some of our attempt to spin out the model to encompass the complexity of Systems Levels may have stretched the model beyond its limits given what is known and what insights can be mustered in the attempt to understand behavioral development. These over-extensions of the model will find a natural corrective in the generation of data and in the formulation of new models based upon those data. The goal here has been to propose a model that would permit the asking of integrative and developmental questions of a stronger nature than currently characterizes much of the research on behavioral development. The structural/behavioral model is proposed as a heuristic that will serve to generate a research agenda that stimulates strong developmental questions. In the hands of imaginative investigators it could be used to spin out hypotheses and more formal theoretical statements that could be subjected to confirmation or disconfirmation.

RECAPITULATION

The structural/behavioral model described in this chapter derives from a set of properties proposed to account for the phenomena involved in the behavioral development of the human organism. These properties include the genetic material united at the moment of conception and the prenatal environment that provides the interactant elements that shape the physiological and behavioral characteristics of the developing human fetus. Once birth has occurred a functional environmental surround provides the supportive elements that foster the development of universal and non-universal behaviors. Two types of universal behavioral repertoires are posited: Universal I type behaviors involving highly probable, almost inevitable behaviors in the normal human organism in a normal environmental surround; Universal II type behaviors that are also highly probable, have longer developmental courses, are variable in rate of development as a function of environmental experience and are subject to the possibility of broader or more limited elaboration under different environmental circumstances. Universal II type behaviors are highly canalized in that they are developmentally guided, especially the broad outlines of their topographical characteristics, by the inherent genetic and biological features of the human organism.

In addition to the Universal behavioral repertoires, it has been proposed that large portions of the human behavioral repertoire can be represented as non-universal behavior shaped by specific learning opportunities and the larger environmental organization of experience represented by culture. Non-universal behaviors, as well as the Universal II type behaviors, are influenced developmentally by periodic reorganization of behavioral and structural systems characteristic of the human organism.

The structural/behavior model, derived from these properties, accounts for developmental outcome at any point in time as the result of an interaction between the organism and the environment. The organism can be described as ranging along two continua: invulnerability (or resilience) to vulnerability (or lack of resilience) and unimpaired to impaired. The environment is described as ranging along a continuum from facilitative of development to non-facilitative of development. The interacting factors form an equation for particular behavioral domains; this equation and the weighting of the variables within a domain may change for different periods or stages of development. It is possible that such change junctures may, in fact, provide a quantitative strategy for defining stages in development within given domains. The structural/behavioral model offers strategies for research that takes into account the role of individual differences. It also involves the notion that the phenomena of development are unlikely to yield any neat picture of continuity or discontinuity. Rather, the structural/behavioral model frames the questions of continuity and discontinuity as one related to processes over time and with respect to different behavioral domains rather than as one involving particular behaviors or developmental phenomena.

Finally, an elaboration of the structural/behavioral model was described to demonstrate how it incorporates ideas related to stages, structures and systems; how it focuses on processes and mechanisms and how it permits investigators to propose stronger developmental questions than the standard developmental theories.

REFERENCES

Bandura, A. (1977). *Social learning theory.* Englewood Cliffs, NJ: Prentice-Hall.

Bransford, J. D. (1979). *Human cognition: Learning, understanding and remembering.* Belmont, CA: Wadsworth.

Bronfenbrenner, U. (1979). *The ecology of human development: Experiments by nature and design.* Cambridge, MA: Harvard University Press.

Brown, A. L. (1982). Learning and development: The problems of compatibility, access and induction. *Human Development, 25,* 89–115.

Brown, A. L., Bransford, J. D., Ferrara, R. A., & Campione, J. C. (1983). Learning, remembering and understanding. In P. H. Mussen (Ed.), *Handbook of child psychology* (Vol. III, pp. 77–166). J. H. Flavell & E. M. Markman (Eds.), *Cognitive development.* New York: Wiley.

Cairns, R. B. (1983). The emergence of developmental psychology. In P.H. Mussen (Ed.), *Handbook of child psychology* (4th Ed., Vol. I, pp. 41–102). W. Kessen (Ed.), *History, theory, and methods.* New York: Wiley.

Cicchetti, D., & Aber, J. L. (1986). Early precursors of later depression: An organizational perspective. In L. P. Lipsitt & C. Rovee-Collier (Eds.), *Advances in infancy research* (Vol. 4, pp. 87–137). Norwood, NJ: Ablex.

Emde, R. N., Gaensbauer, T. J., & Harmon, R. J. (1976). Emotional expression in infancy. A biobehavioral study. *Psychological Issues, A Monograph Series* (Vol. 10). New York: International Universities Press.

Emde, R. N., Kligman, D., Reich, J., & Wade, T. (1978). Emotional expression in infancy: I. Initial studies of social signaling and an emergent model. In M. Lewis & L. Rosenblum (Eds.), *The developmental of affect* (pp. 125–148). New York: Plenum.

Erikson, E. H. (1980). *Identity and the life cycle.* New York: Norton.

Fischer, K. W. (1980). A theory of cognitive development: The control and construction of hierarchies of skills. *Psychological Review, 87,* 477–531.

Fodor, J. A. (1983). *The modularity of mind.* Cambridge, MA: MIT Press.

Freud, S. (1953). Three essays on the theory of sexuality. (1905.) In J. Strachey (Ed.), *The standard edition of the complete psychological works,* Vol. XVII. London: Hogarth Press.

Gholson, B., & Beilin, H. (1979). A developmental model of human learning. In H. W. Reese & L. P. Lipsitt (Ed.), *Advances in child development and behavior* (Vol. 13, pp. 47–81). New York: Academic Press.

Gowen, J. W. (1952). Humoral and cellular elements in natural and acquired resistance to typhoid. *American Journal of Human Genetics, 4,* 285–302.

Hebb, D. O. (1980). *Essay on mind.* Hillsdale, NJ: Lawrence Erlbaum Associates.

Horowitz, F. D. (1978). *Toward a functional analysis of individual differences.* Presidential address to the Division of Developmental Psychology, meeting of the American Psychological Association, Toronto, Canada.

Horowitz, F. D., Linn, P. L., & Buddin, B. J. (1984). Neonatal assessment: evaluating the potential for plasticity. In T. B. Brazelton & B. Lester (Eds.), *New approaches to developmental screening of infants* (pp. 27–50). New York: Elsevier.

Hull, C. L. (1943). *Principles of behavior.* New York: Appleton-Century-Crofts.

Hull, C. L. (1951). *Essentials of behavior.* New Haven: Yale University Press.

Kendler, T. S. (1979). The development of discrimination learning: A level of functioning explanation. In H. W. Reese & L. P. Lipsitt (Eds.), *Advances in child development and behavior* (Vol. 13, pp. 83–117). New York: Academic Press.

Kessen, W. (1960). Research design in the study of developmental problems. In P. H. Mussen (Ed.), *Handbook of research methods in child development* (pp. 36–70). New York: Wiley.

Kuhn, T. (1970). *The structure of scientific revolutions.* Chicago: University of Chicago Press.

Kuo, Z–Y. (1967). *The dynamics of behavior development.* New York: Random House.

Lewin, K. (1954). Behavior and development as a function of the total situation. In L. Carmichael (Ed.), *Manual of child psychology* (2nd Ed., pp. 918–983) New York: Wiley.

Linn, P. L., & Horowitz, F. D. (1983). The relationship between infant individual differences and mother-infant interaction during the neonatal period. *Infant Behavior and Development, 6,* 415–427.

Marx, M. H. (1976). Formal theory. In M. H. Marx & F. E. Goodson (Eds.), *Theories in contemporary psychology* (2nd Ed.). New York: MacMillan.

McCall, R. B. (1977). Challenges to a science of developmental psychology. *Child Development, 48,* 333–334.

Moss, M. (1985). *The relation of neonatal behavior to later cognitive behavior.* Master's Thesis, The University of Kansas.

Oyama, S. (1985). *The ontogeny of information.* Cambridge, MA: Cambridge University Press.

Papoušek, H., & Papoušek, M. (1983). *The evolution of parent–infant attachment: New psychobiological perspectives.* Unpublished paper presented at Second World Congress on Infant Psychiatry, Cannes, France.

Papoušek, H., & Papoušek, M. (1984). Learning and cognition in the everyday life of human infants. In J. S. Rosenblatt, C. Beer, M.-C. Busnel & P. J. B. Slater (Eds.), *Advances in the Study of Behavior* (Vol. 14, pp. 127–163). New York: Academic Press.

Papoušek, H., & Papoušek, M. (1985). *Precursors of control beliefs, their determinants and significance during human infancy.* Unpublished paper presented at meetings of Society for Research in Child Development, Toronto, Canada.

Reese, H. W., & Overton, W. F. (1970). Models of development and theories of development. In L. R. Goulet & P. B. Baltes (Eds.), *Life-span developmental psychology* (pp. 115–145). New York: Academic Press.

Rozin, P. (1976). The evolution of intelligence and access to the cognitive unconscious. In J. M. Sprague & A. N. Epstein (Eds.), *Progress in psychobiology and physiological psychology* (pp. 245–279). New York: Academic Press.

Sameroff, A. J. (1983). Developmental systems: Contexts and evolution. In P. H. Mussen (Ed.), *Handbook of child psychology* (4th Ed., Vol. I, pp. 237–294). W. Kessen (Ed.) *History, theory and methods.* New York: Wiley.

Sameroff, A. J., & Chandler, M. J. (1975) Reproductive risk and the continuum of care-taking casualty. In F. D. Horowitz (Ed.), *Review of child development research* (Vol. 4, pp. 187–244). Chicago: University of Chicago Press.

Scarr, S., & McCartney, K. (1983). How people make their own environments: A theory of genotype-environment effects. *Child Development, 54,* 424–435.

Stella, M. E., & Etzel, B. C. (1980, September). *Visual attention patterns during errorless and trial-and-error learning of normal and atypical children.* Paper presented at the annual meeting of The American Psychological Association, Montreal, Canada.

Stella, M. E., & Etzel, B. C. (1986). Stimulus control of eye orientations: Shaping S+ only versus shaping S− only. *Analysis and Intervention in Developmental Disabilities, 6,* 137–153.

Stella, M. E., Hathaway, V., Villalba, D., Navarete, T., & Etzel, B. C. (1981, April) *Visual attention patterns of normal and atypical children under two training conditions: Trial-*

and-error compared to criterion-realted cue instructions. Paper presented at the meeting of The Society for Research in Child Development, Boston.

von Bertalanffy, L. (1968). *General system theory.* New York: Braziller. (Rev. Ed.).

Vygotsky, L. S. (1978). *Mind in society.* Cambridge, MA: Harvard University Press.

Waddington, C. (1966). *Principles of development and differentiation.* New York: MacMillan.

Wohlwill, J. F. (1973). *The study of behavioral development.* New York: Academic Press.

Yarrow, L. R., Rubenstein, J. L., & Pedersen, F. A. (1975). *Infant and environment.* New York: Wiley.

Zigler, E. F. (1961). Social deprivation and rigidity in the performance of feeble-minded children. *Journal of Abnormal and Social Psychology, 62,* 413–421.

Zigler, E. F. (1963). Rigidity and social reinforcement effects in the performance of institutionalized and non-institutionalized normal and retarded children. *Journal of Personality, 31,* 258–270.

Zigler, E. F., & Williams, J. (1963). Institutionalization and the effectiveness of social reinforcement: A three year follow-up study. *Journal of Abnormal and Social Psychology, 63,* 197–206.

6 Using the Model for Developmental Research

Chapters in developmental psychology or child development textbooks can be organized in terms of "ages and stages" or topically in terms of physical, intellectual, social, and emotional development. Neither strategy is wholly satisfactory to any textbook writer, let alone to the readers. The ages and stages approach is necessarily redundant; the topical organization is necessarily repetitive in tracing topics developmentally. These problems are inevitable in a science where the knowledge base is woefully incomplete and where theories are chaotically supplemented with a variety of mini-theories designed to deal with particular phenomena, behavioral domains, or variables. In some ways the most exciting and productive recent sources of knowledge advancement are to be found in studies of particular variables and phenomena. In this summary chapter a number of the topics, variables, and phenomena of current interest are considered and related to the structural/behavioral model of development described in the previous chapter. They are socioeconomic status (SES), early experience, cognition and intelligence, affect and emotion, social and moral development, and life-span perspectives. These have been chosen from many that might be discussed because of their relatively high profile in the current literature and because they are the kinds of phenomena that must be accounted for in a model of behavioral development that strives to provide a structural/behavioral approach that is relatively encompassing of what will account for developmental outcomes.

SOCIOECONOMIC STATUS

Socioeconomic status is often defined in terms of maternal or parental education, sometimes by father occupation. It is a variable that typically accounts for large portions of the variance in studies of developmental outcome (usually IQ), often the majority of the variance. For this reason, it is typically a subject-selection criterion. Failure to select for or analyze this variable would be considered a major flaw in developmental outcome research as well as in normative and experimental research.

For all the robustness of SES and its frequent use in developmental research, there is little understanding of how it functions to affect behavior and development. There is some indication that maternal behavior varies as a function of SES. Variables such as access to medical care, nutrition, and life stress factors are also linked to SES. But this does not explain how SES variables enter into developmental process. One of the volatile problems generated by the robustness of SES is that it is confounded by race and ethnic variables. A disproportionate number of black and hispanic populations are included in the lower SES groupings in the United States. Poorer developmental functioning associated with SES is also associated with race and ethnicity.

Every trained behavioral scientist knows that correlation does not imply causality. Yet the robustness of the correlational results and failure to make progress in understanding how the variables associated with SES function in developmental process tend to encourage a shading of discussion from correlation to causality. One aspect of SES findings is often ignored. It involves the fact that comparisons of lower and middle SES groups will typically yield not only mean differences, with lower SES subjects functioning at a lower level, but also larger standard deviations for the lower SES subject groups, indicating greater variability within lower SES groups. Rarely is the fact of greater variability a focus of an investigator's attention in the discussion of results. However, it should be a signal to begin to break down the lower SES group into different ranges of scores to try to determine whether there are some important process differences that produce the greater variability. For example, in observations of maternal responsivity, lower SES mothers as a group are often observed to be less responsive to their children. However, within the lower SES groups there will be mothers who are highly responsive to their children. If maternal responsivity is thought to be an important process variable then differential results would be expected if the lower SES group were analyzed in relation to level of maternal responsivity.

How should SES be treated in the structural/behavioral model? One could develop the following hypothesis: maintaining a child on a developmental trajectory that involves good developmental outcome, let us say, in the cognitive domain, generally requires that there be a higher density of direct reinforcement during the preschool years than during the period of infancy. Using the combinatorial approach, however, one would also predict that for some children environmental input will be less critical to maintaining good developmental outcome levels than for others. We also assume a greater probability of independence from environmental input in middle- than in lower-class children. This is based on the notion that poorer prenatal circumstances for lower-class populations reduce some of the incidence of relative invulnerability in these children. Still, some lower-class and a number of middle-class children will show strong resilience even in the face of minimal environmental input. For those children whose level of developmental outcome is dependent on environmental input, maintaining good developmental outcome will require a shift in environmental input from infancy to the preschool years with respect to density of reinforcement (for our example). Wachs' work on environment and development is very compatible with this kind of analysis (Wachs, in press; Wachs & Gruen, 1982). His ideas about environmental specificity, age specificity, and organismic specificity can, in the manner described here, help break apart the summary variable of SES.

SES differentials may be found in the fact that middle-class parents are more likely to shift environmental input conditions to meet the facilitating needs of the child than lower-class parents. Strong developmental outcome will occur for some lower-class children despite the lack of a shift to a facilitative environmental input. Good developmental outcome will be found in lower-class children whose parents did make the shift. SES, in this analysis, is a grouping variable. The model, however, encourages a process as such, it does not explain very much analysis of SES that not only moves one away from gross generalizations about SES but moves toward an understanding of the processes and variables that results in variable outcomes within SES groups. The overall SES differential may still be found but the specification of individual developmental outcome within SES groups will be more qualified. It is obvious that such an understanding would enable a targeting of intervention programs aimed at fostering good developmental outcome more precisely, both in terms of the children who would benefit and by specifying the kinds of environmental manipulations that would be more accurate with respect to the kinds of effects that could be produced.

The ease with which the model is applied to a process analysis that promises to break down the SES variable into its functional components belies the difficulties that will be encountered in carrying out the research that ought to follow. These difficulties are not particular to SES. They are inherent in any strategy that requires tracking individual mother–infant pairs over a period of time. The problems lay in choosing which phenomena and interactive sequences will be observed. Some of the general descriptive characteristics from studies of SES as a grouping variable provide initial guidelines. Overall, lower SES mothers tend to respond less contingently when interacting with their infants. They tend to be less verbal and to use language that is less complex than their middle-class counterparts. These generalizations offer an idea of where to begin with respect to the environmental side of the interaction. There are far fewer clues as to where to begin on the infant individual differences side of the interaction. This is where independent laboratory studies of individual difference phenomena in response to environmental stimulation may be helpful. The literature on this topic is very small, although some of the current work on temperament (to be discussed later) may have relevance here. Programmatic work in this area would be very useful and is essential in order to go beyond SES in accounting for developmental outcome.

EARLY EXPERIENCE

The discussion of SES has some relationship to the issue of early experience and the question of its pre-eminence in affecting developmental outcome. As already noted, experience in the first two to three years of life has been hypothesized as having particular impact upon developmental outcome. Hebb (1949) proposed early perceptual experience in laying a foundation upon which later learning would occur. Hunt (1961) also claimed that early experience was critical for the development of intelligence. All of these stimulated a great deal of research on the effects of early enrichment. They also became the theoretical basis for mounting the major early intervention programs in the United States designed to prevent the developmental differences commonly observed in lower-class children when compared with middle-class children.

Results from the initial intervention efforts were varied (Horowitz & Paden, 1973), and subsequent reviews of the literature have not produced a very different picture. Some children benefit, some programs appear to be effective. The theoretical basis for the intervention programs has not been refuted by the evidence, but neither has it been particularly sustained. The basic tenets have been challenged (Clarke & Clarke, 1976), and there have been some attempts to discount the importance of experience during infancy. Infancy, it is proposed, is an essentially buffered period during which variations in environmental experience will have little or no effect on early development. All normal infants are thought to achieve the major cognitive milestones (Kagan, Kearsley, & Zelazo, 1978; Scarr-Salapatek, 1976). If experience has an impact on developmental outcome or progress, according to this notion, it will only begin to operate after the first two years.

These discussions of the effect of early experience typically employ models of development that are relatively unidimensional (Horowitz, 1980) and involve wrong emphases. One misplaced emphasis focuses upon the topography of behaviors and gross measures of their achievement without looking at the question of the quality of the behaviors that are being acquired. A second relates to the strength of the developmental question that is being framed. For example, Hunt and his colleagues (Hunt, Paraskevopoulos, Schickedanz, & Uzgiris, 1975) have reported differences of almost 2½ years in the accomplishment of some sensorimotor skills for children reared in different environments. It is true that all the children ultimately demonstrated the same cognitive achievements, but one is tempted to ask whether such large differences really have no subsequent importance in the cognitive development of these children?

This is, however, the wrong question. Using the structural/behavioral model a different question is posed. Actually, a set of questions is involved. They focus on trying to determine whether and to what extent the subsequent combinatorial conditions that would produce different developmental outcomes are affected by different timing of earlier achievements. Additionally, one would want to look at the variability within the group showing mean delayed acquisition to identify those children whose achievements may have been relatively more independent of environmental input. Positions taken on the basis of evidence marshalled for and against the claim for the pre-eminent role of early experience on developmental outcome are artifacts of inappropriately formulated questions.

This is not an entirely fair criticism because it is legitimate to raise the issue of the role of cumulative effects on development and whether or not early occurring effects bear a disproportionate weight in the cumulative totals. On the other hand, unless these issues are embedded in a process analysis of the kind generated with the structural/behavioral model they will not tell us very much. A variety of combinatorial relationships can produce similar outcomes. The possibility of so-called "sleeper effects" (Consortium for Longitudinal Studies, 1983; Lazar, Darlington, Murray, Royce, & Snipper, 1982), and the existence of "U-shaped developmental phenomena" (Strauss, 1982) require more complex analyses than are typically attempted. Inconsistencies in the evidence on the effect of early experience on development should discourage the use of simple cumulative models and assertions that some developmental periods are in and some are out as major determinants of developmental outcome.

The structural/behavioral model makes no a priori assumptions about the special role of one period over another. However, it does not rule out the possibility that some of the dimensions of early behavioral development weight combinatorial relationship possibilities differently in the early years than in later years. At the present time there are two different contentions about the effects of early experience. Hebb's notion of early stimulation as setting the base of early learning is one; Kagan's (Kagan, Kearsley, & Zelazo, 1978) and Scarr's (Scarr-Salapatek, 1970) contention (as it was Gesell's, 1954) that infancy is so highly canalized that variations in early experience will have little significant effect on development is the other. These two different positions are not, actually, completely incompatible. They can be reconciled in the following way. Most of the Universal I type behaviors are probably expressed during infancy. These behaviors, it will be recalled, are "hard wired," require little except a species-typical environment for their appearance and maintenance and have a minimal developmental course. It would therefore be expected that the variations in early experience from one infant to another would have little, if any, effect on Universal I type behaviors.

Universal II type behaviors are the ones that are less "hard wired" but highly canalized so that the probability of their acquisition in a normal environment is very high and the probability of variations in environmental experience deflecting them from their normal developmental course very low. Many Piagetian cognitive achievements in infancy are Universal II type behaviors. What is being referred to as "buffered" or highly canalized involves the criterial topography or form of these behaviors, not their quality or elaboration or the degree to which they rest upon an enriched referential base that determines how broadly they are generalized in the child's interaction with the environment.

Universal II type behaviors are thus both canalized and affected by variations in environmental experience. It is the latter aspect that contributes to subsequent developmental competence in Hebbian terms. During infancy there are many behaviors that are acquired that fall into the non-universal category although they may be less obvious or less catalogued than the behaviors that are universal. Variations in early experience will determine which non-universal behaviors will be acquired and their importance for the child.

Early experience is typically thought of as referring to the period of infancy but in some behavioral domains infancy may be too restrictive a definition for early experience. Freud designated the first six years as the critical early experience period. The acquisition of multiple languages without accent is possible in the early period of life but not later. "Early" in this domain for this purpose is defined as before puberty.

The structural/behavioral model of behavioral development is relevant to the issues of how early experience is conceptualized in several ways. First, individual differences on the dimensions of vulnerability and impairment will modulate the effects of experience generally but also differently at different times of development. It has already been suggested that an empirical determination of stage might be derived by identifying the points at which the form of combinatorial relationships changes. Thus, for the acquisition of the topographical aspects of Universal II type behaviors genetically influenced individual differences may prevail and the relative effect of environmental facilitation may be quite small for the first two years of life. For the acquisition of the qualitative aspects of Universal II type behaviors there may be a heavier involvement of the environmental facilitation dimension for the first three years of life. Then, the increasing elaboration of these sensorimotor behaviors in language may be dominated by the combinatorial relationship of the environmental and the organismic dimension. The point at which the combinatorial relationship parameters change could specify the point of stage demarcation. It remains to be empirically demonstrated how early experience should be defined in different domains of development. It is expected that demonstration of early experience for later development or functioning will involve different amounts of time and different numbers of stages for the various domains. Early experience is, thus, not a topic to be investigated generically.

COGNITION AND INTELLIGENCE

The most common measure of developmental status or developmental outcome has been IQ. The debate over this measure, its meaning and its use is extensive. It has been the centerpiece of the nature-nurture controversy. The Piagetian emphasis upon cognitive development has been, in many ways, somewhat orthogonal to the discussions of intelligence although Piaget's genetic-epistemological approach to intelligence through cognition should have entered the discourse long ago. Recent developments in the cognitive sciences, in information processing, in linguistics, in the neurosciences have, in many ways, bypassed Piagetian cognition. This is partly because the cognitive sciences, until recently, have not had a particularly developmental orientation. Siegler's (1983) review of information processing from a developmental point of view highlights the need for a fuller developmental treatment. Gardner's (1983) proposals concerning the existence of multiple intelligences and Sternberg's (1985) triarchic theory of human intelligence both open up interesting developmental issues.

Sternberg's theory is made up of three sub-theories concerning intelligence. The first is that intelligent behavior is defined by the socio-cultural context in which the individual develops and lives. This is very compatible with the structural/behavioral model in which culture is the source of the overriding organization of the environment, determining to some extent the saliency of stimuli and stimulus patterns and the values placed upon different behaviors and different behavioral domains. The culture defines the behaviors that will be considered intelligent and there is a growing consensus on this (Mistry & Rogoff, 1985; Rogoff, 1982).

Sternberg's second sub-theory asserts that a given behavior is not more or less intelligent independent of the context and independent of the point along the continuum of experience with that behavior. A behavior is exhibited at its highest level of intelligence for a particular individual when the individual is required to perform the behavior in a novel situation or is in the process of "automatizing" a performance on a given task. In this latter instance, the manner in which the individual goes about routinizing behavior provides a means for evaluating the level of the individual's intelligence. Thus, performance on a task does not, in and of itself, permit an evaluation of intelligence. One must take into account the novelty of the task for the individual and where on the continuum of experience with the task one finds the individual. If the task is already highly routinized for the individual it will be less revealing of the level of intelligence than if the individual is in the process of routinizing the task. It is not clear where this aspect of Sternberg's theory fits with our model. Perhaps it is on the organismic dimension, made up of the history of experience and the genetic contribution to intelligence.

The third sub-theory is the componential sub-theory that:

> specifies the structures and mechanisms that underlie intelligent behavior. Contextually appropriate behavior emitted at the relevant points in the experimental continuum is intelligent as a function of the extent to which it involves certain kinds of mental processes: Metacomponents control one's information processing and enable one to monitor and later evaluate it; performance components execute the plans constructed by the metacomponents; knowledge acquisition components selectively encode and combine new information and selectively compare new information to old information, so as to allow learning of new information to take place. This subtheory thus specifies the cognitive processes involved in adaptation to, selection of, and shaping of environments. (Sternberg, 1985, p. xii)

Sternberg considers the first sub-theory to be relativistic, or in our terms, non-universal. The behavior defined as intelligent varies as a function of culture and the individual. This is, as we have noted, entirely compatible with our model. The second sub-theory is only partly relativistic in the sense that the point on the continuum of experience at which novelty and automatization occur varies from individual to individual and from culture to culture but is universal in its existence as an aspect of display of intelligent behavior. This sub-theory is more related to task analysis than it is to the individual except that one needs to know the experiential history of the individual in order to determine if the task is revealing of the intelligence to be evaluated. Its relevance to our model is not clear. The third sub-theory is regarded as entirely universal by Sternberg. The set of mental mechanisms that underlies intelligence, the metacomponential processes, the performance component processes and the knowledge acquisition component processes are the same in all individuals and in all cultures. They are the superordinate dimensions of intelligence in the same manner that culture is the superordinate dimension for the ordering of stimulus patterns and behavior.

If the componential aspects of intelligent behavior are universal then there are two developmental questions of interest. The first, and the more traditional one, is the developmental course of the components and the variables that affect their expression. Sternberg (1985) provides a very full review of the normative evidence that bears upon this question. The second involves the processes responsible for the shaping of the componential mechanisms. What accounts for the evolution of the universal template into the behavioral repertoire of the individual? In a manner similar to the analysis of Piagetian cognitive development we can apply the structural/ behavioral model to this issue quite fruitfully, especially as Sternberg clearly recognizes that the expression of the metacomponents will be seen in different contexts and in different behaviors in different cultures. Further, Sternberg believes that the intellectual skills involved in componential aspects of intelligence can be trained. The structural/behavioral model permits an analysis in terms of the "natural" training of these components in the normal environment and, along with Sternberg, becomes a vehicle for systematic intervention whether it be in the form of normal or compensatory educational programs.

For some individuals environmental facilitation of the components of intelligent behavior will be very dependent on facilitative environmental experience; for others environmental facilitation will be less critical. The intellectually gifted individual may reflect different combinatorial arrangements (Horowitz & O'Brien, 1985). In one arrangement the individual is born with high potential for componential development and requires little in the way of particular environmental help. This is the highly invulnerable individual who even in the situation of a relatively non-facilitative environment will display these capabilities. Another intellectually gifted individual will result only when the proper environmentally facilitating conditions obtain. These may involve direct learning opportunities such as observational and reinforced learning. Or environmental facilitation may occur in a more indirect fashion by heightening general motivation to learn and to use the environment for intellectual performance. In both instances, where environmental facilitation is somewhat irrelevant and where it is more critical, the intellectually gifted individual ends up in the far upper quadrant of the developmental status surface of the structural/behavioral model.

Gardner's (1983) proposal for multiple intelligences provides a different cut of intelligence than Sternberg. Gardner has suggested that there are seven kinds of intelligence: linguistic, musical, logical and mathematical, visual and spatial, bodily kinesthetic, interpersonal, and intrapersonal. It will be interesting to determine whether the componential characteristics described by Sternberg apply equally to the seven domains of intelligence that Gardner has proposed. Gardner regards each kind of intelligence as independent of the other with different individuals having differential amounts of each kind in relation to genetic dispositions and experience. Gardner has claimed that each kind of intelligence has its own form of memory, learning, and perception. This would appear to run counter to Sternberg's notion of universal componential aspects of intelligence but it depends on the nature of the forms of memory, learning, and perception that are involved. Gardner's notion of multiple intelligences relates to our model easily. If true it would mean that the combinatorial relationships between organism and environment would need to be independently identified for each kind of intelligence.

Sternberg's (1985) most recent exposition of his theory is entitled *Beyond IQ* and aptly so. The discussion of intelligence and cognition has moved beyond a single measure or a single process analysis. These developments are more compatible with the structural/behavioral model of development than a conceptual approach to intelligence that is bound up entirely in a single measure. The developmental aspects of intelligence proceed on two fronts. The normative descriptive approach does not require the structural/behavioral model; an understanding of individual development of intelligence, however defined, does—unless one believes that the development of intelligence is entirely the result of the play-out of genetically determined abilities constrained by a universal program.

AFFECT AND EMOTION

Freudian theory, both in its developmental aspect and in its nondevelopmental dimension, focused strongly on the distribution of internal emotional energies, on the organizing power of emotion and on the manner in which internal emotional components regulated the development and maintenance of behavior. It is interesting that except for the early attempts of the Hullians to include drive as a variable in their translation of Freud into social learning theory, social learning theory has all but dropped emotional variables per se in its account of behavior. Instead, adopting the stricter criteria of methodological behaviorism and operant behaviorism, emotional variables are discussed in terms of motivation. In operant behaviorism the sources of motivation are to be found in external stimulus conditions based upon the occurrence of positive reinforcement, negative reinforcement, and punishment. Bandura's (1977) social learning theory adds cognitively based motivation that derives from representational mechanisms that can influence behavior in the absence of external stimulus events. The cognitive content involved in the representational mechanisms is, however, based upon the history of experience with punishment and reinforcement.

More recently, however, emotion has re-emerged as a construct of interest in developmental psychology, particularly in the study of infant behavior. Harkening back to Freudian theory but in the context of both system theory and methodological behaviorism there is a growing body of research on such topics as the development of emotion, the perception of emotion, and emotional availability (Campos, Barrett, Lamb, Goldsmith, & Stenberg, 1983; Emde, 1980). The internal organizing power of emotion as a regulator of behavior is intuitively appealing but operationalizing this construct is very difficult. There are several aspects to current efforts in this area. One involves the observation and measurement of behavior classified as emotional. The radical behaviorist generally does not see any scientific gain from organizing observations in terms of a category such as "emotional" until one can demonstrate that the category operates in a different way than other behaviors. For example, is crying any different than any other salient behavior that functions as a stimulus to caregivers? Crying is a response like any other response and its function is to be understood by analyses that would be applied to any other response.

Those interested in emotion and emotional behavior, however, see crying as an emotional expression that has a more motivating effect on the behavior of caregivers than, let us say, reaching. But, the recent champions of the importance of emotion go beyond this kind of assertion in trying to look at emotional behavior in an organizational, system context in which emotion has a superordinate role in organizing the response repertoire that is very close to Freudian theory. However, the research efforts are being undertaken in the framework of methodological behaviorism with concomitant attention to the reliable measurement of variables. For example, Campos and Emde (Klinnert et al., 1983) and their colleagues have devised a social referencing task in which they evaluate the degree to which an infant checks out the expression on the mother's face before responding directly to a stimulus. Emde (1980) has discussed this in terms of "emotional availability" of the mother, giving her emotional expressions more saliency as a behavioral regulator than her other behaviors. Klinnert (1984) has shown that by 12 months of age, some infants reliably use maternal facial expression to regulate their behavior. In the presence of a remotely controlled moving toy, infants moved closer to their mothers if the mother had a fear expression, further away if she posed a joyful expression, and stayed an intermediate distance if she had a neutral expression.

Social referencing behavior is an extremely interesting phenomenon and easily observed anecdotally in the natural environment. It appears to be providing a very valuable methodological tool to investigate the role of maternal facial signals as regulators of infant behavior. Certainly, facial expressions play an important role in regulating important adult social behavior. What is not so clear is whether the phenomenon is different in kind from other learned behaviors. Although emotions, emotional development, and emotional behavior are all phenomena to be investigated as phenomena it remains to be seen whether the laws that govern these phenomena, either in their acquisition or in their function, are generically different from laws that govern other behavioral phenomena.

Emde and his colleagues, however, go beyond the characterization of emotion as a phenomenon in the behavioral realm. They regard emotional phenomena as internal states that play a superordinate organizing role in the behavioral repertoire and as regulatory mechanisms that affect the individual and the environment (Emde, personal communication, May, 1986). Emde has talked about bio-behavioral shifts that occur developmentally which result in different organizations of the behavioral repertoire (Emde, Gaensbauer, & Harmon, 1976). If that is the case then we have a stage-system analysis in which, in terms of the structural/behavioral model, the set of combinatorial arrangements that control behavioral acquisition would change, thus defining the point of shift. If emotion and affect are simply phenomena in the behavioral realm, which are no different than other phenomena in terms of the laws that govern their acquisition, then they are phenomena that do not contribute in special ways to developmental progress except as individual elements in the changing behavioral repertoire. Emde would clearly disagree with this characterization.

However, there is no reason to assign emotion to one or the other role. In some instances it may function as an element in response acquisition. In other instances it may play an organizing role that shifts the conditions that determine acquisition. The phenomena associated with the domain of emotion appear to range widely from facial expressions of both the child and others, to the use of facial expressions as stimuli, to emotional development involving the capacity to express and experience fear, joy, anger, love, and so on. A sub-set of this last group is involved in the concept of "attachment" or social bonding. It is not yet clear how the current work in social referencing and emotional availability is conceptually related to attachment although recent work in this area can be interpreted as suggesting a weak relationship (Dickstein, Thompson, Estes, Malkin & Lamb, 1984). Although attachment as a concept is heavily rooted in Freudian and ethological theory, its empirical use has been methodologically restricted.

The more recent conceptualizations involving emotional availability and social referencing with their greater measurement potential and more sophisticated theoretical developmental context are likely to incorporate and supersede the attachment literature.

How is this all related to the structural/behavioral model of development? First, emotion in terms of emotional signals and their function in learning/ teaching situations contributes to the environmental facilitation dimension. How caregivers use these stimuli, their salience, and so on, become part of the range of learning opportunities that the environment makes available to the infant. In this sense, these stimuli may have species salience for the human organism but they may function in a learning context in the same manner as all other environmental stimuli. Second, one would expect to find individual differences in sensitivity to these stimuli. It remains to be demonstrated whether or not such individual differences are related to emotional stimuli as a class. For example, do some infants respond to lower levels of intensity of emotional expressions than others, making emotional expressions function as a class of stimuli? Is the perception of facial expression as a stimulus class learned or innate or a highly predisposed learned behavior? The individual differences dimension of this would place the infant at different points along the continuum of vulnerability to environmental facilitation. Autistic children may be highly vulnerable requiring more than ordinary amounts of social stimulation to learn to respond to social stimuli as a class. Or, they may be impaired so that the perception of social stimuli is aberrant or perhaps their function as a class, if they are a class, is not perceived.

The third aspect of the relation of emotion to the structural/behavioral model is, theoretically, the most interesting. If emotion, in some fashion, serves as an organizing element in the behavior then it takes on a stage or system level function. It remains to be seen whether this will be demonstrated or not. Intuitively, the notion has some appeal. Emotion and affect may be significant factors in determining the degree to which a system is open or closed. More rigid emotional organization may facilitate closed system function; more fluid open system function. In this sense the individual difference dimension of emotional reactivity may help to regulate how quickly or easily a set of functions begins to operate in a closed system fashion or remains open. This does imply a good or bad value to closed and open. For some purposes closed system functioning may be more efficiacious; for others open system functioning more useful. How one would test these hypotheses is not clear but their theoretical import is evident.

SOCIAL, PERSONALITY,
AND MORAL DEVELOPMENT

Social, personality, and moral development probably represent the behavioral domains most dominated by non-universal behaviors. The high saliency of social stimuli and the evolutionary survival value of human social bonding patterns are indisputable. All societies are organized to socialize the young, and human social systems have some generic characteristics (some of which are shared with infra-human species). Beyond this, however, the patterns and even the timing of socialization are strongly culture bound. Many of the behaviors classified as social are influenced by cultural contexts.

The social behavioral repertoire is largely a learned repertoire with the possible exception of the initial onset of social smiling. Some social patterns associated with humans appear to have universal characteristics but these can be accounted for in an evolutionary adaptive/survival framework and one need not repair to a genetically innate mechanism. The transmission of social behavior from generation to generation is bound up in the complex processes of cultural transmission that occur in the context of families, schools, and cultures. The chances are that these processes are all forms of learning, subtle and pervasive.

There may be stages in social behavioral development but these are probably defined by the socio-cultural context in which the individual develops, constrained by certain other developmental characteristics such as motor maturity and intellectual maturity. The acquisition of the social behavioral repertoire is easily analyzed in terms of the structural/behavioral model. The environmental facilitation dimension would interact with the organismic dimension in terms of learning processes constrained by culturally determined parameters.

Closely allied to social development is moral development, which represents the acquisition of a socially defined behavioral repertoire that relates to right and wrong, to obligation and commitment, to rights and responsibilities. There has been an attempt to invoke a Piagetian stage model to describe moral development (Kohlberg, 1976) and some cross-cultural generality has been demonstrated (Rest, 1983). The moral development research has been almost entirely on the development of moral judgment behavior. As such, it has a strong relationship to cognitive development and to the development of knowledge about social relationships and social organization. The link between moral judgment and acting morally is not well established. To the extent that moral judgment behavior and moral action are related to both cognitive and social development the same application of the structural/behavioral model can be made to the domain of morality. It is not obvious that morality is not just a special case of some intersecting relationship of social and cognitive development.

Another aspect of morality is the case of exceptional moral behavior. Gruber (1985) has tried to analyze the conditions that produce moral giftedness in individuals. He identified some individuals who have acted with great moral courage or taken on extraordinary moral responsibility. No common pattern in their lives emerged in this retrospective analysis leaving only the exhortation that more research is needed to better understand how moral giftedness comes about. The highly visible expression of moral courage or moral responsibility typically involves an individual in behavior that stands out against or is against the general stream of behavior in the individual's environment. This would suggest that the individual who so acts somehow maintains or wrests independence from the ongoing environmental socialization that keeps others acting differently. This would put the individual on the "invulnerable" end for independence from the environmental dimension. The fact that such behavior appears to be exhibited at various times across the life span means that the conditions that are responsible for the emergence of this behavior may coalesce at different times across the life span. Alternatively, the latent ability may be formed at one period during the life span but exhibited idyosyncratically at another time depending on contextual circumstances.

Personality is not as clearly a "domain" of development as cognitive or motor development. It is, in many ways, a summary term that ranges in precision from referring to specific types of disordered personal functioning to general colloquia characterizations such as friendly, nice, somber. A strong element of temperament is included in most people's definition of personality but the stability of temperamental characteristics, independent of situations, has been difficult to establish. Most recently, for example, there have been reports on the difficulty of finding stability in the characteristic of difficult temperament in infants (Daniels, Plomin, & Greenhalgh, 1984), and as has been noted, Sameroff (Sameroff, Seifer, & Elias, 1982) has taken the position that the temperamental characteristics of the infant can be accounted for in terms of parental perceptions of infant behavior. Mischel (1968, 1973) has maintained that personality characteristics are heavily influenced by situational factors. If this is so then to the extent that temperament is situationally influenced we would expect to find instability.

Despite the considerable methodological problems with regard to the definition of temperament some progress has been made. Most notably, the work of Buss and Plomin and their colleagues in using multiple dimensions of emotionality, activity, and sociability (Buss & Plomin, 1984), with emotionality related to levels of arousal, sociability related to responsivity to a class of rewards, and activity related to the intensity of social stimulation and levels of arousal. Buss and Plomin believe these traits have strong heritability as personality traits although they emphasize the role of environmental matching and mismatching in determining how temperament functions in the regulation of behavior.

The notion is that individuals differ in their constitutional predisposition to respond to certain classes of stimuli, in the ease with which socialization occurs, in general reactivity, and so on. If these predispositions are placed on the organismic dimension of the structural/behavioral model they can also be seen to range on the invulnerable to vulnerable continuum. It is then possible to spin out the combinatorial possibilities with the environmental dimension as the behavioral repertoire is acquired and it is easy to see that similar outcomes will occur under a number of different combinatorial arrangements. If one or more of the elements in the combinatorial arrangement changes, the outcome may change. The focus of the attempt to understand personality development and its stability should be on the continuity of the processes and their combinatorial arrangements. An example of the application of this strategy can be seen in the following example.

The child who initially exhibits inhibition to strong stimuli may be described as having a tendency toward timidity or shyness. This tendency can become stronger and more stable under environmental conditions that reinforce such behavior. It can remain stable in some children relatively independent of environmental circumstances. A child who initially shows no such predisposition may acquire the behavior as the result of having timid and retiring behavior strongly reinforced. The continuity or discontinuity in this personality characteristic is not inherent in the organism except for some very few individuals. Kagan, in his discussion of inhibition, has come to the conclusion that environmental conditions play an important determining role in the actualizing of this biological tendency (Kagan, Reznick, & Snidman, 1986). It is the result of the interaction of the individual and the environment. Even in children who exhibit strong and stable behavior relatively independent of the environment, the model includes the possibility (à la Kuo's 1967 notion of multiple behavior potentials) that with sufficient alteration of environmental circumstances for a particular individual the behavior can be made unstable. The set of possible combinatorial arrangements may change over time and this would constitute the conditions for invoking a stage demarcation for personality characteristics.

LIFE-SPAN PERSPECTIVES

For many years developmental psychology was synonymous with child development. The growth of interest in aging stretched the field from birth to death with major gaps between the end of adolescence and old age.

More recently, developmental psychology has become synonymous with life-span psychology and a concomitant interest in development across the life span including various periods of adulthood. Erickson's ages and stages framework has provided the major theoretical backdrop for dividing up the life span even though there has been no empirical verification of the stages described.

The life-span perspective has stimulated a great deal of research on populations that were relatively neglected previously—adults in their middle years. Many phenomena are now being investigated about which little has been known. Normal life transitions such as marriage, the birth of children, and the formation and dissolution of families are topics of great current interest. The life-span perspective has also rekindled interest in longitudinal research and has sensitized the behavioral science community to the role that historical and contemporary community and world events may play in the development of children (Elder, 1974).

The structural/behavioral model is very suited to life-span analyses for obvious reasons. If one assumes the individual's behavioral repertoire is changing across the life span then the processes that are involved in the combinatorial arrangements that determine response acquisition can be tracked. If there are major periods of reorganization across the life span the model permits these to be incorporated. The non-universal portion of the behavioral domain may increase at rapid rates during some periods of development, less during others. These behaviors are much more fully under the joint control of the combinatorial arrangements of the organismic and environmental dimensions than are the universal behaviors. This would suggest that the focus of research on development and behavior during the middle years should key into the environmental dimension as an interactive factor with the organismic dimension. For example, response to stress will be a function of the individual's learned and constitutional disposition to cope with stress and the nature of the stressful circumstances involved. Universal I and II type behaviors will be minimally involved except as Universal II type behaviors in the cognitive domain might be implicated.

CONCLUDING COMMENTS

The structural/behavioral model is currently a heuristic, although it has the potential for being a theory. It is soft in the sense that a lot of things fit into it. It is not currently designed to be tested directly and proved or disproved. Rather, it is designed to foster a way of thinking about development that reorients the nature–nurture issue and the continuity–discontinuity issue. It is designed to stimulate a developmental perspective that is process oriented while incorporating developmental phenomena.

Some of the discoveries of the last 30 years have led to a kind of "gee-whiz" mentality. As new and often amazing facts have been revealed about what infants could do, about what children could and could not do, their existence seemed to constitute the whole of what we needed to understand. A scientific field certainly needs to know its phenomena and this requires a descriptive approach and a normative approach. But a process analysis must also go forward to understand the principles by which the phenomena come into the behavioral repertoire, develop, are maintained and change. Human behavioral development is probably, in its totality, the most complex phenomenon on this planet. The models proposed to account for the phenomenon must approximate that complexity if they purport to be relatively comprehensive.

One of the dangers inherent in trying to propose a comprehensive model when the data base is not strong is that it will all seem too complex and the prospect of mounting good research and asking the right questions dismally remote. In fact, however, attempts that are more sophisticated than has been typical should be encouraged. We cannot usually ask the most complex questions but we can ask questions aimed at a greater level of complexity. Further, we should try to put together the data base that now exists with respect to particular phenomena from the perspective of the structural/behavioral model. Would such a review of the evidence reveal that some chunks of the puzzle have been fitted together? Would it thereby become apparent that some strategically designed studies would help make connections between pieces of the puzzle that are already available?

Stronger developmental questions need to be asked more consistently. These questions will need, initially, to be focused selectively on a particular behavioral domain and on certain dimensions of organismic or environmental variables where there are good measures. Other dimensions may be important but they may be theoretically or technologically beyond current measurement abilities. Science must always progress in terms of its "state of the art." No science has progressed by beginning with questions aimed at the highest level of complexity that characterizes its phenomena. Conceptualizing research is a matter of mind set. The structural/behavioral model is an attempt to help foster a different kind of mind set in approaching developmental research. In suggesting the form and nature of dimensional relationships it is more than a metaphor, but in lacking specification with respect to the values of variables and the exact properties of the combinatorial relationships, it is currently less than a theory.

A summary of the central theses of our discussion defines the re-orientation of mind set about development and developmental research. One of the themes deals with how we characterize the child. Sometimes the child is an active, organizing learner using and exploring the environment and putting together informational relationships as the result of self-initiated behavior;

sometimes the child is reactive to environmentally arranged learning opportunities, dependent on the scheduling of feedback in a systematic manner. Both characterizations of the child are valid at different points in time, for different kinds of learning, in relation to different domains of behavior.

Another theme deals with how we conceptualize the behavioral system. Some aspects of behavioral functioning and development are highly routinized and mechanized, some are characterized by emergent structures and organizations. The child is active and reactive; the system is open and closed. Development is sometimes quantitative, sometimes qualitative. Still another theme deals with the notion that there are a variety of combinatorial arrangements between organism and environment that determine the course of an individual's behavioral development. These combinatorial arrangements constitute the elements in the basic processes of response acquisition. The combinatorial arrangements are describable and how they work themselves out in the basic processes are knowable. In fact, a lot is known about these aspects already although the data have not marshalled from this point of view.

It is time to stop characterizing development in only one way. Contrary to some prevailing opinion, the organismic and mechanistic world views are not irreconcilable. This juxtaposition has served its purpose and its time of usefulness is past. Similarly, the active–passive opposition in the characterization of the child should be discarded. In its stead an integrative model is needed that recognizes the multiplicity of processes and characterizations that will be needed to fully account for behavioral development. The structural/behavioral model proposed here is such a model.

There was no attempt to make a systematic assay of the applicability of the structural/behavioral model to each developmental age period or to each behavioral domain. Partly this is because not enough is known to make an intelligent attempt. But partly the effort was not made because a general model should represent a set of principles sufficiently complex that the variations necessary for relating to different age periods and different behavioral domains can be derived from the structural aspect of the model and/or the principles. In the structural/behavioral model, the principles were discussed in terms of combinatorial possibilities. Specification beyond these aspects would involve realms of unacceptable speculation if, indeed, the reader does not already feel we have ventured into these arenas already.

It is difficult at this point to specify the variables that drive change across age periods. Some of the change will be a function of the cumulative effect of the history of behavioral acquisition, some the operation of genetically determined structural factors involving different weights for different kinds of variables. Organismic variables may play a more central role in the initial expression of the topography of behavioral development during infancy and childhood, waning during the bulk of the adult years, but ascending again during the period of decline in old age. The individual differences that modulate such general statements are, however, extremely important and it should be of high priority in any systematic program of research to map the range of these individual differences.

In the different behavioral domains it is to be expected that the relative influence of organismic and environmental input dimensions will differ and they may well differ in terms of the period of development. One of the most elaborated examples used had to do with motor development. Language development served also as a frequent exemplar. These two domains are useful because each appears to have a strong basic structural topography that is species-typical and requires a species-typical ambient surround. However, there are many examples of non-universal environmental determinants. These appear to shape different repertoires of mature behavior. They also influence qualitative differences and final levels of competence. This is particularly true with language, where it would be hard to define the upper limit of species developmental potential. If non-verbal behavior were added, the discussion of the behavioral system of communication would involve what is likely the most complex aspect of the complex human behavioral repertoire.

It is important to remember that the structural/behavioral model must account not only for the universals in behavior but for the non-universals as well. And, for the qualitative variability that is so apparent in the assessment of developmental outcome. The structural/behavioral model must be thought of as an attempt to accommodate the most complex of possibilities even as some less complex hypotheses are the ones actually investigated. This is particularly the case with respect to qualitative aspects of developmental progression and behavioral development. Not much has been said about how cumulative values with respect to quality get factored into a developmental outcome equation, but they are undoubtedly extremely important. The cumulative account probably begins prenatally.

Similarly, not much attention was directed at the question of how different domains of behavior affect one another and the developmental import of this. Domain interaction has been most studied with respect to cognition and language and a clear picture has not yet emerged. Piaget's descriptions of infant development emphasize an inextricable link between motor and cognitive development. Some children who have significant motor impairment will exhibit normal cognitive development so motoric components are not necessary elements for all aspects of early cognitive development. Perhaps this is an example of the principle of equifinality.

The most important effects of a model or theory are measured in the research it generates, the questions it stimulates, and the data it is capable of integrating and accommodating. The structural/behavioral model involves a certain degree of ecumenism because there is every indication that multiple research strategies are needed to achieve a full picture of behavioral development. Normative data, as long as they are culturally qualified, provide a useful general base against which to look at process. Experimental analyses give some sense of the relevant process variables, how they interact, and how they might be weighted relative to one another. These strategies provide access to phenomena related to a particular behavior, a particular process. A model or theory of development, however, if it is to have any generative value with respect to developmental questions, cannot be built on one phenomenon taken as a prototype of developmental process. It is probable that there are a number of prototypes. Similarly, a particular research strategy may be very productive, but is unlikely to be sufficient for probing a variety of different kinds of questions. If development has multiple determinants then combinations of strategies will be necessary. The strong developmental questions will most likely be answered with multivariate techniques. The model we have proposed is best tested as a model in the context of multivariate research stimulated by strong developmental questions. The time is not always right, in the course of scientific progress, to mount such research. Often, one needs to have many smaller studies of isolated phenomena before one can attempt an integration of data. Such an integration, liberally sprinkled with intuitive hunches and insights, is needed in order to form and test the strong developmental questions. Unless we can make such attempts and risk failures from which we can learn, we will have a psychology of child behavior but we will not have a developmental psychology. The structural/behavioral model was designed to stimulate progress in our understanding of behavioral development. It is hoped it will serve this purpose.

REFERENCES

Bandura, A. (1977). *Social learning theory.* Englewood Cliffs, NJ: Prentice-Hall.

Buss, A., & Plomin, R. (1984). *Temperament: Early developing personality traits.* Hillsdale, NJ: Lawrence Erlbaum Associates.

Campos, J. J., Barrett, K., Lamb, M. E., Goldsmith, H. H., & Stenberg, C. (1983). Socioemotional development. In P. H. Mussen (Ed.), *Handbook of child psychology* (4th Ed., Vol. II, pp. 783–915). M. M. Haith & J. J. Campos (Eds.), *Infancy and developmental psychobiology.* New York: Wiley.

Clarke, A. M., & Clarke, A. B. D. (1976). *Early experience: Myth and evidence.* New York: Free Press.

Consortium for Longitudinal Studies. (1983). *As the twig is bent: Lasting effects of preschool programs.* Hillsdale, NJ: Lawrence Erlbaum Associates.

Daniels, D., Plomin, R., & Greenhalgh, J. (1984). Correlates of difficult temperament in infancy. *Child Development, 55,* 1184–1194.

Dickstein, S., Thompson, R. A., Estes, D., Malkin, C., & Lamb, M. E. (1984). Social referencing and the security of attachment. *Infant Behavior and Development, 7,* 507–516.

Elder, G. H. (1974). *Children of the great depression.* Chicago: University of Chicago Press.

Emde, R. (1980). Emotional availability: A reciprocal reward system for infants and parents with implications for presention of psychosocial disorders. In P. M. Taylor (Ed.), *Parent–infant relationships* (pp. 87–115). New York: Grune & Stratton.

Emde, R. N., Gaensbauer, T. J., & Harmon, R. J. (1976). Emotional expression in infancy. A biobehavioral study. *Psychological Issues, A Monograph Series.* (Vol. 10). New York: International Universities Press.

Gardner, H. (1983). *Frames of mind: The theory of multiple intelligences.* New York: Basic Books.

Gesell, A. (1954). The ontogenesis of infant behavior. In L. Carmichael (Ed.), *Manual of child psychology* (pp. 335–373). New York: Wiley.

Gruber, H. (1985). Giftedness and moral responsibility: Creative thinking and human survival. In F. D. Horowitz & M. O'Brien (Eds.), *The gifted and the talented: Developmental perspectives* (pp. 301–330). Washington, DC: American Psychological Association.

Hebb, D. O. (1949). *The organization of behavior.* New York: Wiley.

Horowitz, F. D. (1980). Intervention and its effects on early development: What model of development is appropriate? In R. R. Turner & H. W. Reese (Eds.), *Life-span developmental psychology: Intervention* (pp. 235–248). New York: Academic Press.

Horowitz, F. D., & O'Brien, M. (1985). Epilogue: Research and developmental perspectives. In F. D. Horowitz & M. O'Brien (Eds.), *The gifted and the talented: Developmental perspectives* (pp. 437–454). Washington, DC: American Psychological Association.

Horowitz, F. D., & Paden, L. Y. (1973). The effectiveness of environmental intervention programs. In B. M. Caldwell & H. N. Ricciuti (Eds.), *Review of child development research* (Vol. 3, pp. 331–402). Chicago: University of Chicago Press.

Hunt, J. McV. (1961). *Intelligence and experience.* New York: Ronald Press.

Hunt, J. McV., Paraskevopoulos, J., Schickedanz, D., & Uzgiris, I. (1975). Variations in mean ages of achieving object permanence under diverse conditions of rearing. In B. Friedlander, G. Sterritt, & G. Kirk (Eds.), *Exceptional infant* (Vol. 3, pp. 247–262). New York: Brunner/Mazel.

Kagan, J., Kearsley, R. B., & Zelazo, P. R. (1978). *Infancy: Its place in human development.* Cambridge, MA: Harvard University Press.

Kagan, J., Reznick, J. S., Snidman, N. (1986). Temperamental inhibition in early childhood. In R. Plomin & J. Dunn (Eds.), *The study of temperament: Changes, continuities and challenges* (pp. 53–65). Hillsdale, NJ: Lawrence Erlbaum Associates.

Klinnert, M. (1984). The regulation of infant behavior by maternal facial expression. *Infant Behavior and Development, 7,* 447–465.

Klinnert, M., Campos, J. J., Sorce, J., Emde, R., & Svejda, M. (1983). Emotions as behavior regulators: Social referencing in infancy. In R. Plutchik & H. Kellerman (Eds.), *Emotions in early development, Vol. 2, The emotions* (pp. 57–86). New York: Academic Press.

Kohlberg, L. (1976). Moral stages and moralization: The cognitive-developmental approach. In T. Likona (Ed.), *Moral development and behavior: Theory, research and social issues* (pp. 31–53). New York: Holt, Rinehart & Winston.

Kuo, Z-Y. (1967). *The dynamics of behavior development.* New York: Random House.

Lazar, I., Darlington, R., Murray, H., Royce, J., & Snipper, A. (1982). Lasting effects of early education. *Monographs of the Society for Research in Child Development, 47* (1–2, Serial No. 194).

Mischel, W. (1968). *Personality and assessment.* New York: Wiley.

Mischel, W. (1973). Toward a cognitive social learning reconceptualization of personality. *Psychological Review, 80,* 252–283.

Mistry, J., & Rogoff, B. (1985). A cultural perspective on the development of talent. In F. D. Horowitz & M. O'Brien (Eds.), *The gifted and the talented: Developmental perspectives* (pp. 125–144). Washington, DC: The American Psychological Association.

Rest, J. (1983). Morality. In P. H. Mussen (Ed.), *Handbook of child psychology* (Vol. III, pp. 556–629). J. H. Flavell & E. M. Markman (Eds.), *Cognitive development.* New York: Wiley.

Rogoff, B. (1982). Integrating context and cognitive development. In M. E. Lamb & A. L. Brown (Eds.), *Advances in developmental psychology* (Vol. 2, pp. 125–170). Hillsdale, NJ: Lawrence Erlbaum Associates.

Sameroff, A. J., Seifer, R., & Elias, P. K. (1982). Sociocultural variability in infant temperament ratings. *Child Development, 53,* 164–173.

Scarr-Salapatek, S. (1976). An evolutionary perspective on infant intelligence. In M. Lewis (Ed.), *Origins of intelligence: Infancy and early childhood* (pp. 165–197). New York: Plenum Press.

Siegler, R. S. (1983). Information processing approaches to development. In P. H. Mussen (Ed.), *Handbook of child psychology* (Vol. 1, pp. 129–211). W. Kessen (Ed.), *History, theory and methods.* New York: Wiley.

Sternberg, R. J. (1985). *Beyond IQ: A triarchic theory of human intelligence.* Cambridge, MA: Cambridge University Press.

Strauss, S. (Ed.). (1982). *U-shaped behavioral growth.* New York: Academic Press.

Wachs, T. D. (1986). Understanding early experience and development: The relevance of stages of inquiry. *Journal of Applied Developmental Psychology, 7,* 153–165.

Wachs, T. D., & Gruen, G. (1982). *Early experience and human development.* New York: Plenum Press.

Author Index

Subject Index

A

Accommodation, 31–35, 40–41, 63
Acquisition of responses, 65, 72, 77–78, 101, 170
Active-passive dichotomy, 38, 76, 131
Additive relationships, 50
Affect, 188–191
Affective development, 80
Aggression, 80
Alcohol, 142
Ambient surround, 128
Amplification mechanisms, 123
Animal analogs, 13, 114
Anthropology, 81
Applied behavior analysis, 65, 78–79
Arousal, 108, 113
Assimilation, 31, 35, 40–41, 63
Associational learning, 105, 106
Assumption of equivalence of associability, 86
Asymmetries, 34
Attachment, 112, 113, 117, 190
Attention, 163

B

Baldwin, James Mark, 29, 30, 31
  accommodation, 31, 35
  assimilation, 31, 35
  genetic epistemology, 31
Behavior
  analysis techniques, 77
  as stimulus-response pairings, 76
  and development, 6–8, 15–21, 64–65, 66
  laws of, 2
  levels of interactions, 15–21
  maintenance of, 6
  modifies physical phenomena, 20
  potentials, 88–91, 146, 147, 194
Behavioral
  chains, 77–78
  change, 6, 43, 167, 169, 170
  development, 6–8, 66, 103
    mechanistic-organismic, 12
    overdetermined, 85
    patterning, 32
    structure, 36
  disorders, 8
  dispositions, 154

genetics, 140
  neophenotypes, 90
  reorganization, 132
  repertoire, 138
  sets, 152, 155
  technology, 79, 83
  transformations, 14, 126
  variability, 156, 180, 183
Behavioral science, level of codification, 10–11
  paradigms, 9, 10
Behaviorism, 4, 7, 9, 10, 13, 19, 20, 25, 62–91, 137, 161, 171
  and Freud, 65, 80–83
  and intervention, 65, 71, 79, 85
  and logical positivism, 65, 67–68
  and methodology, 66, 67–71, 189
  and nature-nurture controversy, 71–72, 91
  and passive active child, 76
  and social learning theory, 80–83, 120
    and cognition, 81–83
    socio-cultural context, 82
  and stages, 43
  applied behavior analysis, 65, 78–79
  as mechanistic, 65, 70
  as obsolete, 62, 66, 76
  as theory of development, 71–72
  cause-effect, 52
  classical conditioning, 13, 64, 70, 73, 74, 84
    and emotion, 73–74
  conditioning defined, 73
  development, 64, 76, 83–91
    and learning, 80–85, 87
    and social learning theory, 80–83
    as linear, 43
    mechanisms of, 65, 66, 70, 78, 83–91
    outcome, 71–73
    Skinnerian definition, 71–78
  environment, 97–98
  evolutionary perspective and learning, 86–88
    cognitive unconscious, 87
    constraints on learning, 88–89
    preparedness, 86
    prepotent stimuli, 86
  history of, 62, 66–72, 77, 80–81
  Hullian theory, 65, 72, 74–76, 140
    and child development, 74–76
    and deductive theory, 140